The Reformation Era

The Reformation Era

ROBERT D. LINDER

Greenwood Guides to Historic Events, 1500–1900
Linda S. Frey and Marsha L. Frey, Series Editors

GREENWOOD PRESS
Westport, Connecticut • London

Library of Congress Cataloging-in-Publication Data

Linder, Robert Dean.
    The Reformation Era / Robert D. Linder.
        p. cm. — (Greenwood guides to historic events, 1500–1900, ISSN
1538-442X)
    Includes bibliographical references and index.
    ISBN: 978-0-313-31843-6 (alk. paper)
    1. Reformation. I. Title.
BR305.3.L55 2008
270.6—dc22   2007038580

British Library Cataloguing in Publication Data is available.

Library of Congress Catalog Card Number: 2007038580
ISBN: 978-0-313-31843-6
ISSN: 1538-442X

First published in 2008

Greenwood Press, 88 Post Road West, Westport, CT 06881
An imprint of Greenwood Publishing Group, Inc.
www.greenwood.com

Printed in the United States of America

The paper used in this book complies with the
Permanent Paper Standard issued by the National
Information Standards Organization (Z39.48–1984).

10 9 8 7 6 5 4 3 2 1

To Robert M. Kingdon
esteemed mentor, peerless scholar, extraordinary human being

CONTENTS

Photographs follow page 136.

SERIES FOREWORD

American statesman Adlai Stevenson stated, "We can chart our future clearly and wisely only when we know the path which has led to the present." This series, Greenwood Guides to Historic Events, 1500–1900, is designed to illuminate that path by focusing on events from 1500 to 1900 that have shaped the world. The years 1500 to 1900 include what historians call the early modern period (1500 to 1789, the onset of the French Revolution) and part of the modern period (1789 to 1900).

In 1500, an acceleration of key trends marked the beginnings of an interdependent world and the posing of seminal questions that changed the nature and terms of intellectual debate. The series closes with 1900, the inauguration of the twentieth century. This period witnessed profound economic, social, political, cultural, religious, and military changes. An industrial and technological revolution transformed the modes of production, marked the transition from a rural to an urban economy, and ultimately raised the standard of living. Social classes and distinctions shifted. The emergence of the territorial and later the national state altered man's relations with and view of political authority. The shattering of the religious unity of the Roman Catholic world in Europe marked the rise of a new pluralism. Military revolutions changed the nature of warfare. The books in this series emphasize the complexity and diversity of the human tapestry and include political, economic, social, intellectual, military, and cultural topics. Some of the authors focus on events in U.S. history such as the Salem witchcraft trials, the American Revolution, the abolitionist movement, and the Civil War. Others analyze European topics, such as the Reformation and Counter-Reformation and the French Revolution. Still others bridge cultures and continents by examining the voyages of discovery, the Atlantic slave trade, and the Age of Imperialism. Some focus on intellectual questions that have shaped the modern world, such as Charles Darwin's *Origin of Species*, or on turning points such as the Age of Romanticism. Others examine defining economic, religious, or legal events or issues such as the building of the railroads, the Second Great Awakening, and abolitionism. Heroes (e.g., Meriwether Lewis and William Clark), scientists (e.g., Darwin), military leaders (e.g., Napoleon Bonaparte), poets (e.g., Lord Byron) stride across the pages. Many of these events were seminal in that they marked profound changes or turning points. The Scientific Revolution, for example, changed the way individuals viewed themselves and their world.

The authors, acknowledged experts in their fields, synthesize key events, set developments within the larger historical context, and, most important, present well-balanced, well-written accounts that integrate the most recent scholarship in the field.

The topics were chosen by an advisory board composed of historians, high school history teachers, and school librarians to support the curriculum and meet student research needs. The volumes are designed to serve as resources for student research and to provide clearly written interpretations of topics central to the secondary school and lower-level undergraduate history curriculum. Each author outlines a basic chronology to guide the reader through often-confusing events and presents a historical overview to set those events within a narrative framework. Three to five topical chapters underscore critical aspects of the event. In the final chapter the author examines the impact and consequences of the event. Biographical sketches furnish background on the lives and contributions of the players who strut across the stage. Ten to fifteen primary documents, ranging from letters to diary entries, song lyrics, proclamations, and posters, cast light on the event, provide material for student essays, and stimulate critical engagement with the sources. Introductions identify the authors of the documents and the main issues. In some cases a glossary of selected terms is provided as a guide to the reader. Each work contains an annotated bibliography of recommended books, articles, CD-ROMs, Internet sites, videos, and films that set the materials within the historical debate.

Reading these works can lead to a more sophisticated understanding of the events and debates that have shaped the modern world and can stimulate a more active engagement with the issues that still affect us. It has been a particularly enriching experience to work closely with such dedicated professionals. We have come to know and value even more highly the authors in this series and our editors at Greenwood, particularly Kevin Ohe and Michael Hermann.

In many cases they have become more than colleagues; they have become friends. To them and to future historians we dedicate this series.

Linda S. Frey
University of Montana

Marsha L. Frey
Kansas State University

PREFACE

Most historians agree that the period now known as the Reformation along with its sister era now known as the Renaissance marked the end of medieval civilization and the beginning of the modern world. Historically speaking, the two periods, Renaissance and Reformation, are closely related and overlap. Many historians view the Renaissance as the precursor of the Enlightenment and the real beginning of modern times. Many others look to the Reformation, with its disruption of the authority of the Medieval Church, as the midwife to the modern world. This book will regard the Reformation Era as a basically religious movement with important political and social consequences and make the case for it as the beginning point for modern history.

In following their hallowed charge to make sense out of the past, historians usually regard the Middle Ages as having lasted from about 500–1500. Likewise, they generally see the Renaissance as the end time of medieval civilization and the springtime of the modern world, and assign it to the fourteenth, fifteenth and sixteenth centuries. Although there is some disagreement as to exact dates, nearly all historians begin the Reformation Era with Martin Luther's posting of his Ninety-Five Theses on the Castle Church door at Wittenberg in Germany on October 31, 1517. The end date for the Reformation is more problematic, with most historians signing off at the end of the Thirty Years' War in 1648, or with the Restoration of the monarchy in England in 1660. This work will use the latter date because, as will be argued, the last gasp of the Reformation Era came when the Puritan-supported republican experiment failed and England reverted to a monarchy.

In the past, most historians saw the Reformation Era as at best two major movements: one a positive Protestant effort to reform the Church along more biblical lines and the other a Roman Catholic counter-movement that was designed to save the Old Church from the ravages of the Protestant heresy. In retrospect, that view appears to have been flawed since the Radical Reformation did not fit well with the Classical Reform Movements represented by Lutheranism, Calvinism and Anglicanism. In fact, the Classical Protestants themselves long regarded the Anabaptists, the main expression of the Radical Reformation, as dangerous heretics, and the Anabaptists have long resisted the category of "Protestant" often thrust upon them by historians. Nowadays, it is more common to speak of four distinct reform movements outside the Roman Catholic Church in this period: Lutheran, Calvinist, Anglican, and Radical.

In the case of the so-called Counter-Reformation, historians now see more than just an attempt to recapture ground lost to Protestantism. It is true that much of the Catholic Reformation was concerned with counter-reform. However, it is also now widely acknowledged that the Catholic Reformation contained within itself many positive features, such as the Oratory of Divine Love, papal reform, the Catholic mystics, and certain aspects of the Council of Trent, 1545–1563.

Therefore, this book will follow the new trend that sees Reformations within an era whereas in the past it was common to refer to the Protestant Reformation and the Catholic Counter-Reformation. First, the background of the Reformation Era will be examined. Chapters, in turn, will follow on the Lutheran Reformation, the Calvinist Reformation, the Anglican Reformation, the Radical Reformation, and finally the Catholic Reformation. The concluding chapter will assess the impact of the Reformation Era on the modern world.

There are many sound books on the Reformation, as the endnotes and bibliography will demonstrate. This volume will attempt to condense and synthesize the best scholarship available and make the story of the Reformation accessible to general readers, especially to students working on term papers and other similar projects related to the era. Therefore, the narrative account of the Reformation Era will be followed by a series of mini-biographies of significant figures of the period, a collection of excerpts from important primary documents, a glossary of selected terms, an annotated bibliography, and an index.

ACKNOWLEDGMENTS

The author thanks series editor Marsha Frey for her suggestions, comments and corrections. They made this a better manuscript and were invaluable. Her patience and that of Greenwood Press editor Mariah Gumpert were monumental in terms of dealing with the trials and tribulations of the author in completing the manuscript for publication. Gumpert also provided expert guidance in preparing the manuscript. The author also thanks Diane E. Ferguson for her assistance in tracking down sources and documents and critiquing the manuscript. It also is conventional to acknowledge but nevertheless true that any errors in fact or interpretation remain the author's. Finally, my heartfelt thanks to Greenwood Press for allowing me to publish a book that I always had wanted to write.

CHRONOLOGY OF EVENTS

1309–1378   Avignon Papacy, the papal residence moves from Rome to Avignon in France.

1347–1351   The Black Death (bubonic plague) devastates Europe killing as many as two-thirds of the population, including large numbers of parish priests.

1378–1417   Great Papal Schism, two and eventually three popes fight each other for control of the Church.

1414–1417   The Council of Constance condemns the views of English scholar John Wycliffe and his Czech follower, Jan Hus, who is burned at the stake for heresy. It also ends the Great Papal Schism by electing Martin V pope.

1453   The Ottoman Turks capture Constantinople causing the flight of hundreds of Christian scholars to Italy with their libraries.

1455   Johann Gutenberg completes printing the Bible in Latin from movable metal type, the first printing of the Bible in any language.

1480   The Spanish Inquisition authorized by the papacy but under state control attempts to suppress heresy.

1492   Spanish conquer Granada, the last Muslim foothold in Spain. Columbus discovers America.

1498   Dominican monk Girolamo Savonarola burnt at the stake in Florence for heresy.

1502   The Elector Frederick III of Saxony establishes the University of Wittenberg.

1509	Henry Tudor ascends the English throne as Henry VIII and marries Catherine of Aragon.
1512	Erasmus publishes *The Praise of Folly*.
1516	Erasmus issues his edition of the Greek New Testament, which becomes the Textus Receptus of the new biblical scholarship; Thomas More publishes *Utopia*.
1517	Martin Luther posts his Ninety-Five Theses on the door of the Castle Church in Wittenberg.
1518	Ulrich Zwingli introduces a reformation along biblical lines in Zurich.
1520	Papal bull *Exsurge Domine* gives Luther 60 days to recant or be excommunicated.
1521	Luther appears before the Emperor Charles V at the Diet of Worms and refuses to retract his theological views; Elector Frederick III of Saxony spirits Luther away to the Wartburg Castle to ensure his safety.
1524–1525	Peasants' War in Germany.
1525	First glimmerings of the Anabaptist Movement in Zurich; Luther marries Katharina von Bora in Wittenberg.
1526	William Tyndale publishes his English New Testament at Worms, the first such translation directly from the biblical Greek.
1527	Luther pens "A Mighty Fortress Is Our God," his most enduring hymn.
1528	Enemies dub Luther's followers "Protestants" (protesting against the emperor's attempts to suppress Protestantism in the Empire) at the Diet of Speyer; Luther and Zwingli fail to reach agreement concerning the correct interpretation of the Eucharist at the Colloquy of Marburg.
1529	Philip Melanchthon presents the Augsburg Confession, a statement of Lutheran beliefs, at the Diet of Augsburg; Turks lay siege to Vienna.
1533	Henry VIII appoints Thomas Cranmer Archbishop of Canterbury; Cranmer dissolves Henry's marriage to Catherine of Aragon and Anne Boleyn becomes queen;

Calvin embraces Protestantism in Paris; Jacob Hutter joins Moravian Anabaptists, who become known as Hutterites.

1534–1535   Fanatical millennial enthusiasts, supported by many Anabaptists, seize Münster in western Germany.

1534   Luther completes his translation of the Bible into German; the Act of Supremacy in England by Parliament makes Henry Supreme Head of the Church of England; Ignatius de Loyola founds the Society of Jesus.

1535   A joint Catholic-Lutheran military force captures Münster and ends the millenarian uprising; Henry VIII orders Thomas More beheaded.

1536   Authorities in Brussels burn Tyndale at the stake for heresy; Calvin publishes the first edition of his *Institutes of the Christian Religion*; Menno Simons breaks with the Roman Church; Denmark and Norway become Lutheran; Henry VIII dissolves 376 monasteries and convents.

1540   Menno publishes his *Foundation of Christian Doctrine*; the pope authorizes the Society of Jesus as a monastic order.

1541   Geneva recalls Calvin to reform the Genevan Church; the Regensburg (Ratisbon) Colloquy fails to heal the Catholic-Lutheran breach.

1545–1563   The ecumenical Council of Trent meets sporadically in three sessions in order to reform the Roman Catholic Church and stave off Protestantism.

1549   Cranmer produces his first Book of Common Prayer for the Church of England.

1552   Cranmer issues his second and much more Protestant Book of Common Prayer.

1553   Geneva City Council executes Michael Servetus.

1554–1558   Mary I restores the Roman Catholic Church as the state religion in England.

1555   Bishops Hugh Latimer and Nicholas Ridley burn at the stake in England; the Peace of Augsburg in Germany.

1556   Archbishop Cranmer burns at the stake in Oxford.

1560s	"Puritans" first identified as Protestants who desire a more complete and thoroughgoing reformation of the Church of England.
1560	Protestant refugees in Geneva publish the Geneva Bible, a translation into English, which becomes the standard English edition of the scriptures for two generations.
1563	Parliament approves the Thirty-Nine Articles as the official doctrinal statement of the Church of England; John Foxe publishes his *Actes and Monuments of These Latter and Perilous Dayes* (commonly known as *Foxe's Book of Martyrs*)
1603	James VI (Stuart) of Scotland becomes concurrently James I of England.
1604	James I chairs the Hampton Court Conference.
1605	Gunpowder Plot fails when Guy Fawkes and other Roman Catholic conspirators attempt to blow up Parliament.
1611	Church of England publishes a new Authorized Version of the Bible (popularly known as the King James Version).
1618–1648	Thirty Years' War rages intermittently on the Continent.
1620	English Separatists (dissenting Protestants often called "the Pilgrims") land at Plymouth Rock on Cape Cod in Massachusetts.
1633	King Charles I names William Laud as Archbishop of Canterbury.
1642–1648	Tensions between Parliament and the Crown bring about the English Civil War; the Parliamentarians win, as most Puritans side with Parliament; Oliver Cromwell emerges as a dominant military and political leader on the parliamentary side.
1649–1660	The Parliament establishes the English Commonwealth.
1649	The Rump Parliament brings Charles I to trial for treason, a high court appointed by the Army Council convicts and beheads him on 30 January.

1653–1658   Cromwell assumes the office of Lord Protector.

1658   Cromwell dies.

1660   The Army takes control of England and allows the election of a new Parliament that invites Charles II, son of the executed Charles I, to restore the Stuart Monarchy.

CHAPTER 1

THE ROAD TO REFORMATION

"We are at the dawn of a new era!" Martin Luther exclaimed following his appearance before the Holy Roman Emperor Charles V (1519–1556) at Worms in 1521.[1] "Luther at Worms," penned the English Roman Catholic historian Lord Acton, "is the most pregnant fact in our history. . . . The great fact that we have to recognize is that with all the intensity of his passion for authority, he did more than any single man to make modern history the development of revolution."[2]

Although few modern historians of the Reformation Era any longer would agree completely with Lord Acton, his main point that the modern era began with Luther's challenge of medieval authority still carries a great deal of weight. The Reformation, along with the Renaissance, is still regarded by most scholars as the hinge on which all modern history turns.

The History of the History of the Reformation

Histories of the Reformation began to appear in the first generation following Luther's posting of the Ninety-Five Theses in 1517. The first polemical account was that of Johannes Cochlaeus, whose *Commentaries on the Acts and Writing of Luther* containing a vicious attack on the Protestant Reformer and his theology appeared in 1549. Johann Sleidan followed with his more balanced work, *Commentaries on Religion and the State in the Reign of Charles V* in 1555. However, even Sleidan, who had observed the Reformation from both sides of the religious divide, could not avoid a Protestant bias as he selected and omitted certain facts.[3]

While partisan histories abounded in the centuries following the Reformation, some historians continued in the tradition of

Sleidan and at least tried to write objective history, attempting to understand the past for its own sake rather than to defend an ideological position. The growth of ecumenical understanding among Christians since Vatican Council II (1962–1965) in the twentieth century led to a significant decrease in partisan histories as scholars of all persuasions, religious and non-religious, have shown greater understanding and appreciation of other points of view.

Interest in the Reformation increased greatly in the 1960s in the wake of religious revivals in the United States and elsewhere in the world, especially as new research and new methodologies resulted in considerable revision of previously held beliefs. For example, historians no longer write about a single Reformation because they recognize that the era experienced multiple reform movements that differed too much from each other to be included under a single label. Many also now recognize the positive achievements as well as the shortcomings of the Medieval Church, and a few even question the necessity for the Reformation Movement at all. New approaches to Reformation scholarship and new areas of research have greatly expanded an understanding of the period and corrected some past mistakes. However, there remain a number of unanswered questions as historians continue to debate interpretations and to investigate new topics neglected by previous generations, such as how the Reformation affected ordinary people and the role of women in the Reformation Era. Moreover, every generation needs to see such important movements as the Reformation in its own context and on its own terms.[4]

The New Social History that rose to prominence in the second half of the twentieth century has particularly influenced Reformation studies in the recent past as scholars have become more concerned with how the various reform movements affected people's lives. Earlier studies usually focused on the theological and political aspects of the Reformation and used traditional sources such as the writings of the Reformers, the correspondence of the political and ecclesiastical elites, the decisions of imperial diets, church councils and popes, and city chronicles. Many scholars seeking to understand ordinary folks in this period now turn to publications that were designed to influence public opinion, such as broadsides, pamphlets and popular woodcuts and paintings. In addition, these historians examine autobiographies, personal letters, local city and church archives, council minutes, wills, and records of church courts, consistories and ecclesiastical visitations in order to understand better the impact of the Reformation and answer questions that previous historians tended either to ignore or to answer by inference rather than hard evidence.

The main result of this new research in social history is increased awareness of the human drama of the period. The older emphasis on theology, politics, high culture and foreign policy has been joined by a focus on health, demographics, crime, families and women. Moreover, bitter rivalries, broken friendships, vitriolic attacks of Reformers on other Reformers, as well as the courageous martyrs who were victims of prejudice and hatred, are all part of the human drama of the era. Reformation history is exciting precisely because it contains heroes and heroines on all sides of the conflict as well as its share of villains. However, even the most impressive characters, like many of the all-too-human major figures of the modern era, had their share of weaknesses.

Further, recent studies have also questioned some of the standard terminology used in earlier works, such as "the Reformation," already noted. Increasingly, historians of the period prefer to use the word "Reformations" because it indicates that there was no unified movement that can be subsumed under a single rubric. Some modern-day historians are even reluctant to use the term "Protestant" to describe the new cluster of churches that arose outside of and in opposition to the older Medieval Catholic Church. They often prefer the word "Evangelicals," literally "followers of the gospel," which is usually how the Reformers and their followers described themselves. Another new term used in place of "Protestant" is "Reformation churches." Even the term "origins of the Reformation" has been called into question by some revisionist historians because it suggests that a reformation was bound to occur, and this, in turn, can lead to studying the Late Middle Ages largely to uncover factors that make the Reformation inevitable. Since nothing in history is "inevitable," and since standard usages of the past often still serve well the needs of the present, this work will take such matters as recent challenges to standard terminology into consideration without violating the canons of common sense.

In any event, the Reformation resulted in a lasting division in a Church that, at least in Western Europe, had retained its essential unity for more than a thousand years. This fact alone makes this era of immense importance. Moreover, the legal existence of more than one Christian Church was difficult to accept after a millennium of religious unity, and this fact was only reluctantly acknowledged when it became evident that neither dialogue nor suppression could restore the Church's unity. Religious divisions, as well as political, economic, and social factors, led to military conflict that vexed Europe between 1550 and 1648. At a local level, parishes, villages, guilds, and families also experienced strife as religious disagreement forced many of those who made spiritual choices in this period to seek a new life elsewhere. This produced the great migratory trek to other places that still continues for many people of European descent even today. Further, these terrible conflicts helped over the long term to undermine some of the most positive aspects of the reform movements and eventually lessened rather than increased the impact of Christianity upon society.

The Medieval Background

To paraphrase William Inge, the twentieth-century Dean of London's St. Paul's Cathedral, "In religion nothing fails like success."[5] By the thirteenth century, the Western Christian Church had reached the zenith of its power and had succeeded, at least externally, as never before. After a long struggle, it had not only gained independence of action from the secular states of Europe but also came to dominate most of them. Moreover, the Church controlled intellectual and cultural life and built countless chapels and cathedrals. It also constructed an elaborate scholastic theological system and a sacramental scheme that covered all aspects of human life.

Further, the Church developed a huge and efficient bureaucracy to administer its vast landholdings, to supervise endowments, to control appointments to office, and to administer justice in ecclesiastical courts. Its legal apparatus functioned so efficiently and fairly that many Europeans sought justice there rather than in local and national courts. In the Late Middle Ages, the Church possessed as much as one-third of the wealth in various countries. All of the foregoing translated into enormous power and prestige.

Church historians view Pope Innocent III (1198–1216) as the most powerful pontiff in the history of the Roman Catholic Church. Most Europeans, kings and peasants alike, regarded him with awe as he ruled over his far-flung ecclesiastical regime—a veritable papal monarchy—with an iron hand. He presided at the triumphal Fourth Lateran Council in 1215. This ecumenical council of the Church made momentous decisions affecting the activities of both church and state. For example, it declared the teaching of transubstantiation (the conversion of the whole substance of the bread and wine into the body and blood of Christ, only the external appearance of the bread and wine remaining, at the hands of the priest at the altar during the Mass) to be dogma, that is, now necessary to be believed. It also henceforth prohibited clergy from participating in the practice known as the ordeal, which judged guilt or innocence in legal matters, thus driving the English to embrace more fully the jury system. There were many more significant changes.[6]

Innocent III, as "the true emperor" of a spiritual world, now claimed "plenitude of power in both spiritual and temporal things." Medieval people thought of Christendom (the totality of the Christian World) as a single entity and the pope as its head, holding the keys to Christ's Kingdom and wielding the spiritual sword. The Holy Roman Emperor was nominally the chief political authority and wielded the secular sword. The pope claimed that the spiritual sword was superior to the secular sword because the Church was responsible for the eternal well-being of princes, kings and emperors. Therefore, Innocent III accepted entire kingdoms, such as Naples and England, as vassalages subject to his feudal lordship.

In 1302, Pope Boniface VIII (1294–1303), in his papal bull *Unam Sanctam*, issued in the heat of a dispute with King Philip IV (1285–1314) of France concerning jurisdiction over the French clergy, claimed for the Church effective possession of both the spiritual and the secular swords. He boldly asserted that "it is altogether necessary to salvation for every human creature to be subject to the Roman pontiff."[7] Thus, he made as great claims for papal authority as were ever promulgated.

The Babylonian Captivity of the Church

But Boniface VIII was no Innocent III, and his attempt to check secular power failed. Previously dreaded ecclesiastical weapons like the interdict and excommunication did not bring the French king to heel. Therefore, Boniface issued a papal bull, an official church document of great weight, ordering Philip to cease his anti-Church behavior. The French king not only ignored the bull but also humiliated the pope by sending an army to Rome that took him prisoner. Following Boniface's death in 1303, the French monarchy dominated the papacy for 68 years (1309–1377), a period called by the great Italian humanist Petrarch "the Babylonian Captivity of the Church," recalling the 70 years during which the Jews were captive in ancient Babylon. The French army literally carried the College of Cardinals off to the papal territory of Avignon in France where it would, for the most part, remain for two generations electing a succession of French popes. The Avignonese Papacy gained a sordid reputation for corruption during this period, leading to the charge oft repeated in the literature of the time that "everything is for sale in Avignon."[8] Most grievous during the Avignonese period, Christian Europe chose sides, some supporting the French-dominated papacy and others, led by the Germans and the English, opposing it.

The Great Papal Schism

Gregory XI (1370–1378), the last French Avignonese pope, returned to Rome in 1377, largely at the pleading of St. Catherine of Siena, who addressed him as "my sweetest daddy."[9] An effort was now made to restore the Chair of St. Peter to its historic resting place in Rome. However, the election of Gregory's successor in 1378 fractured the papacy for nearly 40 years. The cardinals' choice of the Italian Urban VI (1378–1389), under duress of a local mob, provoked the counter-election of a Frenchman, Clement VII (1378–1394), who returned to Avignon. Again, loyalties were divided along the political frontiers of Europe, now more firmly than ever. Since France was for Clement, England supported Urban, which meant that Scotland naturally was for Clement. The age of the Great Papal Schism (1378–1417) had begun. The situation was fraught with problems. How could anyone be sure of the validity of any of the judgments and administrative acts that determined the distribution of offices and property or be certain through which line the true saving sacraments were passed? But the real scandal was ideological, exposing the implausibility of the two claimants to be the true Bishop of Rome and St. Peter's successor as Vicar of Christ on earth. Nevertheless, each pope persisted in asserting that he was that true vicar and the other man a false pontiff.

A herculian attempt to end the schism came in 1409 at the Council of Pisa when a third pope was named and the other two popes, the one in Rome and the one in Avignon, were declared deposed. Unfortunately the third pope, John XXIII (1410–1415, now an antipope in official Roman Catholic thought), could not physically unseat either the Roman or the Avignonese pontiff, and, therefore, became a kind of roving pope-at-large. Moreover, he turned out to be a scoundrel and a brigand, thus further degrading the image of the papacy in the eyes of most Christian Europeans. Finally, at the Council of Constance in 1417, Martin V (1417–1431) was chosen to replace all three pretenders to the papal throne. He was able to re-claim Rome as his seat and gradually re-established legitimate authority there. Except for Avignon, the other popes gave up. The Avignonese antipopes maintained their claims until 1429, when they, too, capitulated. Finally, Christian Europe was at papal peace, but at great cost. The erosion of papal prestige during this period had a withering effect on popular piety and spirituality.

The Conciliar Movement

Since the competing popes were unwilling to resign, the only solution was to call a church council of the bishops on the theory that councils ranked above popes. Two German professors at the University of Paris, Henry of Langenstein and Conrad of Gelnhausen, asked the princes to call a council, just as the Roman Emperor Constantine I had once called the Council of Nicea in 325.

French conciliarists Pierre d'Ailly and Jean Gerson further argued that a council was necessary to re-establish the unity of the Church. Sharp critics of the Church such as philosopher Marsiglio of Padua, Franciscan theologian William of Ockham, and the Oxford University don and clergyman John Wycliffe went so far as to deny the divine origin of the papacy. Wycliffe even urged lay people to read the Bible in English and said that if the clergy, by their evil lives, showed that they were not in a state of grace, the secular rulers should take away their property. Pressure mounted until the cardinals on both the Roman and the Avignonese sides of the divide joined to summon a general council of the Church. Consequently, a series of reforming councils was held, at Pisa in 1409, at Constance from 1414 to 1418, at Ferrara-Florence in 1438–1439, and a competing antipapal council at Basel, from 1431–1449.

As indicated, these councils eventually ended the Great Papal Schism but they did not succeed in reforming the Church. Finally, in 1460, Pope Pius II (1458–1464) reasserted papal supremacy by declaring in his bull *Execrabilis* that it is a detestable thing to appeal to a council over the head of a pope. Still worried, he warned: "Dangerous times are before us. Storms threaten everywhere. The waves of Basel have not subsided. We won through force, they say, and not by convincing arguments."[10]

The Renaissance Papacy

Pius II was one of the first "Renaissance Popes" who occupied the papal throne from 1447 until well into the sixteenth century. During this period, the papacy survived the Great Papal Schism and once more secured itself in the Western World. A single petrine line with its seat at Rome had been restored and even a measure of prestige and wealth had been re-established. But the sagging reputation of the papacy itself would suffer further damage under the assault of a line of popes who were little more than Renaissance "princes of the church": worldly, urbane, sophisticated, talented, and corrupt but seldom religious. Some popes, such as Nicholas V (1447–1455) and Pius II, were accomplished scholars and connoisseurs of rare books and manuscripts. It was Nicholas who began what is today the fabulous Vatican Library. Some were like Innocent VIII (1484–1492), an easygoing, congenial man who was the first pope to dine in public with his mistresses, and who was a real *"papa"*[11] as the father of 16 children.

The papacy reached its nadir with the reign of Alexander VI (1492–1503) who virtually bought the papacy with bribes and then attempted to gratify his ambitious relatives who swarmed to Rome from Spain. His unruly sex life was legendary but he tried to take good care of his several natural children. Among them was Cesare Borgia whose political ruthlessness and amoral pragmatism provided Niccolò Machiavelli with his model for Machiavelli's classic analysis of practical politics, *The Prince*. Cesare murdered numerous of his own enemies and those of his father, perhaps even his own brother Giovanni, whose body was found floating down the Tiber River. Lucretia Borgia, another papal offspring and the most cherished of Alexander's daughters, became a byword for immorality and the alleged perpetrator of numerous poisonings of papal enemies and personal suitors whose attentions had become tiresome to the beguiling Lucretia.

Pope Julius II (1503–1513), successor and sworn enemy of Alexander VI, was a great warrior who led papal armies into battle, sacking Bologna and lesser cities. Like most of his predecessors, he filled the College of Cardinals with relatives and unworthy candidates who subordinated the religious functions of their office to worldly and temporal aims. In any event, Julius made the Papal States of central Italy a leading power in European politics. Leo X (1513–1521), Julius' successor, was the pope who greeted Luther's protests in Germany with disdain and lack of empathy. Leo was of the Medici family, the rich Florentine bankers who had controlled that city for several generations during the fifteenth century. Also, like many of his Medici relatives, Leo loved and patronized the arts but wasted a great deal of his personal and papal wealth on his fondness for gambling. A worldly and wily man, he had little understanding of theology or piety. By Leo's time, the reputation of Rome and the papacy was nearly beyond redemption.

Popular Religion

Ironically, at the very time when the institutional Church was least able to satisfy peoples' religious needs, Europe experienced a great surge of faith and piety. In 1348 and 1349, the bubonic plague, known as the Black Death, struck and wiped out an estimated one-third of the European population. Wars, droughts, famines and disease made life uncertain and miserable. The masses thought more intensely of the "other world" and embraced a mostly fear-driven piety. Pilgrimages, fasting, the rosary, relics, new saint cults and prayer brotherhoods grew to be fashionable. Endowed Masses for the souls of the dead, bequests, indulgence sales, and other evidences of intense concern. that involved "the buying" of religious comfort increased. Blatant superstition also flourished.

In Bohemia in the fifteenth century, the followers of Jan Hus, who had been burned at the stake as a heretic at the Council of Constance in 1415 for what foreshadowed Protestant views, unleashed a full-scale rebellion against the Roman Church. The once-virile scholastic theology of the thirteenth century declined in rigor and a new surge of mysticism and an emphasis on an interior religion of the heart took its place.

Outrage against financial exploitation by the Roman See reached major proportions in the fifteenth century. From 1447 onward, at each meeting of the Diet of the Holy Roman Empire, the imperial consultative body, the grievances of German states against abuses and papal profiteering were aired. Contemporaries noted that the word ROMA was an acrostic for the Latin apothegm *radix omnium malorum avaritia*—"avarice or love of money is the root of all evil."[12]

At the same time, many parish priests, monks, nuns and lay people were honest, sincere and God-fearing. Nothing better illustrated the growing tension between a corrupt papacy and the rank-and-file religious of the time than the clash between Pope Alexander VI and the Dominican monk Girolamo Savonarola over control of Florence in 1494–1498. Assigned to Florence in 1490, Savonarola eventually awakened the spiritual impulses of Florentine Christians with his dynamic preaching and his condemnation of Florence's secular Renaissance culture. He called for repentance on the part of the city-state's leaders and championed the cause of the poor and oppressed. As time passed, he also denounced the powerful Medici family because it corruptly controlled the political life of the city and sponsored much of its secular Renaissance culture. After a show-down prompted by the invasion of Italy by a large French army in 1494, Savonarola and his followers drove out the Medicis and replaced their regime with one more attuned to biblical Christian principles—in short, with a theocratic republic. In the course of events, Savonarola's Florence became a French ally.

The pope watched these developments with a jaundiced eye, for he planned to lead an alliance, the goal of which was the expulsion of the French from the Italian peninsula and the unification of the various Italian states under papal leadership. Tensions between the pope and Savonarola increased dramatically when the Dominican preacher began to denounce Alexander and his corrupt papal court. Unhappy with the prospect of a French ally on his flank and troubled by the preaching of "the meddlesome friar," Alexander threatened to place the city under an interdict if he were permitted to preach again. Although Savonarola denied the validity of the ban since, as he put it, Alexander was the representative of Satan and not Christ, the people of Florence became frightened. Moreover, four years of hard preaching and demanding moral standards had taken their toll. Some of the more wealthy citizens were especially impatient with the friar's ideas.

At the pope's behest, in May of 1494, the Franciscans arranged an ordeal in which one of their number and a follower of Savonarola would march through a fire. When the flames were kindled for the test, an argument broke out between the two groups and a sudden rainstorm quenched the fire. The incident helped to discredit Savonarola, who was tried for heresy. He was subsequently tortured, confessed all of his errors in defying papal authority, found guilty and executed. His body was burned and his ashes thrown into the Arno River so no potential relic would survive. Thus, papal power triumphed over monastic piety with a vengeance. Many observers wondered if perhaps the next great outburst of religious concern would have to go outside the Church.

Such incidents made the low moral level of the popes and the hierarchy of the period stand out even more sharply. Renaissance Christian humanists, like the great Desiderius Erasmus of Rotterdam, led a chorus of criticism and pointed out the stark contrast between papal immorality and abuse on the one hand and of the piety of the ordinary clergy and the laity on the other. Sebastian Brant, one of these Christian humanists, wrote:

> St. Peter's ship, I fear I'm thinking,
> Will very shortly now be sinking![13]

Social and economic conditions invited revolutions and wars. The nobility, the artisans and the peasants were ready for change. The recently invented printing press (1456) poured out not only learned books but also revolutionary pamphlets. It was into this highly inflammable situation that the sparks of Luther's criticism fell. The situation immediately preceding Luther's break with Rome was highly dangerous for the Old Church.[14]

Europe in 1500

As far as the institutional Church was concerned, the Renaissance Papacy was at flood tide in 1500. The three popes of Luther's youth and young manhood were Alexander VI, Julius II and Leo X. Therefore, rumor and fact conveyed the essence of the papacy of the period to the faithful at large: secular, flippant, frivolous, sensual, magnificent and worldly. By 1500, the papacy clearly had lost its moral authority to lead Christendom. The masses knew all of this and looked elsewhere for spiritual leadership. The common saying of the day was: "The closer to Rome, the worse the Christians."[15]

The rise of the early nation-states was underway by 1500, as well. National feeling was beginning to be a major factor in fundamental loyalties. Many German, French and English people, for example, were now being tugged between loyalty to the monarch or the pope, especially from the thirteenth century onward as the pope played an increasingly important role in European politics. Could loyalty to king and pope any longer coincide? How were the faithful, or the papacy for that matter, to regard the spectacle of an alliance in 1536 of the Christian king of France with the Turkish sultan against the Holy Roman Emperor? These sorts of questions were beginning to tear the Church apart at the seams. The rise of the nation-states had the political world in turmoil.

It was also a time when humanism was in full tide. Humanism was an intellectual movement based on the study of the classics of the Ancient World. Its watchword was *ad fonts*, meaning "back to the sources" of Western culture. Humanism also was of two sorts, the first of which, the original movement, arose in fourteenth-century Italy and focused on the secular classics of the Ancient World. Italian scholars "rediscovered" and intensely studied long forgotten Greek and Roman manuscripts. Unlike the Aristotelian-Scholastic mentality that dominated the High Middle Ages, the humanist point of view was human-centered, historical and above all critical. It was critical not only of long-standing Scholastic assumptions in philosophy and theology but also of many of the patent abuses and venerable traditions of the institutional Church.

As the humanist movement spread to Northern Europe in the fifteenth century, it took on a second, more Christian cast. There, humanists were more concerned with Ancient Christianity than with Ancient Greece and Rome. Also historically and critically oriented, the northern scholars closely studied the Christian classics—like the New Testament and the Church Fathers—and found the contemporary

Church to be wanting. They pointed out discrepancies between New Testament teachings and current Church beliefs and practices. Some, like Erasmus, relentlessly used ridicule and irony, not as a tool of destruction but as a means to reform a Church they still dearly loved. However, in the process, they also created increasing skepticism of papal leadership and provided fuel to feed the flames of Protestant criticism of the Old Church following Luther's break with Rome in 1521. The humanists had introduced the problem of the conflict of authorities into the intellectual mix. Should sixteenth-century Christians follow the teachings of the New Testament or the often-variant teachings of contemporary popes? The humanist movement had the intellectual world in turmoil.

Moreover, by 1500, monastic life in many places was in a state of deterioration or spiritually dead. Once a vibrant movement, many religious establishments had fallen on evil days. Whereas at one time in the Middle Ages, many of the best Christians could be found in monastic orders, by the end of the fifteenth century, the common complaint was that the monks and nuns in endowed houses exhibited lives of loose morality and religious indifference. The decline of monastic life removed a major alternative of spiritual comfort for many pious Christians. Monastic decadence had the spiritual world in turmoil.

Worst of all, the main link between Church and people, the parish priesthood, was in a state of moral disorder. During much of the Middle Ages, especially before the fourteenth century, the relationship between parish priest and his flock had been extremely close and beneficial. Many caring, godly men could be found serving the spiritual, social, and even economic needs of their flocks. This began to change after the devastation of the Black Death when many of those priests who survived to minister in the post–Black Death world were those who had deserted their stations in order to save themselves while the more dedicated clergy remained at the side of their ailing parishioners only to perish themselves in the end. By the sixteenth century, many if not most parish priests were poorly trained and indifferent. Many recited the Latin Mass with no understanding of the words they intoned. There was an increase in religious profiteering at the expense of the faithful. This was most irritating when it involved charging fees for the sacraments—for baptism, for marriage, and even for burial. Some complained that almost every religious ministration had a price tag. As Erasmus put it in his classic work, *The Praise of Folly*:

> Then the mob of priests, forsooth, consider it a sacrilege to fall
> short of their prelates in holiness. O brave! They war on behalf

of their right to tithe in the best military manner, with swords, darts, stones, and force of arms. How keen-sighted they are, to elicit from the writings of the ancients something by which they can terrify the poor people and convince them that they owe more than their just tithes! Of course it does not occur to them that many things may be read in many scriptures touching the duty which they, on their side, should discharge as a debt to the people. Nor does their shaven crown in the least remind them that a priest ought to be free from all worldly desires and ought to set his mind upon nothing but heavenly things. These amiable men, on the contrary, say that they have well cleared themselves of their obligations if they somehow mutter those little prayers which, so help me, make me wonder whether any God hears or understands them, since the priests themselves barely hear them and do not understand them, even while they echo them with their mouths. But the priests have this much in common with the profane, that all alike watch for the harvest of profits, nor is a single one of them ignorant of the laws on this subject.[16]

In short, a declining parish priesthood had the everyday lives of ordinary Christians in late medieval Europe in turmoil.

This was the context of Luther's spiritual experiences in late fifteenth- and early sixteenth-century Germany. Those experiences in this context led him to question first the corrupt practices of his Church and then the belief system of the Church itself. His increasing skepticism concerning his Church's ability to meet the spiritual needs of the faithful, as German historian Heinrich Boehmer put it, led Luther to embark upon "the Road to Reformation" that eventually became the main highway of Protestantism beginning in 1521.[17] The next chapter will consider the mile markers along that road and the extension of that highway.

Notes

1. Quoted in Lewis W. Spitz, *The Renaissance and Reformation Movements,* rev. ed., 2 vols. (St. Louis, MO: Concordia Publishing House, 1971), 2:301.

2. John Emerich Edward Dalberg-Acton, *Lectures on Modern History* (London: Macmillan, 1956), 101 and 105.

3. Ingeborg Berlin Vogelstein, *Johann Sleidan's Commentaries* (Lanham, MD: University Press of America, 1986), 12; and *Two Contemporary Accounts of Martin Luther* (New York: Palgrave Macmillan, 2004). The latter book contains both Cochlaeus' life of Luther and that of Luther's friend Philip Melanchthon.

4. For example, see Carter Lindberg, *The European Reformations* (Oxford: Blackwell, 1996); James D. Tracy, *Europe's Reformations, 1450–1650* (New York: Rowman and Littlefield, 1999); Diarmaid MacCulloch, *The Reformation: A History* (New York: Viking, 2003); and R. Po-Chia Hsia, "Reformation on the Continent: Approaches Old and New," *The Journal of Religious History*, 28, no. 2 (June 2004):162–170.

5. William R. Inge, *Outspoken Essays* (London: Longmans, Green and Company, 1919), 41.

6. Norman P. Tanner, ed., *Decrees of the Ecumenical Councils*, 2 vols. (Washington, DC: Georgetown University Press, 1990), 1:572–630.

7. Henry Bettenson and Chris Maunder, eds., *Documents of the Christian Church*, 3rd ed. (Oxford: Oxford University Press), 127.

8. Guillaume Mollat, *The Popes at Avignon* (New York: Thomas Nelson and Sons, 1963), 279–281.

9. F. Thomas Luongo, *The Saintly Politics of Catherine of Siena* (Ithaca, NY: Cornell University Press, 2006), 72, 76, 166.

10. *A Source Book for Mediaeval History*, O. J. Thatcher and E. H. McNeal, trans. (New York: Charles Scribner's, 1905), 332.

11. *"Papa"* is the Italian word for pope, father and/or daddy.

12. Cited in Spitz, *The Renaissance and Reformation Movements*, 2:313. Also see F. R. H. Du Boulay, *Germany in the Later Middle Ages* (New York: St. Martin's Press, 1983).

13. Sebastian Brant, *The Ship of Fools*, trans. William Gillis (London: The Folio Society, 1971), 279.

14. One of the best overviews of Europe on the eve of the Protestant Reformation can be found in De Lamar Jensen, *Reformation Europe*, 2nd ed. (Lexington, MA: D. C. Heath and Company, 1992), 1–51.

15. Quoted in Spitz, *The Renaissance and Reformation Movements*, 2:315.

16. Desiderius Erasmus, *The Praise of Folly*, trans. Hoyt Hopewell Hudson (Princeton, NJ: Princeton University Press, 1941), 101–102.

17. Heinrich Boehmer, *Road to Reformation: Martin Luther to the Year 1521*, trans. John Doberstein and Theodore Tappert (Philadelphia: Muhlenberg Press, 1946).

CHAPTER 2

Martin Luther and the Beginning of the Protestant Reformation

According to Martin Marty, the dean of twentieth-century American church historians, Martin Luther was always "hungry for certainty." That hunger drove him first to seek personal peace with God and later to lead an international reform movement within the Christian Church that has endured to the present day. In the process, with the exception of Jesus Christ, he would become the most written about person in human history.[1]

Martin Luther was born and grew to young manhood on the fringes of Christendom in central Germany, far from the brilliance and grandeur of the Renaissance papal court.[2] His father, Hans, was the eldest son of a land-owning peasant. Since it was the custom in that part of Germany for the youngest son to inherit the land, Hans left the family farm to pursue an occupation elsewhere. Marriage to Margaretha Lindemann, the daughter of a successful middle-class family in Eisenach, helped his fortunes. Hard work, a degree of shrewdness and some well-timed loans eventually brought Hans economic and social advancement.

Martin Luther first saw the light of day on 10 November 1483, in the small Saxon town of Eisleben. The Luthers had their second son baptized the next day and, according to custom, gave him the name of Martin, the saint on whose feast day the baptism took place. A year later, the Luther family moved to the nearby town of Mansfeld, the center of a flourishing copper-mining industry. It was there that Martin grew to young manhood in what can be described as a marginally middle-class home dominated by a peasant-like frugality and discipline.

As an adult, Luther remembered some harsh discipline he experienced as a child. Several psychological historians have used scattered comments Luther made about his early life in an effort to explain his later rebellion against the Church. However, the sometimes painful experiences he cited were typical of child discipline in late fifteenth-century Germany.[3] Moreover, there is plenty of evidence that Luther's parents loved him dearly and that they were proud of the fact that he was a gifted student who did well in school. He also demonstrated considerable musical ability, and sang and played the lute well. Moreover, he had a good sense of humor. His upwardly mobile father duly noted his intellectual acumen and made certain that he was well educated, first at Mansfeld and later in the much larger city of Magdeburg. After a year at Magdeburg, Martin was off to Eisenach where his mother's relatives lived and where he spent three happy years making lasting friendships and receiving an excellent further education.

At the age of 17, Luther's ambitious father sent him off to Erfurt, one of Germany's oldest, largest and best universities. He earned his bachelor's and master's degrees there in 1502 and 1505, respectively. Old Hans then urged his son to seek a law degree, apparently hoping that Martin would continue to elevate his family's status. Yielding to his father's wishes, Luther began legal studies at Erfurt in May 1505. The 21-year-old Luther's future direction seemed set until he had an experience later that year that changed the course of his life and propelled him down the road to the Reformation.

If anything set off young Martin Luther from other young Germans of the period, it was the intensity of his religious interest and the fervor with which he did most things. He was an especially sincere young Christian in a country where at this time in history the people were known for their religious devotion. Luther's parents emphasized religion in the home while he grew up, some said even to the point of superstition. In any case, young Martin maintained a lively devotional regimen all during his school days up to and including his university years. In so doing, he indicated the first signs of a restlessness that sought certainty as he duly tried to follow the religious prescriptions of his Church. He also had several close brushes with death during his university days, including 1505 when an outbreak of the plague in Erfurt claimed the lives of two of his university examiners. He later commented that it was at about this time that he experienced intense spiritual turmoil and spent a great deal of time thinking about death and how to prepare for it.

It was in this context that he had the first of what Luther called his *Anfectungen*, a difficult to translate German word meaning roughly "a trial" during which the struggling Christian felt the withdrawal of grace or sensed abandonment by God. It might be a trial sent by God to test a person, or an assault by the Devil to destroy an individual's faith. It was all the doubt, panic, despair, desolation and desperation that occasionally invade the human spirit. This situation was considered not only a serious moral deficiency but also a grievous sin, for it called God's goodness into question.[4] This, in turn, set off the alarm bells of the soul because during the later Middle Ages God was depicted more and more as a stern judge who sat on the heavenly throne weighing the deeds of frail and sinful humans in the balances. The main emphasis increasingly became justice rather than grace and mercy. To be sure, God was still portrayed as a loving Father, but more often as the wielder of the thunder and the lightning. How could frail and sinful human beings satisfy such a God? The Almighty Father might be softened by the intercession of his somewhat more approachable Son, who also was frequently thought of as a dreaded adjudicator unless mollified by his more understanding mother, Mary. In any case, life was often short, difficult and depressing, and young Martin Luther was frequently disheartened by what he saw all around him and by his own spiritual doubts about whether or not he was able to satisfy such a fierce and demanding God.

This was the spiritual context of Luther's Christian development. The historical context of his first *Anfectung* was a sultry July day in 1505 when an unexpected encounter with death led to his decision to become a monk. As he returned to Erfurt after a visit with his parents at Mansfeld, a lightning bolt suddenly struck him to the ground as he took shelter under a tree during a thunderstorm. In that single flash he saw in his mind's eye the drama of human existence. Luther later maintained that his whole life passed before him and he saw his own sinfulness in contrast with the purity and majesty of God. He glimpsed God the all-terrible judge, Christ the inexorable savior, and the leering fiends of the nether world who sprang from their lurking places in pond and wood that they might seize his wretched body and cast him into hell. It is little wonder that he cried in terror to his father's saint, the patroness of miners and the mother of the Virgin Mary: "St. Anne help me and I will become a monk!" She did, and he did! Two weeks later, on 17 July 1505, against his father's wishes, Luther entered the Augustinian cloister at Erfurt.[5]

Luther's Spiritual Crises

The meaning of Luther's entry into the monastery is simply that the great revolt against the Medieval Church that eventually engulfed Christendom arose from a desperate attempt by a loyal son to follow the way that the Church prescribed. He went to the monastery like thousands of others before him, and even more than others, in order to make his peace with God. Thus, Luther's reform movement was not initiated by the moral indignation of a Savonarola directed against the Renaissance Papacy but by the personal anxiety of a solitary Christian about his own soul's salvation. Moreover, Luther's hunger for spiritual peace foreshadowed the fact that the quarrel that eventually developed between the German monk and his Church was basically religious because Luther was above all else a man of religion. In the end, perhaps Luther was too devout a Catholic.

In any event, Luther seems to have had at least three more of these profound religious crises or trials as he made his way along the road to his final break with the Roman Church.[6] The second came two years later, in May 1507, at the celebration of Luther's first Mass as a young priest. Luther took his place at the altar and began to recite the introductory portion of the Mass until he came to the words, "We offer unto thee, the living, the true, the eternal God." It was while pronouncing these sacred words that he experienced another moment of profound terror. He later recorded that this incident occurred because he still felt full of sin in the presence of the infinite, holy God. The fear of the Holy, the dread of Infinitude, struck Luther like a new lightning bolt. He later said that it was only through enormous self-discipline that he was able to hold himself at the altar to the end. This experience convinced him that even as a priest and monk, he did not have assurance of his personal salvation. At this point, he turned to other means of settling his inner turmoil: fasting, repeated confessions, mysticism, and even self-flagellation. There never was a better monk than Luther. He confessed and confessed, and there were never such dull confessions. Nevertheless, peace with God did not come. The unrest continued, as he drove his ecclesiastical superiors to distraction.

A third *Anfectung* occurred in November 1510 when Luther made a trip to Rome on business for his order. His vicar and father confessor, Dr. Johan von Staupitz, a good and wise man, sent Luther on his way, thinking that a trip to the Holy City would help the young monk in his quest for religious peace. Brother Martin made the usual pilgrimages to the famous churches and shrines of Rome in an attempt to comfort his troubled soul. But instead of being helped spiritually, he was sadly disappointed in what he saw. Julius II was pope, Savonarola had been dead for only 12 years, and the capital of Christendom was full of great wealth, splendor, corruption, vice and sin, but not peace, holiness and piety. Then, while climbing the steps of the *Scala Sancta* located in front of the Lateran Palace, Luther had another of his great emotional crises. It was said that anyone who crawled up the steps on hands and knees, repeating a *Pater Noster* (an "Our Father") for each one, could find personal spiritual peace and at the same time release a soul from purgatory. In the midst of his effort, Luther said that he suddenly realized the emptiness of all of his works of merit, especially those he had most recently completed in Rome. He felt that he was still a lost sinner in the sight of God. This incident crystallized his conviction that he could not find salvation and peace by performing the works of merit prescribed by the Church. He returned to Germany determined to search the Bible for an answer to his spiritual misery.

Luther's fourth and final major spiritual crisis most likely occurred during the years 1517–1518, when he was a lecturer in biblical theology at the newly established University of Wittenberg.[7] Shortly after his return from Rome, von Staupitz asked Luther to take his place at the university, and Luther moved to the village of Wittenberg, where he would spend the remainder of his life. Luther had qualified for this post by earning his ThD (Doctor of Theology) degree in 1512.[8] It was while teaching there that he came to his new understanding of justification through grace by faith in Christ—or, as Luther would put it, his rediscovery of St. Paul's teaching on this matter. Though historians continue to debate the dating of his "Reformation breakthrough," it is clear that it emerged from Luther's scriptural studies as he prepared for his lectures at the university.

Even though medieval scholars read the Bible with reverence and intensity, biblical studies had not been an important part of Luther's theological education at Erfurt. In addition, the most commonly used exegetical method tended to obscure the real meaning of the biblical text. Only a few theologians insisted that the literal sense of scriptures be given priority. In any event, influenced by humanists like Erasmus, Luther, as a part of his own quest for certainty of salvation, examined the Bible wanting to know what it really meant. Like Erasmus, he asked what the scriptures meant to those who read them in the days when they were written and what continuing meaning did they have for people in his day?

It was while a young university professor that he discovered that righteousness before God is not what the sinner achieves but what the sinner receives as a free gift from God. The promise that salvation was no longer the goal of life but the foundation of life freed him from preoccupation with his own spiritual miseries and readied him for life in the real world. Luther reversed the medieval piety of achievement: from good works make the sinner acceptable to God, to God's acceptance of the sinner prompts good works. Thus, it was as a university professor that Luther experienced what is commonly known as his evangelical conversion, one in which he placed his faith in Christ for his personal salvation and spiritual peace.

His own account of his fourth *Anfectung* is revealing. It is usually referred to as his "tower experience" because he once stated that it happened in his study in the tower of the Augustinian Monastery in Wittenberg as he invested huge quantities of intellectual sweat in an attempt to understand what it was that St. Paul meant by the phrase "the righteousness of God" and "justification by faith" in the New Testament Book of Romans. Luther described the impact of his discovery as opening to him a new understanding of the entire Bible:

> My situation was that, although an impeccable monk, I stood before God as a sinner troubled in conscience, and I had no confidence that my merit would satisfy him. Therefore I did not love a just and angry God, but rather hated and murmured against him. Yet I clung to the dear Paul and had a great yearning to know what he meant.... Night and day I pondered until I saw the connection between the justice of God and the statement that "the just shall live by his faith." Then I grasped that the justice of God is that righteousness by which through grace and sheer mercy God justifies us through faith. I felt myself to be altogether born again and to have gone through the open doors into paradise. The whole of Scripture took on a new meaning, and whereas before the "justice of God" had filled me with hate, now it became to me inexpressibly sweet in great love. This passage of Paul became to me a gate to heaven.[9]

Although Luther would have other bouts of spiritual anxiety in the future, he now believed that he had found the key to spiritual peace. Following his "tower experience," he spoke and wrote of salvation being a matter of *sola fides,* meaning by faith in Christ alone, a phrase that became a watchword of the Protestant Reformation. He also emphasized that this act of faith delivered him from the penalty and power of sin and resulted in a changed life.[10] In this manner, Luther became an "evangelical," a "Gospel person," from the New Testament Greek word *"evangelion,"* meaning "gospel" or "good news."[11]

The Indulgence Controversy

If Luther had kept his experience of grace to himself, there might never have been a Protestant Reformation. Or perhaps his teachings might have been subjected to theological discussion and eventually accepted by the Church, just as many other such teachings had been debated and eventually domesticated into the body of Church doctrine in the Middle Ages. It is certainly true that in the autumn of 1517, few people in Europe had heard of Martin Luther. The main celebrities of the day were Erasmus, Michelangelo, Pope Leo X, King Henry VIII of England (1509–1547), King Francis I of France (1515–1547) and the Holy Roman Emperor Maximilian I (1493–1519). Dr. Martin Luther was an obscure, unpublished professor in a third-rate university in the backwater village of Wittenberg in central Germany. All of this would change thanks to the dramatic events of late 1517 and early 1518.

At about the same time as his evangelical conversion experience, Luther became engaged in a major confrontation with the papal indulgence sellers of the period. This clash would make his name a household word throughout Europe. Luther's personal discovery became a public event with his criticism of indulgence practices by means of his "Ninety-Five Theses." Like numerous Medieval Church teachings, the practice of granting indulgences (from the Latin *indulgeo,* meaning "to grant") developed over a period of time and then degenerated into a spiritual farce. Originally a congregational event, the power to impose private penance was gradually taken over by bishops and popes, and made into a church-wide teaching during the time of the Crusades.

Indulgences are based on the concepts of "the treasury of excessive merit of the saints," purgatory, and papal power that could make the treasury of merit available to ordinary sinners. According to the Medieval Church, a practicing Christian might escape hell but purgatory, a place of temporary abode, awaited those who still needed to be purged of their unconfessed and/or overlooked sins in order to settle their spiritual accounts and make them fit to stand in the presence of a Holy God. Hell was where spiritual punishment for sin takes place and was permanent. Purgatory was where temporal (a temporary, but indeterminate time-based) punishment for sin takes place. The medieval papacy assumed the power of remitting the temporal punishment for sins after the guilt had been forgiven on the basis of sincere repentance and by application of the merits of Christ, Mary and the saints.

Eventually time off from purgatory was promised to crusaders, pilgrims and donors to the Church. In 1476, the papal bull *Salvator noster* extended the remission of temporal punishment in purgatory to include both the living and the dead. For many, purgatory became a sort of "debtors' prison," and an indulgence was a pardon. Whatever the case, in all of this, a formula was to be followed: contrition, confession, and then contribution. It proved to be a lucrative source of income. Unfortunately, by the sixteenth century, the income was all that mattered. Contrition and confession were usually quickly passed over or neglected altogether in order to get to the contribution.

By Luther's time, most indulgence selling had become routine huckstering. In 1515, Pope Leo X issued a plenary indulgence and collaborated with various bishops and archbishops in order to finance various church schemes and relieve personal debt. Among others, the pope made arrangements for the preaching of this particular indulgence in the lands of Albrecht of Hohenzollern,[12] who was the Archbishop of Mainz. The two churchmen agreed to split the proceeds between themselves. The sale was carefully organized. The archbishop chose Johann Tetzel, a Dominican monk who was one of the most effective indulgence hawkers of the day, to lead the effort in his own territories. Tetzel entered towns with fanfares of trumpets and drums and the flag and symbols of the papacy. He preached to large crowds, stretching the doctrine of indulgences to the limit and beyond as he offered direct access to heaven for both the living and for the dead in purgatory. He also used Madison Avenue–like jingles in his preaching, such as: "As soon as the coin in the coffer rings, the soul from purgatory springs." According to some reports, Tetzel's extravagant claims for the power of an indulgence included remission of sin even if one had raped the Virgin Mary. Another claim, according to popular lore, backfired on Tetzel, much to his dismay. A knight apparently bought an indulgence on the understanding that it covered future sins and then robbed Tetzel.[13]

Luther Invents E-Nail

In any event, Tetzel never took his traveling indulgence road show to Luther's parish because Frederick, Elector of Saxony (1486–1525), prohibited him from entering his lands, which included

Wittenberg. However, Tetzel was just over the border, and some of Luther's parishioners went to hear him. When they returned with indulgence scripts in hand, they expected to receive absolution without any show of contrition or commitment to a change in their way of living. This enraged Luther and led him to draft his "Ninety-Five Theses," a document that not only attacked indulgences but also the entire papal penitential system, including papal authority.

On the evening of 31 October 1517, Luther, according to the custom of the day, nailed his theses on the Castle Church door in Wittenberg in order to invite theological debate on their propositions. However, this is not what really ignited the uproar over papal and ultimately Church authority in Christendom. The theses were written in Latin, the official theological language of the period, and most Wittenbergers could not even read German.[14] What ignited the ensuing controversy was not the act of nailing a theological treatise to a church door but two other developments related to this act.

Luther's E-Nail (Ecclesiastical Nail) touched off an uproar first as a copy of the theses was sent to Tetzel's superior, Archbishop Albrecht,[15] and then as the document was translated into German, printed and circulated throughout the empire. Much like modern e-mail, once the process of the distribution of Luther's attack on papal authority began, it surged throughout the German-speaking world and beyond. Through Albrecht, news of Luther's document reached Rome. Through the recently invented medium of printing, word of his defiance of the papacy reached first the literate public and then the masses. Luther almost immediately became a German hero because he had unknowingly touched the nerve of far-reaching political and ecclesiastical discontent. Luther's E-Nail soon, at least in the eyes of the papacy, became like an electronic virus of the sixteenth century.

In any case, Luther's theses were different from all such documents calling for theological debate that had preceded him in the centuries before. First, they were forged in anger and, like many such angry documents written by intelligent people, were eloquent, bold, crisp, forceful and persuasive. Theological debate in the Middle Ages was an intimate affair that took place among scholars. The language was scholarly and restrained and understood by few outside of academic circles. Luther's theses stood in stark contrast with the traditional approach. Second, they had wide appeal. They were stated with clarity and could be understood in part by almost everybody who read or heard them. Third, the complaints contained therein were legitimate. Luther verbalized what many within the Church believed, learned and unlearned, and what they spoke behind closed doors concerning the increasingly corrupt business of forgiving peoples' sins for money. Luther now articulated the accumulated complaints of decades. Fourth, the availability of the new printing trade made it possible to publish the theses in large quantities for widespread circulation. Luther's words were magnified by the printing press, thus making the Reformation the first mass-media event in history. The printing press—Luther called it "God's last and greatest gift"—launched Luther onto the international stage and sent him down the road to Reformation. The sum total of these four factors made Luther's clarion call for reform different from anything like it before in Western religious history.

It was at this point that Luther's newly formed evangelical theology gained traction. Because of his recovery of St. Paul's teaching of salvation by faith in Christ, Luther had not only secured a sense of certainty concerning his personal salvation but also established himself in a strong ideological position as he looked to the future. Two things now confronted him: First, there was the extraordinarily difficult conflict with the established ecclesiastical system and its head, which he increasingly called into question; and, second, there was the development and application of his new theological understanding in theory and practice, a task undreamed of in magnitude and scope in 1517 and impossible to predict.

The "Wild Boar in God's Vineyard"

Events accelerated rapidly as the establishment attempted to silence Luther. The papacy responded not by looking into Luther's charges concerning the abuse of indulgences but by attempting to silence him so that the fire he had lit would not become a conflagration. A series of theological debates and papal interventions followed that widened rather than narrowed the gap between Luther and the Church of Rome. In 1520, Luther unleashed a flurry of radical tracts in which he called for the German nobility to reform the Church because the clergy had become indifferent to this need, attacked the entire medieval sacramental system, and outlined the doctrine of justification and its implications for Christian living. By the end of 1520, it was clear that Luther had broken with the Church. It is, therefore, not surprising that a papal bull of excommunication was issued that year. On 15 June 1520, the lines were drawn with these papal words:

> Arise, O Lord, and judge thy cause. A wild boar has invaded thy vineyard.... We can scarcely express our grief over the ancient

Tensions between Luther and other reformers escalated during the Peasants' War (1524–1525) as the radical millenarian Thomas Müntzer joined the last phase of the conflict with the rallying cry that "the godless have no right to live." The extremely volatile mix of late medieval apocalyptic fervor and oppressive social and economic conditions coupled with the Reformation motif of "the freedom of the Christian" and Luther's critiques of papal authority, fueled the peasants' social and religious expectations for political and economic liberation. It all badly misfired at their disastrous defeat at Frankenhausen in 1525. As for Luther, after first siding with the peasants' grievances, he then turned against them as they demonstrated their growing disregard for law and order. Consequently, many German peasants deserted Luther and found support and comfort among various Anabaptist groups.

Despite the negative impact of the peasants' uprising of the mid-1520s, the Lutheran Reformation continued to spread. Wittenberg became a center of missionary activity as students studying at the university returned to their homes, carrying with them Luther's ideas. During the 1520s almost all of northern Germany became Protestant. From there Lutheran preachers spread the message to the Scandinavian countries, where rulers converted and nations followed, the process being completed by the 1540s. Iceland, Lithuania and Estonia also became Lutheran during this period. Lutheran state churches appeared in all of the foregoing areas, thus linking religion and politics and compromising Reformation spirituality. In the beginning, faith was the primary consideration. However, as time passed, heartfelt faith and nominal adherence stood side by side and made politics and religion in those areas complicated matters. Furthermore, before Luther's death in 1546, his ideas appeared in nearly all other European countries and caused considerable commotion. Few areas were left untouched.

The Emperor Charles V's military preoccupations with France (the Habsburg-Valois Wars, 1521–1559) and the invasion of Eastern Europe by the Ottoman Turks continually frustrated his efforts to eliminate the Reformation movements in his realm apart from his hereditary lands, the Low Countries. Charles also needed the support of the growing numbers of German Protestant princes in his military campaigns. The Protestant princes presented a confession of their faith to the emperor at the Diet of Augsburg in 1530. Composed by Melanchthon, the Augsburg Confession did not sway the Catholic emperor to rescind the Edict of Worms, but it did become the foundational document for Lutheran churches up to the present.

The rejection of the Augsburg Confession led the Protestant princes to form a defensive military alliance, the Schmalkald League,

heresies which have been revived in Germany.... As for Martin himself, good God, what office of paternal love have we omitted in order to recall him from his errors? ... Now therefore we give Martin Luther sixty days in which to submit, dating from the time of the publication of this bull in his district. Anyone who presumes to infringe our excommunication and anathema will stand under the wrath of Almighty God and the apostles Peter and Paul.[16]

Angry mobs that resented a German hero being condemned by Rome often resisted those who tried to distribute the bull in Germany. Then, on 10 December 1517, at Wittenberg, Luther, shaking with emotion, threw a copy of the papal decree into a bonfire. When news of this dramatic act of defiance reached Rome, the pope excommunicated Luther and urged the young, newly elected Holy Roman Emperor Charles V to issue a mandate against him. However, the German constitution and Charles' coronation oath upheld the right of Germans to a trial by impartial judges. Thus, Luther was promised safe conduct to a hearing at the Diet of Worms in southwestern Germany in April 1521. The Diet, a consultative assembly of imperial electors, German princes and representatives of the various imperial free cities, met periodically to render advice and consent to the emperor in the governance of his empire.

Luther arrived in Worms on 16 April, a world away from his monastic cell and classroom. Moreover, instead of a hearing, the ecclesiastical authorities presented him with a stack of his writings and asked him to recant their errors. His brief answer that he could not go against his conscience unless convinced by scripture and clear reason included the memorable words: "Here I stand, I cannot do otherwise. God help me. Amen."[17] The die was cast. The end result of this confrontation was the Edict of Worms, issued by Charles V on 26 May 1521, after Luther had departed from the city. The edict declared Luther to be a heretic and an outlaw, both capital crimes, and authorized his seizure and delivery to imperial authorities. Fortunately for Luther, he had powerful supporters, including his own prince, the Elector of Saxony, known among Lutherans as Frederick the Wise. The Elector sequestered Luther in the Wartburg, one of his castles, for safekeeping. During the six months of what some called his "castle arrest," Luther translated the New Testament into German.

Pigtails on the Pillow

Luther returned to Wittenberg in 1522, in order to restore peace after an outbreak of radical iconoclastic behavior accompanied by violence. After taking care of this matter, he settled down to defend his reformation and to deal with problems associated with his challenge to established authority. As he did so, his previously busy life became even more frantic. The order that he restored to his city was not reflected in his own personal existence—that is, until he met Katie.[18]

In 1525, Luther married an ex-nun named Katharina von Bora, who had fled the Wittenberg convent in 1523 with 11 others. All the others had married or left Wittenberg, except for Katharina who stubbornly refused to marry a man Luther had suggested. However, she volunteered to marry Luther or one of his colleagues, Nikolaus von Amsdorf. Katharina's dogged determination paid off, and she and Luther were married on 13 June 1525. Luther was 42 years old and Katharina 26. After a slow start, affection grew and Katie, as he came affectionately to call her, turned out to be the perfect partner and companion. She was strong in areas where Luther was weak. Luther was never any good with money. He thought money was for spending, and his income was limited because he refused to accept any payment for his preaching or his publications, which could have earned him a great deal. Katie had to find ways to bridge the gap between earnings and expenditure. She did this by running a farm, gardening, breeding pigs, brewing beer, and taking in lodgers. In 1532, the Elector of Saxony gave Luther the Augustinian monastery together with its lands. It was a three-story building with 40 rooms on the ground floor alone, so the Luthers had plenty of room for children, students and guests, and the house was always filled with chattering, eating people. Moreover, Luther had a habit of bringing home his students and other guests for dinner, often without first consulting Katie. She put up with it all, and more. After these meals, the students often took notes while Luther reminisced and told stories, resulting in the famous "Table Talks" that disclose so much of Luther and his home life. They also reveal that Katie took part in these discussions as an equal, and that she gave as good as she got.[19]

Marriage brought many changes to Luther's way of living. As he himself observed, "Before I was married the bed was not made for a whole year and became foul with sweat. But I worked so hard and was so weary I tumbled in without noticing it." Katie put an end to that lifestyle. There were other adjustments for the middle-aged former monk as well. Luther later noted, "There is a lot to get used to in the first year of marriage. One wakes up in the morning and finds a pair of pigtails on the pillow which were not there before."[20] And Luther liked it. The couple had six children, three boys and three girls. They also adopted 10 or 11 other children and raised them as

their own. Luther loved his children dearly and was a good father to them despite his busy life. He named his first son Hans, after his father. When Magdalena, his second daughter, died in his arms in 1543 at age 14, Luther could hardly bear the grief. It remained with him the rest of his life. As he laid her away, he said, "You dear little Lena, you will rise and shine like the stars and the sun. How strange it is to know that she is at peace and all is well, and yet to be so sorrowful."[21]

In some ways, Luther married to prove that he practiced what he preached—that not allowing priests to marry was a medieval invention, and that marriage was a positive good and to be praised rather than denigrated, as was often the case in the Middle Ages. In so doing, he established a model that nearly all Protestants after him followed. Luther's marriage was in many ways patriarchal by modern standards. However, it was also about companionship, and Katie ran the home and always had a major voice in Luther's life and ministry. This determined the tone of Protestant domestic relations for the next 400 years and is still important today. It created a new avenue for Protestant women to exercise societal influence in the role of the pastor's wife, one that is still not fully appreciated. Moreover, Luther not only included the pastor's wife when he wrote about a sense of "calling," but also expanded this important category to include lay vocations, like teaching, as well.

Why Luther Succeeded: Politics, Printers, Propaganda and Prayer

By the mid-1520s, the early stages of the Lutheran Reformation were over. The next period would witness the spread and consolidation of the Reformation in Germany and the appearance of other reform movements. Over the course of time, Luther gradually changed from reformer to revolutionary. The response to his initial call for reform played a major role in that change as developments at the margins, as in all great mass movements, began to affect the center. Also, politics soon intruded into the process as various territorial rulers opted for the new reform movement or chose to defend the old establishment. The very name "Protestant" itself was a result of the stout "protests" of Luther's political defenders against attempts by the Emperor to coerce Luther back into the Roman fold. As for Luther, Philip Melanchthon's assessment in his Luther biography was undoubtedly correct. He had not intended to start a revolution yet "little by little he was dragged into other subjects."[22]

designed to protect the Protestant movement. It proved viable until its defeat by imperial forces in 1547. However, by that time, the evangelicals had gained sufficient strength that Charles V had no other recourse but to grant official toleration within the empire by the Peace of Augsburg, 1555. This treaty established the principle that the religion of the ruler would be the religion of the territory, effectively making all of Germany outside of Bavaria and Austria officially Protestant. However, the settlement applied only to Catholics and Lutherans and made no provision for other expressions of Protestantism, a condition that made life in Germany more complicated when Calvinism became the official faith of several German principalities in the years following 1555.

Lutheran success was largely achieved by a wave of propaganda heretofore unequaled in the Western world. The primary tools were the religious tract and the woodcut cartoon. The sheer volume of the propaganda effort warrants calling the German Reformation the West's first mass-media campaign. In the early years of the Reformation movement, 1518–1525, the output of pamphlets skyrocketed, increasing 40-fold over previous production figures. By church historian Mark Edwards' calculation, a little over 6 million printed pamphlets appeared in Germany during Luther's lifetime, mostly by Protestants in favor of their cause. This means that there was approximately one exemplar for every two people in the empire. Luther was the most productive Protestant publicist of them all as he issued scores of books and tracts that both promoted his New Testament theology and attacked his opponents, especially the Roman Catholic Church, Anabaptist radicals, and Jews who refused the Gospel. The German Protestants had quickly sensed the value of the new printing technology in the spread of their ideas and turned it to good use to further their interests. In so doing, they demonstrated that the pen was mightier than the pope![23]

Moreover, a cursory glance at the content of the religious cartoons of the period is revealing alike for the methods and the selection of themes for popular dissemination. The external abuses of the Roman Church were easy to lampoon. The familiar theme of the contrast between Christ and the pope was exploited with great skill. Monasticism, images, relics and magic were heartily mocked. Lucas Cranach the Elder and Albrecht Dürer, two great woodcut artists and early Lutheran sympathizers, contributed their expertise to this propaganda war, thus assuring a high-quality Protestant product. Poetry and music also became weapons. Hans Sachs, the shoemaker poet of Nuremberg, for example, composed the popular pro-Luther poem "The Wittenberg Nightingale." Further, Luther himself wrote many hymns including "A Mighty Fortress," that became a kind of anthem of Protestantism. Before Luther's death a large number of hymns were available in a series of different editions for every occasion, and the Lutheran Church soon acquired a reputation as a "singing church." Luther also supplied his church with a liturgy that encouraged prayer. Thus, attractive ideas, well-written pamphlets, shrewd exploitation of the new printing technology, the use of the literary arts and, good Lutherans would say, prayer all contributed to the success and spread of the Lutheran Reformation.[24]

The Effects of the Lutheran Reform

Luther's last years were marked by bouts of depression and increasing physical ailments. During the last decade of his life he suffered from attacks of dizziness, a running sore on his leg that never healed, kidney stones, gout, constipation and hemorrhoids. These problems combined with the pressure of overwork, endless controversy and constant personal attacks made him a grumpy old man. He died in February 1546, after mediating a quarrel between two of his feuding noble followers. Katie followed him four years later, dying with words that would have made Luther happy: "I will cleave to the Lord Christ as a burr to the cloth."[25]

Luther and his movement have been blamed for much and given credit for much. Both views contain merit. The impact of Luther and the Lutheran Reformation on European life was enormous. Luther dominated his age as few others have done, but at the same time there was an unaffected naturalism about him. Open and frank to a fault, he was always himself and displayed his innermost sentiments for all to see.

To Protestants, he became the consummate hero, the man who formulated basic evangelical theology for the churches from that day forward. First, his view of salvation through grace by faith in Christ became foundational to Protestant theology. Second, his substitution of the authority of the Bible for the authority of the Church also permeated all of Protestantism from that day forward. Third, his teaching of the priesthood of the believer, by which he eliminated the priest as middleman between the believer and God, became fundamental to all Protestant thinking. Fourth, he replaced the Seven Sacraments of the Medieval Church with the two that he believed had New Testament foundations: baptism and Holy Communion. Moreover, for Lutherans and for Protestants in general Luther remained a great hero whom God used for the liberation of his church from papal oppression.[26]

To the Church of Rome, Luther continued to be a "wild boar in God's vineyard" until the mid-twentieth century when Vatican Council II invited a second look at the German Reformer, which finally tempered Catholic views. Nineteenth- and twentieth-century German nationalists found Luther useful as they portrayed him as "the Eternal German" or a German Wundermann. Luther's Magisterial Protestantism, meaning one that embraced the state as a partner in religious reform, suited many modern leaders who supported such a view, and his doctrine of Law and Gospel encouraged conservative politics. Some historians believe that his sharp distinction between the venues of state (Law) and church (Gospel) helped inspire the development of a conservative monarchy in Germany, perhaps even twentieth-century German fascism. In Luther's view, if the magistrate were a Christian, then church and state could cooperate for the good of both. If the magistrate were not a Christian, then church and state should be separate and operate in their respective spheres. In any event, like many before him, Luther extended the command to honor father and mother to include reverence for all in authority, such as bishops, teachers and magistrates.

In society, Luther established a new emphasis on marriage as primarily a means of companionship that modeled godly living. In economics, Luther was a conservative and sided with the agrarian elements in society against the growing power of the capitalists, somewhat ironic in light of his own father's acquisitiveness and thirst for upward mobility. In education, on the other hand, he was a progressive as he embraced the historic Protestant drive for an educated clergy and laity in order that all could read the Bible for themselves. In so doing, Luther urged compulsory universal education for both girls and boys. Science also flourished under Lutheran auspices.

Luther even became a film celebrity of sorts as the modern motion picture industry produced several quality Luther films, the latest of which in 2003 became something of a box office hit.[27] However, even the best of these films could not capture the real Luther whom historian Geoffrey Elton described as often "furious, violent, foul-mouthed, passionately concerned."[28]

In the end, Luther's greatest contribution to modern history was his challenge to the dominant authority of the Medieval Church of his day. As he did, he not only shattered the theological and cultural unity of Western Christendom but also opened the door to the further questioning of societal authority in the following centuries. This largely unintended challenge to established authority and its results is the main theme of the Lutheran Reformation. This challenge, in turn, encouraged freedom and made the world a far more dangerous place in which to live. Things would never be the same again. Moreover, ironically, in the long term this development also strengthened Christianity by emphasizing that true faith could only flow from freely made decisions to embrace and follow Jesus Christ. This, in turn, struck a blow at the nominalism (being a Christian in name only) that for so long had plagued the Church, which in turn helped elevate the quality of religion in Western society.

Only a man who hungered for certainty and who wrote so much with such great passion could produce so many different results and interpretations of his work. There is a great deal of Luther from which to pick and choose, if one wishes to do so. However, there can be no doubt that he deeply impacted his own world as well as posterity. One of those upon whom he left his mark was the leader of second-generation Protestantism, John Calvin, whose movement is the subject of the next chapter.

Notes

1. Martin Marty, *Martin Luther* (New York: Viking, 2004), 1–51; and Lewis W. Spitz, *The Renaissance and Reformation Movements*, rev. ed., 2 vols. (St. Louis, MO: Concordia Publishing House, 1987), 1:355.

2. Almost everything known about Luther can be found in Martin Brecht, *Martin Luther*, trans. James L. Schaaf, 3 vols. (Philadelphia: Fortress Press, 1981–1993). Roland H. Bainton's *Here I Stand: A Life of Martin Luther* (Nashville, TN: Abingdon Press, 1950) is a nicely written introductory biography of Luther and still a good place to begin a study of the German Reformer and the Reformation. Also see Brecht's one-volume life of Luther: *Martin Luther: Theology and Revolution*, trans. Claude R. Foster, Jr. (New York: Oxford University Press, 1991).

3. The best of several psychoanalytical interpretations of young Luther is Erik H. Erikson, *Young Man Luther* (New York: Norton, 1962). John Osborne followed Erikson's lead and wrote one of his best-known "angry young man" plays, "Luther," that PBS-TV has telecast frequently in the USA. See Osborne's "Luther: A Play" (London: Faber, 1971). Most historians have questioned Erikson's methodology as well as his interpretation. For example, see Roland H. Bainton, "Psychiatry and History: An Examination of Erikson's *Young Man Luther*," *Religion in Life*, 40 (1971):450–478.

4. Bainton, *Here I Stand*, 42; and Brecht, *Martin Luther*, 1:76–80.

5. Bainton, *Here I Stand*, 34.

6. These *Anfectungen* are sketched in Bainton, *Here I Stand*, 34–67; and laid out in detail in Brecht, *Martin Luther*, 1:76–237.

7. There are differences among Luther scholars concerning when Luther made what he regarded as his rediscovery of St. Paul's teaching concerning salvation by faith in Christ and experienced evangelical conversion. Bainton, for example, places it sometime in 1515–1517. *Here I Stand*, 60–67. Here I follow Brecht, *Martin Luther*, 1:221–237.

8. The ThD was the most prestigious doctorate of the day.

9. Martin Luther, *Luther's Works*, trans. and eds. Jaroslav Pelikan and H. T. Lehmann, 55 vols. (St. Louis, MO: Concordia, 1955–1975), 34:336–337. Hereafter cited as LW.

10. Most Reformation Protestants understood Luther's conclusion to be a recovery of the New Testament teaching of faith in Christ alone as the Way of salvation. They also believed that, like Luther, it came at a moment of spiritual enlightenment through biblical understanding, and, therefore, was "an experience" of some sort. For a somewhat different but complementary view, see Martin E. Marty, "Luther: The Daily Gift of New Life," *Christian History and Biography*, Issue 86 (Spring 2005):50.

11. Luther, Calvin and most of the other first Protestants never referred to themselves as Lutherans, Calvinists or similar terms but simply as evangelicals or reformers.

12. Albrecht was the brother of the Elector Joachim of Brandenburg, each man a member of the increasingly powerful Hohenzollern family that in the nineteenth century became the Kaisers of a united Germany.

13. Bainton, *Here I Stand*, 74–79.

14. Some historians dispute the fact that Luther actually nailed his "Ninety-Five Theses" to the church door at Wittenberg because Philip Melanchthon, Luther's younger friend and theological confidant, only verified it many years after the event. However, there seems no reason to doubt the tradition that affirms the act, even though Luther most likely posted the document after he sent a copy to Archbishop Albrecht. Brecht believes that the theses were actually posted but in mid-November rather than on the traditional date. Brecht, *Martin Luther*, 1:201.

15. Perhaps Luther naively assumed that Albrecht did not know that his hireling Tetzel was abusing the authority of the Church. If so, he would not be the first or last university professor to make such a mistake.

16. Denis R. Janz, ed., *A Reformation Reader* (Minneapolis: Augsburg Fortress Press, 1999), 327–329; and Bainton, *Here I Stand*, 147.

17. LW, 7:838; and Bainton, *Here I Stand*, 185.

18. Kirsi Stjerna, "Katie Luther: A Mirror to the Promises and Failures of the Reformation," in David Whitford, ed., *Caritas et Reformatio: Essays on Church and Society in Honor of Carter Lindberg* (St. Louis, MO: Concordia Publishing House, 2002), 27–39.

19. LW, 50:47–50; and 54:145, 153, 174–175, 270, 317, 384 and 396.

20. Ibid., 54:191.

21. Ibid., 54:432.

22. Philip Melanchthon, *The Life and Acts of Martin Luther* (London: Unwin, 1845), 6.

23. Mark U. Edwards, *Printing, Propaganda, and Martin Luther* (Berkeley: University of California Press, 1994), 14–28.

24. Bainton, *Here I Stand*, 305–310, and 340–347.

25. E. G. Schwiebert, *Luther and His Times* (St. Louis, MO: Concordia, 1950), 844–845.

26. Robert Kolb, *Martin Luther as Prophet, Teacher and Hero: Images of the Reformer, 1520–1620* (Grand Rapids, MI: Baker Books, 1999).

27. "Luther," the latest of several commercial and quasi-commercial films made about the German Reformer in the last one hundred years, received good reviews and did reasonably well at the box office during its 2003 release. The film starred Joseph Fiennes as Luther.

28. G. R. Elton, "Commemorating Luther," *Journal of Ecclesiastical History*, 35, no. 4 (October 1984):619.

CHAPTER 3

JOHN CALVIN AND SECOND-GENERATION PROTESTANTISM

John Calvin is undoubtedly the most misunderstood of the sixteenth-century reformers. He was one of those major figures of history whose prolific writings and strong theological views caused many people either to love or hate him. Nevertheless, the ghost of this frail Frenchman still haunts the classrooms and corridors of the universities of the world. His influence, particularly on the ideas of the Western world, has been enormous.[1] Like Luther, Calvin passionately endeavored to serve God as he attempted to establish a just society based on the Bible, especially in Geneva. Moreover, the movement that he founded became international in nature and has endured to the present day.

Luther to Zwingli to Calvin

However, before Calvin ever saw Geneva, the Reformation came to the Swiss canton of Zurich thanks to the efforts of a learned city priest named Ulrich Zwingli. In the spread of the Protestant Reformation, Zwingli became the middleman between Luther and Calvin. But first, the great Erasmus, as Zwingli's role model, had a hand in the Swiss reformer's intellectual and spiritual formation that, in turn, played a role in determining the nature of the Reformation in German-speaking Switzerland.[2]

At about the same time Luther was unleashing his attack on the authority of the Medieval Church in Germany, Zwingli began a similar but independent reform movement in Switzerland. Born on 1 January 1484, and like Luther the son of an ambitious and upwardly mobile peasant, Zwingli attended several universities where he studied the works of Erasmus and other humanists before his ordination to the priesthood in 1506. Urbane, well-educated, a skilled musician, popular with the women, Zwingli observed first-hand many of the corrupt practices of his day including simony (the buying and selling of church offices), the abuse of indulgences and the sexual temptations of the priesthood. He became an eloquent preacher and a noted scholar-pastor, eventually attracting the attention of his superiors who nominated him as chief pastor of the Great Minster in Zurich. He preached his first sermon there on his 35th birthday, New Years' Day, 1519, and announced that he would begin a series of expository sermons on Matthew's Gospel the next Sunday. Thus, he abandoned the Church's lectionary and immediately revealed his commitment to the Reformation principle of *sola scriptura*. By 1525, through persuasion and after a series of officially sanctioned debates between Protestants and Catholics, the Zurich City Council declared the canton's state church "reformed."

However, Zwingli did not escape controversy as Zurich Anabaptists on the left challenged him for maintaining a state church and not carrying reforms far enough, and by regional Catholics on the right for abandoning Church authority and replacing it with the Bible. Most important, a summit meeting at Marburg between Luther and Zwingli in 1529 aimed at uniting the two Protestant movements failed. At the Marburg Colloquy, the Lutherans and Zwinglians agreed on 14 of 15 articles of faith but stumbled over the meaning of the Eucharist. They repudiated the Roman Catholic doctrine of transubstantiation and they insisted that the laity be given both the cup and the wafer in communion. However, the two evangelical parties remained apart on whether the Lord's Supper was primarily a memorial of Jesus' death (Zwingli's belief) or a sacrament offering the recipient Christ's real presence in the elements (Luther's view). These differing theologies of the Eucharist continued to divide Protestants in spite of Calvin's later ecumenical efforts to heal the breach. Moreover, even though this difference seems trivial to most modern Christians, it was of great importance to early Protestants in whom had been instilled the awe and importance of the Mass in Christian life and worship. In any event, Calvin and Zwingli's successors in Zurich reached agreement on the Lord's Supper and Calvinism eventually absorbed the Zwinglian Reformation.[3]

In the meantime, unable to achieve imperial recognition at the Diet of Augsburg in 1530, the Zwinglian Reformation was vulnerable to Catholic pressures. In response to Protestant evangelism in the eastern Swiss cantons, civil war ensued. In 1531, at the Second Battle of Kappel, a Catholic army routed Zurich forces and killed Zwingli who participated as a battlefield chaplain. The consequent political resolution that divided Switzerland by confessional allegiance fore-shadowed the fate of Europe.

Calvin's Life: A God-Frustrated Scholar

At the time of Zwingli's death, neither Calvin nor Geneva had yet adopted the Reformation. Calvin was born Jean Cauvin in the Kingdom of France, in Noyon in Picardy on 10 July 1509.[4] Interest-ingly, he became known in the English-speaking world not by his birth name but by a version of his Latinized surname and the Eng-lish equivalent of his given name: John Calvin. Twenty-six years younger than Luther, he was only eight years old when the German reformer published his "Ninety-Five Theses." Therefore, Calvin was very much a second-generation reformer. Although Luther and Cal-vin never met and their personalities were significantly different, the two men seemed to have admired each other. Calvin was sometimes critical of Luther's extreme language, nevertheless he regularly defended the German reformer against his detractors. On the one hand, Calvin considered himself a follower of Luther and not the founder of a rival movement. On the other, he clearly did not con-sider Luther's theology as the final word.[5]

Calvin, like Luther, came from an upwardly mobile family and his ambitious father, Gérard Cauvin, looked for ways to advance his family's fortunes beyond those of his own. At the time of Calvin's birth, his father was the bishop's notary and a leading citizen of Noyon. He wanted his bright son some day to be part of the Church hierarchy. Therefore, when John was 11, his father obtained a Church benefice for him, which provided him with income for fur-ther study at the University of Paris where he could train for an ec-clesiastical career. Young Calvin had completed the arts course, in which he became proficient in Latin and philosophy, when the direc-tion of his studies changed. In contrast to Luther who moved from the study of law into the study of theology, Calvin was about to embark upon the serious study of theology when his father had a quarrel with the cathedral chapter of Noyon and directed his son to leave theology to pursue a law degree, a growing source of wealth in the period.

Therefore, in 1527, the dutiful son moved to the University of Orléans, one of the great centers for the study of civil law, and two years later to the University of Bourges. When his father died in May

1531, Calvin quickly completed his legal studies and returned to the University of Paris to pursue his first love: humanist literature. Moving in humanist circles, he developed great respect for Erasmus and the leading French Christian humanist Jacques Lefèvre d'Étaples, and published his first book in 1532, a humanist commentary on Seneca's *De Clementia.* The Christian humanists called his attention to the need for reform and directed him to some pamphlets by a German reformer named Martin Luther.

It was during this period, probably in 1533–1534, that Calvin experienced in an evangelical sense what he called a "sudden conversion."[6] Trained in law and imbued with humanist learning, Calvin now echoed Luther's understanding of personal salvation through faith in Christ and not by works. Later, in his landmark tome, *The Institutes of the Christian Religion,* Calvin described justification by faith in terms of God's acquittal of the guilty sinner.[7]

Now convinced that God had a different plan for his life, Calvin was caught up in spreading the Gospel in and around Paris as he became openly identified with French reformers. He had to flee Paris in late 1533, as a reaction set in against those calling for change in the Old Church. He became a religious refugee, wandering first through interior France and finally to Strasbourg, where he paused for a time. In the autumn of 1534, he moved to Basel, and there, two years later, published the first edition of his *Institutes,* prefaced by a moving appeal to the French King Francis I for a fair hearing for the evangelical faith.[8]

Further travels took him to Geneva, from whence he hoped to return to Strasbourg to pursue his scholarly studies and to write further in defense of the evangelical faith. It was there in July 1536, when his intimate relationship with the city-state on the shores of Lake Geneva began. Guillaume Farel and Pierre Viret had been preaching reformed doctrines in Geneva off and on since 1532. Only months before Calvin's arrival, the Genevans, with the aid of their Protestant neighbor Bern, had achieved independence from the Duchy of Savoy. The citizens then voted to embrace the Reformation and to expel all clergy who disagreed. With the city in an uproar and faced with the task of institutionalizing reform in Geneva, Farel insisted that God wanted Calvin to remain in Geneva to help with this work. Calvin protested that he was but a shy scholar and only wanted to be left alone to pursue his writing on behalf of the Reformation. However, when Farel passionately announced to Calvin that to shirk this duty would incur God's wrath, Calvin stayed.[9]

The emphasis of Calvin and Farel on church discipline soon alienated the Geneva Council and many of the city's leading citizens.

Exiled in 1538, Calvin eventually returned to Strasbourg and began again to pursue scholarly interests. During this period, Calvin married. Since he had never been ordained and never would be, there was no need for a second thought, except that he declared that his bride should be a help and not a hindrance to his ministry. Always seemingly afflicted with some ailment, he also wanted somebody who could aid in maintaining his health. Idelette de Bure, a widow with two children, was a member of Calvin's congregation. In 1540, Martin Bucer, Strasbourg's main reformer, suggested that Calvin consider her. They married in August 1540, and she became, as Calvin put it, "the best companion of my life." Their only child died shortly after birth. After nine years of marriage, Calvin also lost his spouse, who died at age 40. Calvin was devastated, never recovered and never remarried. In later life some of Calvin's enemies in Geneva tormented him over the fact that he had no living offspring, to which he responded that nevertheless he had many spiritual children in God.[10]

The Elect Take Office

Calvin spent most of his married life in Geneva because in September 1541 he reluctantly left his happy life of productive scholarship and ministry in Strasbourg to return to Geneva. Geneva lurched dangerously close to ecclesiastical anarchy during Calvin's three years in Strasbourg. The City Fathers, eager to establish an orderly reformation, invited Calvin to return as chief pastor of the Genevan Church. Calvin reluctantly agreed to return to the turbulent city, but only after the strenuous intervention of Farel and Viret and only after Geneva agreed to allow him a free hand in reforming the church there. In so doing, Calvin realized that his dream of a tranquil life of scholarship was over. If he pursued his studies in Geneva, which he did, it would always be in the midst of some operational crisis or another and under great stress. As it turned out, his decision to return was a lifetime commitment.

Within six weeks of his return in 1541, Calvin completed and submitted to the magistrates of Geneva his *Ecclesiastical Ordinances*, a blueprint for the reformation of the Church of Geneva. Quickly adopted, the *Ordinances* organized the church along presbyterial lines with four categories of ministry: doctors (teachers), pastors, deacons, and elders. Doctors were responsible for theological instruction; pastors for preaching and the sacraments; lay deacons for social services; and lay elders for maintaining discipline within the church and community. The Venerable Company of Pastors consisted of all of the ministers in Geneva who met weekly as a group, presided over by Calvin, to discuss theology and to maintain their own personal and doctrinal integrity. The institutional organ for church discipline was the Consistory, an ecclesiastical court that included all of Geneva's pastors and elders. The Consistory's main tasks were to resolve disputes among Christians and to supervise public morality. It became a source of controversy during Calvin's time in Geneva because of its power to excommunicate. Excommunication meant exclusion from quarterly communion services, and the ban lifted when the person showed signs of repentance.

Slowly but surely Calvin placed his stamp on the Geneva Republic. Since it was a republic and governed by the votes of its citizens, Calvin always had to work by persuasion and through the elected magistracy. He never held any elective office other than that of an ordinary pastor. His power lay in his preaching skills and the fact that he served as a spiritual advisor to the City Council. His goal was to make Geneva a just and holy commonwealth based on the Bible. However, he understood that this was to be done with the support of the legitimately elected magistrates and within the political framework of the Geneva Republic.

Challenges to Calvin's ecclesiastical and moral authority came from a variety of sources, including the City Council, which resisted Calvin's insistence that the church retain exclusive control over the power of excommunication. Opposition also came from those who resented what they considered meddling in their personal lives, accentuated by two major public controversies in the period 1551–1553. The first was Jerome Bolsec's sharp criticism of Calvin's doctrine of predestination. The charge that the reformers were unclear about a point of scripture was not a narrow theological challenge because Protestantism rested upon popular confidence in its biblical basis. Calvin's response was to reiterate that predestination is an expression of unconditional grace, meaning that God chooses the sinner, not vice versa. Bolsec, therefore, was tried by the City Council for heresy and banished from Geneva.

The second controversy centered on the trial and execution of Michael Servetus for repudiating the doctrine of the Trinity, a capital crime according to Roman Law under which most of Continental Europe operated. Already notorious throughout Europe for his written attacks on the Trinity, Servetus escaped execution in France where he had been condemned by the Catholic Church for heresy, and for some unknown reason headed for Geneva where he had prepared the way for his coming by hostile correspondence with Calvin.

When someone in Geneva recognized him, Servetus was arrested and ordered tried for heresy by the City Council. From a political perspective, the Genevans were in a bind if they did not prosecute Servetus because the city had gained a reputation as a haven for heretics. However, the real motive behind his trial was theological. Calvin gave evidence for the prosecution as a legal expert because he was a trained lawyer. Servetus was convicted and sentenced to death by fire. Calvin's personal pleas for him to recant fell on deaf ears and his request to the Council that he be spared the stake and instead be beheaded was ignored. After a lengthy trial, Servetus was executed outside Geneva on 27 October 1553, the only individual to die for heresy in Calvin's Geneva.[11]

Although modern historians have sometimes stressed the Servetus affair as a sign of tyrannical government, Calvin's Protestant contemporaries did not think so. Thousands of religious refugees poured into Geneva beginning around 1550. They came from nearly every province in France as well as from England, Scotland, the Low Countries, Spain, Germany, Poland, and Bohemia. Most eventually returned home, and when they did, they took Calvinism with them. However, many remained and helped swell the population with Calvin supporters.

Many of the refugees, especially from France, were well-educated professionals who brought with them considerable wealth. Calvin's political strength grew dramatically in the early 1550s when large numbers of these refugees were granted bourgeois status, including the right to vote. The balance of power in Geneva shifted decisively in the February 1554 election when Calvin's supporters won an overwhelming victory. From that time forward, resistance to Calvin's reforms gradually dissipated as his opponents discredited themselves through conspiratorial activities and disobedience to new city legislation regulating the economic, social and moral behavior of inhabitants. A few were executed for treason while most were simply exiled. The Elect had taken office and now controlled the Republic of Geneva to pursue a blueprint for the city's transformation into a just and godly society. Who were these Elect?

The Calvinist Signature: Calvin's Dynamic Theology

It was Calvin's dynamic theology that dictated the life of the Elect in this brave new Protestant world. Eventually, it would transform Geneva into what the Scotsman John Knox, Calvin's disciple and temporary religious refugee in the city, would call "the most perfect school of Christ that ever was in this earth since the days of the apostles."[12] Even as Calvin's scholarly plans were often frustrated by the practical demands of his life as pastor and mentor to a republic, an entire library of works flowed from his indefatigable pen, including several revisions of his opus magus *The Institutes of the Christian Religion.*

Originally a manual for new believers and an explanation of basic Protestant beliefs for outsiders, the *Institutes* eventually was expanded to a fifth and final edition published in Latin in 1559, and a French translation in 1560. By 1559, it had grown into a sophisticated theological work that dealt with some of the most complex doctrines of the faith in significant detail. Thousands of copies in several languages were published in the sixteenth century, and it is still widely reprinted today. The *Institutes* became the most important and widely read theological treatise of the Reformation Era, and is the prime expression of Calvin's ideas.[13]

Like Luther, Calvin replaced the authority of the Roman Church with that of the Bible. Like Luther, he taught that an individual is justified by faith in Christ and not by works. However, unlike Luther, Calvin stressed that the Holy Spirit through the Word of God and at God's initiative induced this faith. This, in turn, led to his doctrine of predestination as he asked why people are saved, in contrast to Luther's emphasis on how humans are saved. In the first edition of his *Institutes* Calvin only mentioned predestination twice, and in so doing stressed how it brought assurance to the people of God. By contrast, the 1559 edition devoted four chapters to this doctrine. The development of this teaching was in part a reaction to the challenge of Bolsec in 1551.

However, predestination was never the center of Calvin's theological system, as it would become for later Calvinists. Calvin believed that it was an ancillary biblical doctrine that explained why some accepted the Gospel and others rejected it. He did not ask why God made his choices because this involved probing the inscrutable judgments of God and that was not the place of mere mortals. Rather, Calvin taught predestination as a pastoral doctrine that was designed to comfort believers because it assured them that their salvation was not dependent on their own efforts. He was also careful not to define the doctrine beyond what he considered the clear teaching of scripture and never tried to place numbers on the Elect. Moreover, he readily conceded that the Elect could be found in all churches including the Roman Church of his day.

Calvin stressed the sovereignty of God, the basic sinfulness of the human race and the need for salvation through faith in Christ.

Based on these common Protestant beliefs, he then probed the question of why God saves humans. He described predestination as "God's eternal decree, by which he compacted with himself what he willed to become of each man."[14] The Elect were those preordained to be saved and the Reprobates were those who earned eternity in hell. The decision rested upon the absolute sovereignty of God and a humanity rendered helpless by its sin. According to Calvin, in the light of human depravity it was amazing that God chose anyone for redemption. It was a God-centered and not a human-centered perspective, one difficult for modern human-centered people to grasp. In Calvin's view, those who placed their faith in Christ were the Elect, and the Elect were those who placed their faith in Christ.

Contrary to the assertions of many modern historians, Calvin did not teach "double predestination." He stressed only the need for the Elect to respond to the Gospel, and freely admitted that only God knew the Elect. Therefore, his pulpit message was similar to that of nearly all Protestant reformers: "Believe in the Lord Jesus Christ and you will be saved."[15] It was later Calvinists who stressed double predestination, often to the point of theological ossification. Also contrary to some modern misconceptions, belief in predestination did not lead to fatalism on the part of Calvinist believers. The Calvinists who embraced the redemptive work of Christ were confident that God had elected them. Moreover, they were certain that they should and would demonstrate their election by godly living. Further, the divine plan, which had compelled many to undergo severe hardships, must also be obeyed in the constant struggle against the forces of evil. They were also confident that in the end the forces of good would triumph over the forces of evil and that they would have a part in that triumph. Thus, their belief in predestination fortified them for the task at hand, which was to struggle mightily against what they regarded as the religious and political tyranny of the age.[16]

Like Luther, Calvin taught that there were two biblical sacraments. However, for Calvin baptism was a covenant between the Lord and parents to raise children in a godly manner until they reached the age when they could make their own decisions for Christ. He also tried to find a middle road between Lutheranism and Zwinglianism concerning the Holy Supper by emphasizing a real spiritual presence in the Eucharist. Further, he believed in a universal invisible church but stressed the local visible church as an assembly of the Elect. For practical purposes, the Elect could identify themselves by confessing Christ, striving to live according to biblical standards of conduct, and participating regularly in the sacraments.

He preferred a form of presbyterian church polity in which ministers and people shared in governing the local congregation and, as in a republic, elected their leaders.

Calvin taught that the institutions of church and state should be separate but interlocking. In Geneva, the elders of the church also served as magistrates in order to facilitate this scheme. It was permissible, even commendable, for the civil authorities to aid and abet religious institutions and religious reform. Moreover, he was not only happy that Geneva was a republic but also preferred the republican form of government although he was careful not to condemn monarchy if it were friendly to his followers. Finally, Calvin and several of his key followers appeared to authorize the right of resistance to tyrants who persecuted those who tried to live according to biblical principles and approved of that resistance as long as it was led by legitimately constituted lesser magistrates. There was much in Calvinist thought that promoted a republican outlook in both church and state.[17]

The Calvinist Vision: A World Based on Biblical Justice

Calvin referred to his branch of the Protestant Reformation as the Reformed Church. In Scotland, it became the Presbyterian Church and in England the Puritan Movement. In any event, Calvinism, as it was later called, quickly spread to nearly every part of Europe and became a major expression of Protestantism in France, the Netherlands, many German cities and states, Hungary, England, Scotland, Northern Ireland, and eventually in North America and Korea. Thus, it became an international movement that rivaled the Roman Catholic Church in extent and influence.[18]

In the years that followed Calvin's introduction of sweeping reforms in Geneva, the city became a veritable Protestant Rome, not in an institutional but in an ideological sense. Geneva was the new center for the evangelical movement and Calvin was its leader. How did this come about? There were four main reasons for this astonishing development.

First, there was Calvin's personal example and inspiration. Calvin was no finished saint nor was he a malicious tyrant. Rather he was a highly gifted and unreservedly dedicated man. He took himself and Christianity seriously and labored long and hard at what he regarded as "the Lord's work." He seldom slept, usually no more than four hours a night. A shy, scholarly and self-effacing man, he lies buried in an unmarked grave because he did not want his followers to venerate his remains. Many hated him, but those who knew him best loved, admired and respected him. He drove himself relentlessly in his attempt to serve the Lord. He preached twice on Sunday and once every day of alternate weeks. He also baptized once a month, regularly visited the sick, carried on an extensive correspondence and sustained heavy organizational responsibilities. Moreover, he enhanced the role of women in church life, consequently Calvinism attracted a large number of female adherents, many of them, like Marie Dentière and Katharina Zell, educated and outspoken on behalf of women. It is little wonder that his example called forth from his followers a dynamic zeal and depth of dedication to their work that has gone unsurpassed until the modern era of fanatical followings of sports and dictators.

Second, Calvin led his international movement through his direct intellectual influence nourished by his many books and his personal preaching and teaching. Like many shy people, Calvin could be eloquent on the platform and powerful in his writing. His most important and widely read book was, of course, his *Institutes*. But there were also his commentaries on the Bible, 47 volumes in one English edition, and his scores of theological treatises, devotional tracts and polemical works. Printing became a major industry in Calvin's Geneva and Calvin its leading author. Beyond Geneva, hundreds of Calvin's works were translated into various European languages, especially English. Calvin's Geneva sermons and lectures were also popular and powerful, and students came from all over Europe to sit at his feet. Calvin and Viret established the Academy of Geneva in 1559 to institutionalize these lectures, and Theodore Beza became its first rector. Calvin stressed education and an educated ministry, a Reformed and Presbyterian tradition that has continued to the present day. In the mid-sixteenth century, hundreds of young men trained in Geneva returned to serve as missionary pastors in their native lands.[19]

France was a special case in point, and Calvin's influence there was enormous. At one time in the sixteenth century, more than one-tenth of the population of that kingdom was Calvinist believers. Once Calvin's leadership was established in Geneva, he and the French exiles living there formulated an effective evangelization program for France. Although French Calvinists were called Huguenots, they preferred the term Reformed. By 1557, more than a hundred pastors sent from Geneva were organizing Reformed congregations roughly patterned on the Geneva Church. In 1559, the first national synod of the Reformed Church in France met in Paris, and adopted a confession of faith for which Calvin provided the first draft. As Reformation ideas began to take root not only in the middle class but also among the French nobility, the Crown initiated a policy of persecution to root out Protestantism because it seemed to the ruling Valois family that it threatened the unity of the kingdom.

The resulting strife, based on a mix of political and religious considerations, prompted the Crown's call for a public Protestant-Catholic debate to sort things out. Any hope that the ensuing Collo-quy of Poissy in 1561 would contribute to peace was dashed when Beza, Calvin's heir apparent in Geneva and leader of the Huguenot delegation, unequivocally rejected the bodily presence of Christ in the sacrament because he and his colleagues believed that it was idolatrous and a rejection of the true Gospel. The Catholic rage at such blasphemy was both a reaction to theological disputation and a generation of religious turmoil in the country. The Crown's efforts to mitigate the failure at Poissy by an Edict of Toleration in January 1562 lasted only two months before armed attacks on Huguenot con-gregations occurred, and the country descended into decades of con-flict fueled by religious animosity and concern for national unity. The most infamous event in the so-called Wars of Religion (1562–1598) was the St. Bartholomew's Day Massacre on 24 August 1572 when thousands of Huguenots were massacred in a frenzy of state terrorism. A generation later, weary of bloodshed and assassinations, the Protestant Bourbon Henry of Navarre converted to Catholicism and became King Henry IV (1589–1610). He then established a pol-icy of limited toleration with the Edit of Nantes of 1598 that lasted until its revocation by Louis XIV (1643–1715) in 1685.[20]

Third, Calvin led his international movement as an advisor and mentor. Some of this was accomplished face to face but it was mostly done by letters. Calvin corresponded with all kinds of people, church and lay leaders, and ecclesiastical, political and social figures. He wrote frequently to Farel and Viret in Switzerland and France, and corresponded with Knox in Scotland, the young King Edward VI of England (1547–1553), Edward's regent Edward Seymour, most of the English reformers, the King of Poland, the Bourbon princes of France, the sister of the French king, and the rulers of many German states. He gave advice by letter to hundreds of pastors in Reformed churches in Spain, Italy, France, Germany, the Low Countries, Poland, Hungary, England and Scotland. There survive more than 5,000 of these letters to 307 different persons or groups, and thou-sands more have been lost. The evidence clearly shows that Calvin devoted most of his literary activity to nurturing, promoting and sta-bilizing Protestantism.

Fourth, Calvin's Geneva provided a model for Calvinist believers all over the world in terms of how to establish and maintain a just biblical commonwealth. Geneva, a city-state of some 10,000 to 15,000 inhabitants during Calvin's day, was heavily influenced by Calvin for 23 years and dominated by French refugees for the last 10 of those years. Nevertheless, at no time was Calvin's control over Genevan life absolute or unquestioned. Geneva was, after all, a republic. However, it is undeniable that the reformer's influence was extensive, and that he exercised it not by political, monetary or military power but by moral persuasion in his role as the pastor of St. Pierre Cathedral and as spiritual advisor to the City Council. Aiding in this was the fact that through compulsory church attendance and other public meetings, Calvin and his ministerial colleagues had access to the hearts and minds of the Genevan people on a daily basis. In short, church attendance was the radio and TV of the age. In any event, under Calvin's aegis, a series of legal reforms based on the Ten Commandments and New Testament principles was introduced and systematically enforced.

Calvin is often castigated by modern historians for the nature and severity of many of these reforms. However, they were increasingly accepted in Geneva as the Elect took office and became overwhelmingly present in the population at large. Blasphemy and swearing disappeared from public discourse, and there were severe penalties for those who committed adultery or engaged in other forms of sexual misconduct. Prostitutes, undesirables and recalcitrant Catholics were banished. Public order was a high priority, the Sabbath was strictly observed, and gambling was limited. However, most of these kinds of laws were on the books before Calvin came to Geneva. The difference was that now they were enforced.

But beyond these moral restrictions, Calvin's Geneva also introduced new laws curbing economic injustice and establishing a public school system and a civic welfare program. For example, Calvin was progressive in his economic views and at the same time in tune with the city's commercial life. He tried to see to it that new economic legislation cut through traditional Medieval Church restrictions on usury but still hedged his position in an attempt to secure reasonable interest rates and thus ensure economic justice. He also supported laws that protected the economically disadvantaged, forbade taking interest from the poor, and embodied the Golden Rule.

Consequently, by the time Calvin died in 1563, Genevans enjoyed great personal security because there was no crime in the streets. Moreover, there were no beggars and no homeless people in Calvin's Geneva, and economic justice was a high priority. The city-state had become, in essence, a biblical republic that translated Bible morality into civil codes. Discipline, order and justice were the hallmarks of Christian life in Geneva following Calvin's time there.

The Geneva experiment made a profound impression on visiting believers from foreign lands. Therefore, Knox, after his return to Scotland, tried to transform Edinburgh into the "perfect school of Christ" that he had observed as a religious exile. Similar experiments were attempted, with varying degrees of success, in Amsterdam, Boston and elsewhere. In any case, Geneva, the Protestant "city on a hill," was there for all to see and emulate for the next century and beyond.[21]

The Impact of Calvinism on the Western World

By early 1564, it was obvious that Calvin was seriously ill. Since he had returned to Geneva in 1541, he had suffered chronically from catarrh, asthma, indigestion and migraine headaches. Over the last decade of his life he also consulted physicians about arthritis, gout, tuberculosis, intestinal parasites, hemorrhoids, a malarial-like fever, pleurisy and bowel irritation. By the winter of 1563–1564, he was in such bad shape that his attendance at the weekly Consistory meetings became increasingly infrequent. He preached his last sermon at St. Pierre on 6 April 1564, and bade farewell from his bed to the members of the City Council on 27 April and to the ministers of Geneva the next day. He asked both groups to forgive him for his periodic outbursts of temper and apologized that his illnesses had sometimes made him a difficult man with whom to deal. He kept writing to the end, until he expired on 27 May, not quite 64 years of age, and was quickly buried in an unmarked grave.

After his death the term "Calvinist" came into common usage to describe those who followed his teachings. Although he objected to such terminology, it nevertheless emphasizes that Calvin's place in human history rests largely upon his ideas. By the time of his death, Calvinism had been established as the most formidable alternative to Roman Catholicism in Europe, bolstered by Calvin's perceptiveness in recognizing the importance of intellectual clarity and ecclesiastical organization to the survival of a movement. Historians are not all of one mind concerning the nature of the continuing impact of Calvinism on the Western world but the vast majority of them acknowledge that it is extensive.

First, in the course of stressing the doctrinal component of his intellectual legacy, Calvin's successors placed a new emphasis on predestination, which in turn sparked some of the most intense disputes over exactly what it meant and how much it should be emphasized. It also served as a benchmark in controversies with Arminians, those who stressed free will in matters of God's plan of salvation. In so doing, Calvin's second- and third-generation followers placed an emphasis on this doctrine which is largely lacking in Calvin's thought but which attracted many looking for the comfort and security of inclusion among the Elect.

Therefore, Calvin's theological system attracted large numbers of followers, especially among the clergy, who then popularized it for their flocks, because it seemed to explain so much. Given his premises, Calvin's theology was a vigorous and coherent explication of both how and why sins are forgiven. Moreover, successive generations could consult his *Institutes* where these explanations, along with almost all aspects of theology, are systematically arranged. No other reformer left behind such a legacy. Moreover, the genius of Calvin's theology was such that it could become the official doctrine of the Presbyterian, Reformed and Congregational churches while at the same time seeping into the theology of the Church of England and many Baptist churches in a modified form.[22]

Second, Calvin deeply influenced the course of political thought in the Western world. He did this in several ways, especially in terms of trends toward democracy, the right of resistance and the development of civil religion. Calvin clearly had republican preferences in both secular and ecclesiastical government, and supported elected political processes in both. Some historians have argued that his views also supported the development of democracy, at least in its embryonic forms. In any event, it is clear that his thought provided plenty of opportunity for generational followers to exploit it to support democratic ideas and movements.[23]

In addition, Calvin and his colleagues authorized resistance to established authority if that authority proved to be hostile to the preaching of the Gospel, as Calvinists understood it, provided that they were led in their resistance by duly constituted lesser magistrates. The St. Bartholomew Day's Massacre of 1572 precipitated an intense debate among Calvinists over the limits of civil authority and over natural human rights as a basis for the right of resistance. This seemed to signal to Calvinists in Scotland, England and America that they, indeed, could resist the Powers That Be if they were deemed inimical to the Gospel and human liberty. In North America on the eve of the American Revolution, the emergence of a covenantal understanding of human rights was linked with Calvin's appeal to natural law to promote the notion of all humanity being created equal, with certain inalienable human rights to life, liberty and the pursuit of happiness.[24]

Moreover, a secularized version of Calvinism provided core beliefs for English and American civil religion, especially the concept of each of those countries as "an elect nation," chosen by God to bring the blessings of the Gospel and political enlightenment to the world. This idea grew out of the Calvinist emphasis on predestination and election—being chosen by God. Calvinism regarded this doctrine as giving religious inspiration and moral legitimatization to the international expansion of the movement. Thus, election was not understood merely to refer to individuals, but to the communities to which they belonged. These Calvinist communities had been chosen by God and set apart in order to achieve God's purposes. It was natural for Calvinists, who among Protestants emphasized the Old Testament, to notice and exploit the obvious parallels between their own situation and that of Ancient Israel. The Israelites were the chosen people of God in the Ancient Near East and the Calvinists were their successors in the early modern world. With the coming of Queen Elizabeth I (1558–1603), many Calvinist writers regarded England as having been granted most favored nation status in the eyes of God. The English Congregational Puritans transferred this perception to North America beginning in 1630 as they proposed to establish their biblical commonwealth as a "city upon a hill" in the New World.

The early history of North American colonization, whether by English or Dutch Calvinists, was widely regarded as the entry of God's chosen but exiled people into a new promised land. Thus, the unquestioned premise of the first New Englanders was that they had entered into a covenant with God to establish a holy commonwealth. The Great Awakening of the first half of the eighteenth century seemed to confirm this, and by the time of the American Revolution, the errand of God's chosen people in the American wilderness had become the destiny of the new American Republic itself. This meant that a secularized Calvinism made it possible for a secularized United States to think of itself in religious terms as singled out among nations with its institutions and symbols endowed with sacramental significance. These themes can be traced to America's Puritan past and are still operative in its civil religion to the present day.[25]

Third, many historians and sociologists believe that Calvin and Calvinism profoundly influenced the economic life of the Western world. Calvin's fondness for 1 Corinthians 10:31 ("So whether you eat or drink or whatever you do, do all for the glory of God") and his insistence that all work should be a calling from God helped to highlight its importance in the life of the Elect. He also preached what later became known as the middle-class virtues, each backed by biblical authority: reverence, chastity, sobriety, frugality, industry and honesty. These concepts were foundational to worker productivity. In addition, Calvin stressed that society should be economically just. Moreover, rejecting medieval strictures on usury and allowing Christians to participate in money lending helped to stimulate economic activity among Protestants.

The fact that Calvinism produced a group of productive and reliable people led the prominent twentieth-century German sociologist Max Weber to formulate his well-known thesis concerning the connection between Calvinism and the growth of modern capitalism. In his classic essay "The Protestant Ethic and the Spirit of Capitalism," Weber argued that the Calvinist ethic played an important part in the rise of modern capitalism. Of all the expressions of Reformation Christianity, Weber averred, Calvinism inculcated in its followers an austere, ascetic work ethic that systematically suppressed the pursuit of pleasure. However, in contrast to medieval Catholicism, this "worldly asceticism" encouraged believers to work hard, discipline themselves and find their meaning in life in their secular calling. Among other things, Weber claimed, this attitude tended to inspire economic productivity and generate income that was not spent for "frivolous purposes" but turned into savings or investment capital. There has been endless controversy over the validity of Weber's thesis with various critics pointing out its flaws and finding the origins of modern capitalism in various other religious movements of the early modern period. Nevertheless, it is intriguing to note that English Puritans were inclined to act this way, especially in the seventeenth century, and that Protestant nations tended to reflect this work ethic and be places where capitalism flourished.[26]

Finally, Calvinism left its mark on education and intellectual life through the insistence by Calvin and his followers on the value of education for all believers, women included. Calvinists stressed the education of ministers in particular and provided institutions of higher learning for that purpose, beginning with the Academy of Geneva in 1559, followed by universities and colleges like Leiden, Heidelberg, Harvard, Yale, and Princeton. Calvin also modeled scholarship "for the glory of God" to latter-day Christians.[27]

The intense man who sacrificed ease, scholarly honors and personal inclination for a pastoral ministry in a difficult city did so because he believed it was God's will. His prime goal was undoubtedly to do God's will, and if Calvin too often identified the divine purpose with his own wishes, that error does not detract from the sincerity of his consecration. Little wonder that his ideas and example heavily influenced the Reformation in England, the subject of the next chapter.

Notes

1. Robert Bellah et al., *Habits of the Heart: Individualism and Commitment in American Life* (Berkeley: University of California Press, 1985), 306.

2. This sketch of Zwingli's life is based on G. R. Potter, *Zwingli* (Cambridge: Cambridge University Press, 1977), the standard biography of the reformer in English.

3. Ibid., 316–342.

4. This account of Calvin's life is based on T. H. L. Parker, *John Calvin: A Biography* (Philadelphia: Westminster Press, 1975) and Alister E. McGrath, *A Life of John Calvin: A Study in the Shaping of Western Culture* (Oxford: Basil Blackwell, 1990).

5. Robert D. Linder, "The Early Calvinists and Martin Luther: A Study in Evangelical Solidarity," in *Regnum, Religio et Ratio*, ed. Jerome Friedman (Kirksville, MO: Sixteenth Century Journal Publishers, 1987), 103–116.

6. Unlike Luther, Calvin seldom talked about himself, especially his early years. Consequently, there is not much information about his conversion experience, the time of which is problematical. Most historians place it around 1533–1534, but Parker argues that it came earlier, most likely in 1529 or 1530. See Parker, *John Calvin*, 22 and 162–165; and McGrath, *Life of John Calvin*, 69–75.

7. John Calvin, *Institutes of the Christian Religion*, ed. John T. McNeill, trans. Ford Lewis Battles, 2 vols. (Philadelphia: Westminster Press, 1960), 1:728–729.

8. Ibid., 1:9–31.

9. Parker, *John Calvin*, 51–53.

10. Ibid., 101–102.

11. Andrew Pettegree, "Michael Servetus and the Limits of Tolerance," *History Today* 40, no. 2 (February 1990):40–45.

12. Carter Lindberg, ed., *The European Reformations Sourcebook* (Oxford: Blackwell, 2000), 249.

13. The best introduction to Calvin's theological ideas is François Wendel, *John Calvin: Origins and Development of His Religious Thought* (New York: Harper and Row, 1963).

14. Calvin, 1:926.

15. Acts 16:31.

16. McGrath, *Life of John Calvin*, 208–218.

17. Calvin, 2:1485–1521.

18. Menna Prestwich, ed., *International Calvinism, 1541–1715* (Oxford: Clarendon, 1985).

19. McGrath, *Life of John Calvin,* 175–193; and Robert M. Kingdon, *Geneva and the Coming of the Wars of Religion in France, 1555–1563* (Geneva: Droz, 1956). The Academy is now the University of Geneva.

20. Mack Holt, *The French Wars of Religion, 1562–1629* (Cambridge: Cambridge University Press, 1995); and Raymond A. Mentzer, "The French Wars of Religion," in Andrew Pettegree, ed., *The Reformation World* (New York: Routledge, 2000), 323–343.

21. E. William Monter, *Calvin's Geneva* (New York: Wiley, 1967); William G. Naphy, "Calvin and Geneva," in Pettegree, 309–322; Elsie McKee, *John Calvin on the Diaconate and Liturgical Almsgiving* (Geneva: Droz, 1984); Jane Dempsey Douglas, *Women, Freedom and Calvin* (Philadelphia: Westminster Press, 1985); Jeannine Olson, *Calvin and Social Welfare: Deacons and the Bourse française* (Selinsgrove, PA: Susquehanna University Press, 1989); and Philip Benedict, *Christ's Churches Purely Reformed: A Social History of Calvinism* (New Haven, CT: Yale University Press, 2003).

22. Alister E. McGrath, *Iustitia Dei: A History of the Christian Doctrine of Justification,* 2 vols. (Cambridge: Cambridge University Press, 1986), 2:39–50.

23. Robert M. Kingdon and Robert D. Linder, eds., *Calvin and Calvinism: Sources of Democracy?* (Lexington, MA: Heath, 1970).

24. Robert D. Linder, "Pierre Viret and the Sixteenth-Century French Revolutionary Tradition," *Journal of Modern History,* 38, no. 2 (June 1966):125–137; James Torrance, "Interpreting the Word by the Light of Christ," in Robert Schnucker, ed., *Calviniana* (Kirksville, MO: Sixteenth Century Journal, 1989), 255–267; and Robert M. Kingdon, "Calvinism and Resistance Theory, 1550–1580," in James Henderson Burns, ed., *The Cambridge History of Political Thought, 1450–1700* (Cambridge: Cambridge University Press, 1991), 193–218.

25. Perry Miller, *Nature's Nation* (Cambridge, MA: Harvard University Press, 1967); and Sydney Ahlstrom, *A Religious History of the American People,* 2nd ed. (New Haven, CT: Yale University Press, 2004), 6–7.

26. Georgia Harkness, *John Calvin: The Man and His Ethics* (New York: Abingdon Press, 1958); and Max Weber, *The Protestant Ethic and the Spirit of Capitalism,* intro Anthony Giddens (Gloucester, MA: Peter Smith, 1988).

27. Paul Grendler, "Education in the Renaissance and Reformation," *Renaissance Quarterly,* 43, no. 4 (Winter 1990):774–824.

CHAPTER 4

THE REFORMATION AMONG THE ENGLISH-SPEAKING PEOPLES

Of all the sixteenth-century reform movements, the English Reformation was the most complex. Sometimes also called the Anglican Reformation, it eventually had to do with more than the Church of England or even England itself. The English Reformation and the Reformation in all parts of Britain were exceptional in the extent to which reform was contested, both at the time and ever since. As historian Patrick Collinson pointed out, the history of religious change was important yet different in England, Wales, Scotland, and Ireland. In the seventeenth century, these four areas came under the rule of the same monarch, and their religious and political history became one of interactions, so much so that no sense can be made of one case without reference to all of the others.[1] Eventually the results of the English Reformation would reverberate throughout what became the British Empire.

Nothing better illustrates the complexity of the Reformation in England than the fact that in 1521, King Henry VIII published his negative response to Luther's *Babylonian Captivity of the Church*, by way of a book dedicated to Pope Leo X titled *Defense of the Seven Sacraments*. A grateful papacy thereupon bestowed upon Henry the title "Defender of the Faith," an official royal appellation from that day to the present. Ten years later, the king was at loggerheads with the pope and on the brink of a permanent rupture between Canterbury and Rome.[2]

This break with the Roman Church cannot be understood apart from medieval English history. Before Henry I (1100–1135) died without male heirs in 1135, he designated his daughter Matilda as his successor and had his barons swear loyalty to her. However, his effort to achieve a peaceful female succession failed and instead led to 19 years of civil war. A major confrontation between King John (1199–1216) and Pope Innocent III over control of the English Church in the early thirteenth century resulted in John's humiliation and England's becoming a papal fief accompanied by the requirement of an annual payment to the pope by the English monarch. In the fourteenth century, the sharp attacks of John Wycliffe, an Oxford University don and priest, on papal authority created enormous tension between Wycliffe and his noble supporters on the one hand and Rome on the other. Moreover, the Lollards, Wycliffe's lay preacher followers, continued to spread his Protestant-like teachings throughout England long after his death, with elements lingering into the early sixteenth century in Yorkshire and Kent. From 1455–1485, the War of the Roses between two competing branches of the royal family, the Houses of York and Lancaster, disturbed the peace and finally resulted in the Lancasters ascending the throne as the House of Tudor in the person of Henry VII (1485–1509). When his son followed him as Henry VIII, the Tudor's claim to the throne was still shaky and the political situation in England still unstable. The same period witnessed significant growth in English national feeling. Therefore, in the early sixteenth century, Henry VIII and English society wanted above all else security and order under a strong national monarch.

"The King's Great Matter"

There is little doubt that Henry VIII was the key figure in the coming of the Reformation to England. He towered over his generation of English people as few others have before or since. As a young man, he looked every inch a king: tall, handsome, muscular, well proportioned, and nothing like the swollen sovereign of the portraits of his last years. Henry was also a good dancer, an excellent athlete and horseman, a composer and fine musician with a pleasant voice. He was in addition well educated, especially in the humanities, and highly intelligent with a good grasp of theology and fluent in several languages.

The issue that brought Henry VIII into direct confrontation with the papacy was what Stephen Gardiner, the king's secretary and Bishop of Winchester, dubbed "the King's great matter," Henry's desire for an annulment of his marriage to Queen Catherine of Aragon.[3] This "matter" was, in turn, related to Henry's determination to maintain order while at the same time protecting his dynasty. Catherine, daughter of the powerful King Ferdinand II (1479–1516) and Queen Isabella (1479–1504) of Spain, had come to England in 1501, betrothed to Henry's older brother Arthur, heir apparent to the throne. An Anglo-Spanish alliance had inspired the match and since political concerns persisted after Arthur's unexpected death, Henry was designated to take his brother's place. However, canon law forbade marriage with the widow of one's brother, though it was possible under certain conditions to receive a papal dispensation to overturn this rule. After a royal petition of the papacy and certain "considerations"—most likely a monetary donation to the papacy—changed hands, a dispensation was granted removing the impediment of affinity existing between Henry and Catherine and the two were married.

Catherine, who was six years older than Henry, had a number of children but only one, Mary, survived infancy. At some point, Henry began to doubt the legitimacy of the dispensation and thereby his marriage. There was talk of an annulment as early as 1514. By 1526, when Catherine was 41 and Mary 10, it was evident that Henry would have no male heir by Catherine. Since Henry had sired a male bastard, the evidence seemed to put the blame for the lack of a son on his wife. With the memory of Matilda and the recent triumph of the Tudors in mind, the peace of the realm seemed to be threatened since that peace depended on an orderly succession to the throne. In Henry's view, the chances that Mary would be accepted were slim to nonexistent.

In the meantime, Henry had developed a passion for one of the ladies-in-waiting at court, the clever and vivacious Anne Boleyn. Henry had fallen madly in love with her sometime before 1527. Had she wished, she might have served as his royal mistress, as had her sister before her. But she aspired to the throne and this, combined with Henry's desire for a legitimate male heir, made marriage a necessity. There is no doubt that Henry's sex life was unruly and that he panted after Anne. However, it also seems clear that he was more concerned with the succession than with lust since plenty of outlets for that could be found at court. In any event, before marriage to Anne could take place, the king had to dispose lawfully of Queen Catherine.

Henry claimed that a study of the Bible had convinced him that God was punishing him for having violated the law of God in marrying his deceased brother's wife. A literal reading of Leviticus 20:21[4] suggested that he was under a divine curse. Henry wanted a male heir and hoped that the youthful Anne Boleyn would serve that purpose. He, therefore, in 1527 appealed to Pope Clement VII (1521–1534) for an annulment. Henry's request placed the pope in an ecclesiastical and political bind. If he granted an annulment, he would further undermine papal authority, already under attack on several fronts, by reversing a previous pope's action. The political dilemma stemmed from the fact that Clement was virtually a prisoner of the Emperor Charles V who had just sacked Rome and whose troops were still in the immediate area. Charles happened to be Catherine's nephew and was adamantly opposed to Henry's plan to rid himself of her. Therefore, the pope's tactic was to stall for time.

Cardinal Thomas Wolsey, Lord Chancellor and the man who really ran England, albeit under Henry's watchful eye, was charged with extracting the desired decision from the pope. When he failed, it cost him his job and ultimately his life. Sir Thomas More, a brilliant Christian humanist and devout Catholic, succeeded Wolsey. Since More opposed the king's plan to dispense with Catherine, Henry finally conceded that he would not have to be involved. However, this meant that the king's highest official remained aloof from the major political issue of the day. In the end, Henry lost patience with More and removed him from office. Eventually, More's refusal to recognize the king's right to be Head of the Church of England also cost him his life.

In any event, tired of the papal game and exasperated by the inability of his underlings to accomplish his goals, Henry took the initiative in 1532. His solution was, after a long and convoluted process, to obtain a favorable response through the English ecclesiastical courts. In this, he was aided and abetted by Thomas Cranmer, his newly appointed Archbishop of Canterbury, and Thomas Cromwell, recently named to a half dozen key posts in the Henrician government. Cranmer was a prominent Cambridge trained scholar of a Protestant persuasion who probably would have preferred the Ivory Tower had he not been catapulted into public life by "the King's Great Matter." Cromwell was an administrative genius and a convinced Protestant who was able to handle enormous amounts of business with great efficiency. Always working carefully through Parliament, the institution that represented the important people of the realm and that had to approve any new taxes, Henry used a series of parliamentary acts, capped by the Act of Supremacy of 1534, to achieve his ends.[5]

In January 1533, Henry secretly married Anne Boleyn; in May, Cranmer's archiepiscopal court declared that Henry's marriage to Catherine was invalid; in June, Anne was crowned queen of England; and in September she delivered not a son but another daughter whom they named Elizabeth. When the Supremacy bill was passed a year later making the king the Supreme Head of the Church of England, the first stage of the English Reformation was complete.

The Quest for Orderly Reform: Henricians and Elizabethans

Henry wanted Rome out of his realm, but not Catholicism. Therefore, the Parliament's Act of Six Articles in 1539 affirmed pre-Reformation orthodoxy, creating what amounted to an English Catholic Church without a pope. The most disruptive event of the Henrician Reformation was the suppression of the English monasteries in two steps, the smaller ones in 1536 and the larger ones in 1539. The initial bill of dissolution helped set off the only major rebellion against Henry's break with Rome, the so-called Pilgrimage of Grace, which Henry put down with guile and force in 1537. The monastic closures involved a huge transfer of property from the Church to the Crown and, beginning in 1539, the government sold or granted these lands to laymen and universities, all of whom thenceforth had a vested economic interest in maintaining the Henrician Settlement.

By the time the Pilgrimage of Grace began, both Catherine and Anne were dead. Catherine died of natural causes early in 1536 and Anne on a bogus charge of adultery by means of the chopping block later in the same year following her miscarriage of a second child, this one a male. Eleven days following Anne's execution Henry married Jane Seymour, daughter of a powerful Protestant family, who in October 1537 delivered the long awaited male heir, named Edward. Jane had served the king and his kingdom well, but it cost her life as she died of puerperal fever 12 days following Edward's birth. Henry married three more times in the remaining decade of his life but he never had any more children. The future of the dynasty and of the English Reformation now lay in the hands of his three offspring: Mary, Elizabeth and Edward.

In the meantime, both Cranmer and Cromwell attempted to make the Henrician Settlement more Protestant. Working closely together, they introduced evangelical teachings into the initial doctrinal statements of the English Reformation, the Ten Articles of 1536 and the Bishops' Book of 1537. A royal order of 1538 that an English Bible be placed in every parish church was another important step in making England more Protestant.

Without diminishing the significant roles of the various Tudor monarchs in the reform of the English Church, the planting of Protestantism in England benefited greatly from a residual Lollard

anticlericalism, humanist interest in reform, and Continental Reformation ideas spread by young Cambridge scholars, pamphlets and
Bible translations, and by English students returning from study in
the centers of the Swiss Reformation. Survivals of Wycliffian Lollardy
have already been mentioned. John Colet, Dean of St. Paul's Cathedral and a trained humanist, castigated clerical worldliness and
called for a reformation of clerical behavior and more attention to
biblical teachings. Other Christian humanists echoed his sentiments.
During the 1520s, groups of students and teachers at Oxford and
Cambridge began to discuss Luther's works. The group of 50 or
more scholars that met at the White Horse Inn in Cambridge in this
period included many of the future Protestant leaders and martyrs of
England: Cranmer, Robert Barnes, John Frith, Hugh Latimer, Nicholas Ridley, Thomas Bilney, John Foxe, who later wrote the influential
Book of Martyrs, and probably William Tyndale.

Tyndale was in many ways the most remarkable of England's
earliest Protestants. It was he who was responsible for a new English
translation of the Bible that was to play a critical role in the early
English Reformation. A learned man who knew at least seven languages, and an independent-minded Christian, Tyndale believed that
the key to reform rested in making the Bible available to the people
of England in their own language. Failing to find official support for
his project in England, he journeyed to the Continent where he
eventually set up shop in Antwerp and produced a fresh English
translation of the New Testament based on Erasmus' scholarly Greek
text. Numerous copies of the New Testament and portions of the
Old Testament were smuggled into England. Some were seized and
burned but many made it to their destinations. On the Continent,
Catholic authorities and English agents relentlessly pursued Tyndale
until he was finally apprehended in 1535. He was imprisoned, tried
and condemned as a heretic. In October 1536, at age 41, Tyndale
was first strangled and then burned for his Protestant beliefs. Back in
his native England, his English Bibles were increasingly in demand.[6]

In the meantime, the top-down imposition of ecclesiology continued under the children of Henry VIII: a more Continental-type
Protestantism under Edward VI, a return to the Roman Church
under Mary I (1553–1558), and a comprehensive general English
Protestantism under Elizabeth I beginning in 1558. Henry's successors continued the Erastian arrangement that he started, thus making
the Church basically a subdivision of the State. Reformation theology
of a Zwinglian variety that stressed justification by faith alone and
biblical authority developed during the reign of young Edward VI.
Archbishop Cranmer provided an exquisitely crafted Book of

Common Prayer in 1549 (revised in 1552) and a statement of faith known as the Forty-two Articles in 1553. The Prayer Book retained much of the old liturgy and terminology of the Eucharist while the new theological statement left little doubt that the Church of England now embraced the essential doctrines of the Protestant Reformation. In doing this, Cranmer demonstrated great moderation in balancing traditional and Reformed rites and beliefs.

The tide was reversed with the accession to the throne of the devout Roman Catholic Mary I following Edward's untimely death in 1553. Determined to redeem her mother's memory and re-establish her mother's faith to the land, Mary immediately restored ecclesiastical ties with Rome. Believing that the faith of English Protestants was shallow and that most English people were basically loyal to the old faith, she expected to accomplish her task of bringing the English Church back into the Roman fold with limited opposition. She was wrong.

Ironically, her efforts to restore Catholicism strengthened Protestant resolve. Her marriage to Prince Philip of the House of Habsburg (later Philip II of Spain) in 1554 linked her faith to foreign influence and her efforts to restore Church properties alienated their current owners. Her persecution of leading Protestants created the host of martyrs celebrated in Foxe's martyrology.[7] Among the nearly 300 who perished at the stake during Mary's reign were Archbishop Cranmer and Bishops Latimer, Ridley, and John Hooper. Hundreds of others would have perished but they managed to flee the country ahead of the martyrs' flames. Among these Marian Exiles was John Knox, a resident of England at the time, who, after a sojourn in Calvin's Geneva, returned to his native Scotland to consolidate the Reformation there along Calvinist lines. Others, such as Thomas Sampson, Laurence Humphrey and Edmund Grindal would return to lead the Puritan movement during the Elizabethan period.

Mary died without issue in 1558, and the throne passed peacefully to Anne Boleyn's daughter, the Protestant Elizabeth Tudor, the last of Henry VIII's surviving children. Ironically, the English Reformation had begun because Henry felt that he needed a male heir to assure a peaceful succession, but the English people readily accepted the legitimacy of both his daughters. Elizabeth, in fact, proved to be an outstanding ruler who dealt with a particularly difficult situation in an impressive manner. England had experienced three religious changes in 11 years, and the wars of religion were already beginning to plague the Continent. Elizabeth was faced with the challenge of arriving at a religious settlement that would unite a divided country and protect England from open civil and/or religious conflict.

The pendulum of reform swung to the middle with Elizabeth I, whose long reign facilitated the establishment of English Protestantism and molded the Church of England into the comprehensive institution that it still claims to be today. Elizabeth herself was much more suited to rule than was either of her siblings. Historians differ concerning just how much she contributed personally to the government of England. However, all agree that she served as an important symbol of the new era, every inch a queen and every inch English, a true daughter of her father, Henry VIII. They also concur that she was a remarkable woman who presided over England in an exciting era when the nation became thoroughly Protestant and the leader among Protestant nations. She ruled wisely and well.

By the time she ascended the throne at age 25, Elizabeth was an experienced and worldly-wise young woman. She reminded people of her father, moderately tall and well formed, with reddish hair, an olive complexion, striking expressive blue eyes and a dignified bearing. She was shrewd, calculating, dissembling, capable of playing coquette or the cold administrator, with the self-confidence and will to make quick decisions and nerves of steel to carry them out. Her greatest strength was her ability to choose talented and loyal men to advise her and carry out her policies. For example, William Cecil, later Lord Burghley, was a moderate but convinced Protestant who served Elizabeth during nearly her entire reign, first as Secretary of State and then as Lord Treasurer. He counseled her to act decisively but with moderation and discretion. Elizabeth appointed only Protestants to her Council of State, men more devotedly Protestant and more favorable to Puritanism than she herself was. Her personal faith is still a matter of debate but most historians agree that she was a moderate Protestant with a taste for pomp and ceremony. She was satisfied to establish an ecclesiastical regime that accepted pomp with no pope.

The Elizabethan Settlement, as it is now called, adopted what most Anglicans proudly allude to as a *via media*, that is a "middle way" between the old Roman Catholic Church and the newer forms of Protestantism. It was calculated to be an English form of Christianity to which the overwhelming majority of the people could give their allegiance. The Settlement settled much. The Elizabethan Church of England retained traditional vestments and an English liturgy with sermons and prayers conforming to the Thirty-nine Articles adopted in 1563. This theological statement revised the former Forty-two Articles, especially concerning the theology of the Eucharist, a perennial focal point of dispute. The Thirty-nine Articles denied the Catholic doctrine of transubstantiation on the one hand

and Zwinglian symbolism on the other, while remaining open to a range of Lutheran and Calvinist interpretations, and might even be celebrated as something close to the old way in the hands of a careful and shrewd priest.[8]

Rather than the Supreme Head, Elizabeth was now Supreme Governor of the Church of England, a somewhat less ominous title, according to the Supremacy Act of 1559. As such, she appointed moderate clergy who conformed to her program of ecclesiastical realpolitik. Significant support came from such scholars as John Jewel and Richard Hooker. Hooker, in particular, defended the Settlement with considerable force and logic in his massive eight-volume *Treatise on the Laws of Ecclesiastical Polity*, written between 1593–1600. In response to those elements within the Church of England who criticized the relegation of the Church to what amounted to a department of state (Erastianism) with the queen as its Governor, Hooker based his rational argument on the harmony of natural law. He contended that to erect a barrier of separation between church and state, as some radical reformers wanted, would destroy English unity and deprive the Church of the natural and necessary patronage and protection of the Crown. Therefore, he insisted that the two bodies, church and state, be "under one chief Governor."[9]

The Elizabethan Settlement left the Church of England basically Reformed in its theology, Catholic in its ecclesiology, and Episcopal in its polity. It also allowed clergy to marry, and Cranmer's marriage service in the Book of Common Prayer elevated attitudes toward matrimony, sex and love. Further, the Settlement maintained most of the gains for women, small though they may seem to modern people, because women already had a growing status in pre-Reformation England and forms of Christocentric piety had already developed in the Late Middle Ages that had much in common with Protestantism. In fact, several historians have argued that this Christocentric devotion served as a comforting bridge in a time of spiritual ferment that enabled many Catholic women to make a smooth transition to Protestantism.[10]

When Elizabeth I died in 1603, her Settlement had been secured and significant progress had been made in church reform. England was undoubtedly a Protestant nation despite lingering vestiges of the old faith and superstition, and an imperfect understanding of doctrinal truths on the part of many in the pews.[11] Elizabeth had successfully responded to Catholic challenges on the right by executing her double cousin and Catholic rival for the throne, Mary Stuart, Queen of Scots (1561–1567), in 1587, and by turning back an attempted invasion of England by the vaunted Spanish Armada in

1588. Thwarting the goals of a growing number of concerned Christians on the religious left, however, proved more difficult. This group, dubbed "Puritans" sometime in the 1560s, wanted a more comprehensive reformation. While Elizabeth lived, she managed to contain their restless quest for a more clearly Protestant Church, mostly through her personal charm and guile. However, when she disappeared from the scene, "all heaven broke loose."

Order Challenged: The Puritans Seek a "Further Reformation"

Many historians believe that the real English Reformation was played out in the century following Elizabeth's ascent to the throne.[12] This entailed the Puritan attempt to accomplish what they called "a further reformation," a quest that began immediately following the return of the Marian Exiles from their Continental places of refuge in the years after 1558.[13]

Who were the Puritans and what was Puritanism? Historians have long struggled, with only limited success, to define these terms with precision. The word "Puritan" originated as a term of derogation used by their enemies. The early Puritans referred to themselves simply as "the godly," a clue concerning why they were unpopular in some quarters. In any case, Puritans shared some things in common, such as their Calvinist theology, but even that was gradually modified to fit the English context. All shared a concern to make the English Church "more Protestant." Almost all Puritans wanted a more completely reformed national Church that included a clergy that had experienced a spiritual conversion in a personal manner. They also wanted a national culture based on the Bible that included dedicating Sunday to worship and rest, and a growth in educational provisions so that everybody could read the Bible and other godly books for themselves. They also advocated a system of social welfare for the poor. However, they differed among themselves concerning what kind of Protestantism it was that they desired: Lutheranism, an English version of Calvin's teachings, or something more radical.

As the century wore on it became apparent that most Puritans had embraced a form of Calvinism that included belief in election to salvation and that, as in Calvin's Geneva, the Elect should take control. Eventually many Puritans came to think that they could win the entire nation to Christ and thereby establish an "Elect Nation." This Elect Nation then would be used by God to convert the world to Christ, a view later called postmillennialism. This concept of an

Elect Nation was later secularized and domesticated into the body of beliefs of English civil religion.[14]

Equally important, Puritans eventually embraced church polity from across the spectrum: episcopal, presbyterian and congregational. At first, Puritan leaders tried to work within the episcopal system of the Church of England, but to no avail. Then, later in the sixteenth century, many concluded that they could never achieve their goals with government-controlled bishops at the top of a hierarchy that blocked their plans to change the Church. Most of these leaders adopted a presbyterian church polity that allowed for more independence for the local congregations to run their own affairs and choose their own leaders while providing for synods at different levels with some kind of National Synod or Assembly at the top to resolve disputes. Eventually, in the first half of the seventeenth century, many Puritans lost confidence in both the episcopal and presbyterian systems and became congregationalists who tried to establish autonomy for each local body of believers without reference to any hierarchical arrangement. Beginning in the 1580s, some of those with congregationalist inclinations left the established church altogether to create independent and, therefore, illegal congregations. These Independents, also called Separatists, became increasingly troublesome to the central government and the established church as the issues of the day finally led to civil war in the 1640s.

As noted, Elizabeth's goal was a unified, orderly society. Almost everybody at the time agreed that there could be but one true religion and that the church should be maintained by the state. The continence of an ordered society was as yet inconceivable without the Christian Church, and the Church was yet inconceivable except as a single comprehensive institution that was uniform in faith and worship. Since Elizabeth's subjects could not agree as to what form of Christianity should be enforced as true, her policy was to maintain at least the semblance of uniformity without at the same time disrupting her government. Her main objective was to rule England without undue strife. She knew that her people would permit her to do this provided that they also were allowed to go about their business with as little interference as possible.

Therefore, without troubling to be either logical or zealous, Elizabeth made herself secure. Her religious settlement was based on two principles: independence from Rome, and an English Church broadly Protestant in belief. As head of the nation, she asserted her control over ecclesiastical government and insisted that her bishops be men upon whom she could depend to follow her lead. The only religious test she insisted upon was willingness to swear allegiance to herself as the Supreme Governor of the Church. She also saw to it that uniformity was enforced by fines, and in some extreme cases, imprisonment, for those who failed to attend church services regularly.

The Queen rejected Catholic attempts to regain control of her Church because the pope had branded her as illegitimate. Consequently Catholics began to be known popularly as "papists" in Protestant England. She also resisted Puritan attempts to take over her Church because they represented a Calvinistic form of Protestantism that she believed was too extreme in keeping with her political and religious goals. For their part, the Puritans were a growing and increasingly well-organized minority that opposed Elizabeth's religious settlement. Who were these Puritans and what did they want?

Collinson provides the best insights into the nature of the Puritan Movement and its goals. He noted that the Puritans intended "to complete the English Reformation," and in so doing, Puritanism became something like "a church within the Church, with its own standards and nascent traditions, and even its own discipline and spiritual government." Most important, the Puritans wanted "to purify" the Anglican Church of all traces of what the Puritans regarded as the corruption that had survived from the days of the Roman connection. In other words, they wanted to get rid of everything they deemed papist and make the Church of England biblical to its core. Hence the source of their name "Puritan," and hence it was certain that the movement would have both ecclesiastical and political consequences. In summary, the Puritans were "the hot Protestants," that is, the more serious type of English Christians in this period.[15]

Perhaps no Englishman represented the Puritan spirit and intent better than Hugh Latimer, Bishop of Worcester from 1535 to 1555, who was martyred during Mary I's reign. Cambridge educated, Latimer became a dedicated evangelical churchman after his conversion to Christ following a period of Bible study in 1533. He also was one of the most popular of the new Protestant preachers in England. His eloquent denunciations of sin, injustice, corruption and the exploitation of the poor struck a responsive chord in the large crowds who came to hear him speak. According to all accounts, he lived a consistently godly life. Unfortunately for him, by the time Mary came to the throne in 1553, he was one of the best known of the Protestant leaders. He refused to flee to the Continent with many of his more wary fellow-believers when he had the opportunity. Consequently, he was arrested, tried, convicted of heresy, and burned at the stake in 1555. Latimer represented a certain kind of sixteenth-century

English Protestant who thought of himself as more intensely religious, Christian and Protestant than the ordinary churchgoer, and no doubt he was. He also wanted all Christians to be as totally committed to God as he was. He simply could not conceive of a half-hearted follower of Christ, a half-hearted religion or a half-hearted Reformation. As such, he reflected the attitude of those like-minded individuals, clerical and lay, who followed in his wake after Elizabeth came to the throne.[16]

The heirs to Latimer's Puritan spirit were not placated by a reformation that reformed so little. Elizabeth to their dismay did not really cleanse the Church but only swept the religious rubbish under the royal rug. Therefore, the Puritan Movement may be said to have sprung from the shock of their disappointment in finding out that their sovereign mistress was such an untidy religious housekeeper.

Ably led by returned Marian Exiles like university dons Laurence Humphrey, Thomas Sampson and Miles Coverdale, and by newly appointed bishops like Edmund Grindal, Thomas Bentham, Edwin Sandys and numerous others, the Puritans attempted in 1563 to reform the Church of England through the Convocation of the clergy of the province of Canterbury, and lost by a single vote. They then embarked upon a reforming crusade to place a spiritually minded and morally sound preacher in every parish, to abolish clerical robes called vestments, to reject the practice of kneeling at the reception of communion, to stop the practice of crossing oneself at baptism, and to introduce stricter church discipline. The Queen and the Archbishop of Canterbury, Matthew Parker, strongly opposed modification of standard practices and no changes were made.

As the battle for spiritual supremacy within the Church continued, Puritan hopes soared when Grindal was named the new Archbishop of Canterbury following the death of Parker in 1575. Grindal was the only Puritan (some would say "Puritan sympathizer") ever to occupy this important ecclesiastical position in the Church of England. Grindal's Protestant credentials were impeccable. He had been an energetic Bishop of London and Archbishop of York, and an unrelenting opponent of a powerful body of Catholic gentry in the north who persisted in defying royal wishes to comply with the Elizabethan Settlement. However, his very determination to make progress eventually caused conflict with the Queen, especially his sponsorship of "prophesyings" in the Church. Considerably less dramatic than the name suggests, these were gatherings or "exercises" for clergy to practice their preaching skills and their ability to use scripture, with supportive lay people gathered for the public part of the proceedings. Regular prophesyings were widely established and the bishops generally welcomed them, but not the Queen. The reason she disliked them is not clear. Perhaps the name suggested lurid connotations of disorder. In any event, she was not fond of the Protestant stress on preaching anyway, and occasionally rudely interrupted sermons that annoyed her.[17]

Grindal's response was defiance of the Queen culminating in a 6,000-word defense of the prophesyings and of the vital place of preaching in the Church. In this document, he dropped this fatal sentence: "Bear with me, I beseech you, Madam, if I choose rather to offend your earthly Majesty than to offend the heavenly majesty of God."[18] In 1577, the Queen suspended Grindal, placed him under house arrest, and by circular royal letter summarily forbade all prophesyings. Grindal remained suspended and without archepiscopal power until he died, blind and in increasingly ill health, in 1583. Suddenly all of the things that seemed so promising to the Puritans had been undermined. They had lost a friend at Canterbury at about the same time that many of the first generation of Elizabethan bishops who had supported further reform in the Church died. They were replaced by a new generation of hard-line anti-Puritan bishops.

During the 1580s, Puritan leaders realized that they would never accomplish their goals through the hierarchy of the Church. Therefore, they began to concentrate on Parliament, with the objective of electing enough Puritans and Puritan sympathizers to mandate change through parliamentary legislation. This took much longer than they expected. In the interim, the Puritan Underground proved effective in blunting an offensive against Puritanism launched by the new archbishop, John Whitgift, in 1583. Whitgift considered Puritans to be "rebels" and tried to destroy their influence. Driven from their pulpits, most deposed Puritan ministers carried on their program of reform from the shadows using clandestine presses to publish their work. Left largely to their own devices in the countryside, Puritan ministers worked hard to obtain individual conversions to Christ, especially among the gentry, and to encourage Puritan believers to seek election to the House of Commons. Puritanism also spread among the powerful London merchant class during this period as well. In the end, it was the intervention of the Puritan laity and compromises on both sides that prevented Whitgift from accomplishing his purposes.

It was also during the 1580s that Separatism made its appearance. These were those Puritans who had become so frustrated by their failure to reform the Church of England that they decided the only way forward was to separate from the Church. Claiming to be acting according to biblical precedent, they concluded that the national church should be replaced by local congregations that were "gathered communities" of truly converted people who joined these local bodies freely and who were bound together by a covenant. Of little consequence during Elizabeth's reign, these churches grew in number and significance in the first half of the seventeenth century, eventually providing the background for the emergence of the Congregationalist and Baptist denominations. It was also a Separatist church that fled to British North America and landed in Massachusetts in 1620, becoming "the Pilgrim Fathers" of Plymouth Rock fame.

When Elizabeth died in 1603, it seemed as though she had achieved her goal of avoiding religious war in England. However, as the end of her reign approached, many frustrated Puritans became further radicalized with increasing numbers demanding the abolition of the Prayer Book and the replacement of the episcopacy with a presbyterian system of church government. Further, many of these radicalized Puritans found their way into the House of Commons where they agitated for a further reformation of the English Church. This push for religious reform soon shaded off into political reform as well because in order to achieve their religious goals the House of Commons needed to become a more potent institution.

Before she died, the childless Elizabeth pushed through Parliament a succession bill stipulating that she be followed to the throne by her nearest living male Protestant relative. Ironically, this was James Stuart, James VI of Scotland (1567–1625), son of Mary Queen of Scots whom Elizabeth had ordered executed for treason in 1587. He became James I of England (1603–1625) in 1603 while retaining his rule of Scotland as James VI.[19] Since Presbyterian ministers had reared James in Scotland, the Puritans expected him to sympathize with their aspirations. Therefore, they presented him with a formal request called the Millenary Petition because it allegedly contained the signatures of a thousand Church of England ministers. The document reiterated the usual Puritan protests against clerical dress, desecration of the Sabbath and a lack of biblical preaching in the churches.

James not only received the petition but, in contrast to his predecessor, agreed to meet with representatives of those who had signed it at the royal palace at Hampton Court in 1604. While James avoided making major concessions that would threaten the Elizabethan Settlement, he made some minor ones. Most important for the story of English Puritanism, he vetoed the idea of changing the established church from episcopal to presbyterian not only because he despised the strict biblical morality of the Presbyterian ministers who had raised him but also because he aspired to be the powerful monarch in Episcopal England that he could never be in Presbyterian Scotland. However, the king agreed that there should be one uniform translation of the Bible that would be the only version used in all of the churches of the realm. This resulted in what would be popularly called the King James Version, or Authorized Version, of 1611 that became the standard translation in the English-speaking world for the next three centuries.

In any case, James continued to harass the Puritans, fiercely persecuted the Separatists because of their radical nonconformity, and, after initially lifting some restrictions on Roman Catholics, turned on them with a vengeance following the Gunpowder Plot to blow up Parliament House during the traditional "Speech from the Throne" to inaugurate a new Parliament in November 1605. The plot was discovered, and Guy Fawkes, who was the fuse man, and certain Jesuits and Catholic leaders implicated in the affair were arrested, tried and executed. News of the plot resulted in a huge wave of revulsion against the Roman Catholic Church sweeping the land as the Gunpowder Plot quickly became the symbol for Catholic treachery and the justification for the resumption of vigorous Catholic repression. The event also guaranteed that England would be an overwhelmingly Protestant nation well into the twentieth century.[20]

However, as James' reign wore on, disputes between the monarch and the House of Commons with its growing Puritan numbers became more frequent and sharp. There were not only problems of religion but also deep differences over how to finance national interests and a growing constitutional crisis over limitations to royal authority. James had managed to preserve the Elizabethan Settlement but at great cost to his prestige and ability to govern. This coupled with an exotic sex life that came under increasing Puritan criticism meant that his reign did not end happily.

Following his death in 1625, his son Charles I (1625–1649) came to the throne. There perhaps has been no more unhappy monarch in all of English history. For one thing, his father arranged for him to marry a French Catholic princess, Henrietta Maria, and toleration was accorded to her Catholic courtiers. Charles also continued his father's oppressive policies and his feuding with a Puritan-packed House of Commons. It is little wonder that Puritans in the 1630s were convinced that popery was about to be restored to England. One group centered at Cambridge University became so convinced that their doom was at hand that under the leadership of John Winthrop, they decided to leave their homeland for New England in 1630. There they hoped to establish a colony where they were free to follow the dictates of their consciences and to fashion a Christian "city upon a hill" for the entire world to see, note and emulate. During this decade some 20,000 of their like-minded Puritan fellow believers followed. This was extremely important because it robbed the Puritan Movement of 20,000 of its most able people on the eve of a civil war in which the Puritans they left behind had a vital stake. Moreover, it is important to note that these departing Puritans were of the congregationalist type, the most radical branch of the English Puritan Movement.[21]

The story of the coming of the English Civil War (1642–1651) is extremely complex and thousands of gallons of ink have been spilled by historians arguing about its origins, nature and results. Suffice it to say that the Puritans played a major role in both the coming and execution of the conflict. This role was reflected through the influence of many Puritan Members of Parliament, through Puritan clergy support of the Parliament against the Crown in the conflict, and through the contribution of large numbers of Puritan troops to the Parliamentary Army, including many of its officers. The Parliamentary leaders emphasized that they were protecting "the historic rights of Englishmen" against royal usurpation. Most Puritans agreed, but their real aim was the "further reformation" of the English Church that had thus far eluded them.[22]

There is almost nothing any historian can say about the origins and course of the English Civil War that will not produce disagreement from at least a large minority of professional colleagues.[23] For example, they continue to debate who was most responsible for the English Civil War. However, King Charles I cannot escape responsibility for estranging his Puritan subjects in a way that his father had never done. The king was not sensitive to their views and alienated people who wanted to be loyal subjects but who were appalled by his religious policies. The Puritans were unhappy about Charles' unwillingness to back Protestants in their struggle against Catholics in the Thirty Years' War (1618–1648) then raging on the Continent, not even his Protestant son-in-law, Frederick of the Palatinate. They were particularly distressed when Charles promoted people whom they considered to be "Arminians," meaning in this context anti-Calvinists and high churchmen, who emphasized the liturgy, incense and the vestments, to leadership positions in the Church. This was especially true of William Laud, a polarizing figure who was appointed Archbishop of Canterbury in 1633. The Puritans detested Laud because he seemed to threaten everything they stood for and appeared determined to impose pre-Reformation liturgical uniformity on the Church.

By this time the Puritans had strong support among the gentry who sat in Parliament, and they brought their grievances to be debated in the House of Commons. When Charles attempted to stop Parliament from dealing with matters that he considered to be the royal prerogative, the parliamentarians protested that the king was violating their ancient rights. For many who were not Puritans in the Parliament, this became a central issue in the debate and eventually a parliamentary battle cry in the civil war that followed.

Historians differ over whether the English Civil War was a struggle between King and Parliament over constitutional issues, a conflict fought primarily over religious disagreements, or a dispute over matters of greater complexity, including economic factors. Most would at least acknowledge that religious motivations were present and important. Generally speaking, the sides divided up with Parliament and most Puritans in one camp and the king and his supporters and most high church advocates in the other. Neither side wanted a military conflict and both sides suffered terribly from a war that eventually spread to every part of the British Isles. The Puritans were on the winning side but once they had triumphed they were faced with many new problems, including what to do about the divisions that developed among themselves and the enormous difficulty of achieving their vision of a godly commonwealth.

The Civil War (or Wars) was really a series of armed conflicts and political machinations that took place in three distinct phases: 1642–1645, 1648–1649, and 1649–1651. The first two periods pitted the king and his partisans against the supporters of the Long Parliament of 1640–1660, while the third saw fighting between Charles and his followers and supporters of the Rump Parliament of 1648. Parliamentary forces won each of these conflicts. Its victory after the second phase led to the trial and execution of Charles I, the exile of his son and heir apparent, the future Charles II (1660–1685), and the replacement of the monarchy with the Commonwealth of England (1649–1653) and then with a Protectorate (1653–1659) that shaded off into the personal rule of Oliver Cromwell. With the Commonwealth the monopoly of the Church of England on Christian worship came to an end, and the victors consolidated the already established Protestant aristocracy in Ireland.

After the first period of the war, Charles promised to adhere to Parliament's wishes but secretly negotiated an agreement with the Scots to restore him to power by promising them church reform. In the meantime, Parliament continued to recognize Charles as the legitimate ruler of the realm. Furious that Parliament had done this and suspecting the king of duplicity, in December 1648, the army, now controlled by the Puritans, marched on Parliament and conducted "Pride's Purge," so named after the commanding officer of the operation, Colonel Thomas Pride. Troops arrested 45 Members of Parliament and kept 146 others out of the meeting place. Pride allowed only 75 MPs into the building, and then only to do the army's bidding. The army, now led by Oliver Cromwell, ordered this "Rump Parliament" to set up a high court of justice in order to try Charles I for treason in the name of the people of England. Fifty-nine judges, called Commissioners, found Charles guilty, declared him a traitor, murderer and public enemy, and ordered him beheaded on a scaffold in front of the Banqueting House of the Palace of Whitehall in the heart of royal London on 30 January 1649.

Cromwell, as Commander of the New Model Army, Parliament's elite fighting force composed of 22,000 mostly Puritan troops, gradually emerged as the most powerful of the Parliamentary leaders.[24] From heavily Puritan Cambridgeshire, Cromwell had been converted to Christ and the Puritan way as a young man, and thereafter found living within a Church still full of "popish" ceremonies unbearable. He yearned for the pure and unadorned preaching of the Gospel of Christ throughout his nation. When the opportunity came, he stood for the House of Commons from Cambridge and when elected joined the Puritan parliamentary caucus. Politically dominant by 1649, Cromwell made several attempts to fashion a lasting political solution based on a republic. He had proved himself a brilliant cavalry general and played a leading role in bringing Charles I to trial and execution. Now the English looked to him for leadership.

In 1649–1650, he relentlessly and sometimes brutally eliminated opposition to the new regime in Ireland and Scotland. Britain was a Commonwealth during 1649–1653, with executive power vested in a Council of State and legislative authority vested in the Rump. However, when the mostly presbyterian Rump proved unable to provide clear, decisive leadership, Cromwell dissolved it and the three kingdoms of England, Scotland and Ireland became a Protectorate with Cromwell serving as Lord Protector. The enthusiastic parliamentarian, republican and congregationalist was now a benevolent dictator, king in all but name. He died in September 1658 and was succeeded by his son, Richard. However, as the state drifted toward anarchy during 1659, only one solution seemed possible. Therefore, in May 1660, the remnant of the Long Parliament invited the Stuarts to restore their throne in the person of Charles II, and then dissolved itself.

As Lord Protector, Cromwell was constrained to work with and through a Council of State and to meet Parliament regularly. Therefore, his dictatorship was never absolute. He also sincerely sought

God's will as he governed his people. In any case, he often used his power wisely, as when he established a wide measure of religious liberty. The new state church was congregationalist in nature but no one was required to attend it, and almost everyone, Catholics and Jews included, was allowed to worship privately in light of conscience. The Puritan hope was that the free preaching of the Gospel would eventually lead to the conversion to Christ of the overwhelming majority of the people. In any event, membership in the state church was no longer a qualification, as it was before 1649 and from 1660 to the late nineteenth century, for entry into the universities, the professions or public office. Unfortunately for Cromwell, extremists took advantage of religious liberty to espouse their views and sometimes disturb public order, which added to his headaches. His brilliant naval and military reforms, along with the financial measures that underpinned them, appeared to go unnoticed amidst the religious turmoil of the times.

Cromwell desperately wanted to build a godly commonwealth and fulfill Puritan dreams of a thoroughly biblical reformation of the Church. Ironically, in order to do this he had to ride roughshod over those who opposed him, mostly through punishing taxes and occasional imprisonment of the most obstreperous. The Puritans had misread the signs of the times, and not everybody wanted to embrace Christ as Savior and join a national Holy Club based on Puritan values. Moreover, he had always led a minority government with even presbyterian Puritans often opposing his goals. The coalition of interests he represented disintegrated with his death.

As historian John Morrill observed, his achievement was transient and in the short and medium term negative. He gave the English an abiding suspicion of religious enthusiasts and of soldiers in politics, and he escalated the long-term instability of Ireland, where an English colonial elite oppressed the Catholic masses. On the other hand, he had championed genuine religious liberty, the principle of the accountability of rulers to the people, and parliamentary power, and these proved a great inspiration to nineteenth-century reformers, liberals and nonconformists. He is a dominant figure in British and Irish history, and probably the one about whom there is the most disagreement.

Most important for the history of the Reformation, Cromwell represents shattered Puritan dreams. Like all Puritans, Cromwell wanted a Church of England purified of papal trappings and reformed according to biblical principles. Like all Puritans, he longed to see all of his fellow English people converted to Christ. Like all Puritans, he wanted people to live disciplined, godly lives.

Even though many then and now might consider it desirable to have a reformed Church and a converted, highly disciplined citizenry, Cromwell and the Puritans found that this way of life could not be forced on an entire nation. And yet, how could England be God's chosen nation without these attributes? Therein lies the Puritan dilemma. And thus the English Reformation that began with a quest for order under Henry VIII and the Tudors ended with the re-establishment of order with the Restoration of the monarchy in 1660. In between was nearly 150 years of disorder, change and turmoil.

The Impact of the English Reformation on the Western World

Therefore, which was the real English Reformation: The one represented by the Elizabethan Settlement or the one represented by the Puritan longing for a Church of England that was thoroughly cleansed of popery and reformed according to the Bible? The Elizabethan Settlement created a latitudinarian Church, one that embraced a variety of theological emphases and worship styles. Generally speaking, the English Church was and remains moderately Calvinist in theology, Catholic and liturgical in ecclesiology and episcopal in church polity. Moreover, in terms of theology, the worldwide Anglican Communion includes within its ranks convinced evangelicals, adaptable liberals, and devoted Anglo-Catholics. Further, the Anglican Church in England and elsewhere remains closely related to and engaged with the state.

The Puritan Movement still lives on in the Church of England, the Anglican Communion around the globe and in many nooks and corners of the Protestant world. Many former Puritans became adherents of the Evangelical Party of the Anglican Church. Others disappeared into the various new Protestant churches after 1660, such as the English Presbyterian Church and some of the Baptist churches. Other Puritan elements would be absorbed into Evangelicalism when it made its appearance in the eighteenth century. In all these instances, they carried with them the Puritan dream of a global Christian Church purified by biblical truth and filled with godly people, soundly converted and working assiduously for Christ in order to bring the Gospel to the entire world. These two rich religious heritages, one representing comprehension and the other representing a covenanted community, often exist side-by-side in the present-day Church of England. In that sense, perhaps both the Elizabethan Settlement and the Puritan Dream were the real English Reformation.

Therefore, the English Reformation produced a Church with no pope but with an Archbishop of Canterbury as its spiritual leader, a leader with decreasing powers as the years passed. The monarch is still the Supreme Governor of the Church, with even more greatly reduced powers than the Archbishop of Canterbury. However, in most branches of the Anglican Church today much of the pomp, that is the liturgy, clerical garb and ceremonial practices from the days of the Roman connection, remain. On the other hand, Puritan simplicity remains very much a part of the ethos of many nonconformist Protestant churches in Britain today. They continue the tradition of no pope and no pomp.

Both the Church of England and the Puritan Movement have left their marks on English politics. The Church of England, though it no longer enjoys most of the fruits of being the established church of the nation, still maintains many rights and privileges and is still loosely tied to the state. Moreover, it still plays a major role in official English life, such as the coronation and spiritual care of each new monarch. Moreover, there is still the lingering belief among many English people that to be genuinely English is to be Anglican and that the Church of England is foundational to English nationalism. As for the Puritans, Cromwell deeply impacted the course of British politics in ways already mentioned. He led the way to increasingly widespread religious liberty and helped to increase the powers of Parliament, especially the House of Commons that this institution enjoys today. By the same token, his republican experiment set a negative example for those who aspired to make England a republic rather than the constitutional monarchy the country enjoys today.

The economic impact of the Reformation was also substantial. Government-sanctioned Elizabethan privateers roamed the world challenging Catholic Spain and its world empire, and making considerable profit as they did. Moreover, Puritan merchants greatly increased their wealth, as they seemed to substantiate Max Weber's claim that Calvinists make better capitalists. First Puritan and then nonconformist believers tended to dominate the British economy well into the twentieth century.

Reformation influences on English language and literature were enormous. Here mainstream Anglicanism contributed heavily. The sonorous tones of Cranmer's Book of Common Prayer and the beautiful cadences of the King James Version of the Bible are cases in point. Moreover, it is doubtful that the mountaintop of literary development known as the Elizabethan Renaissance could have occurred without the encouragement and freedom provided by Elizabeth and her religious settlement.

Finally, the English Reformation, especially Calvinistic Puritanism, provided the ideological base for the development of both British and American civil religion. A broad national faith that included both the established Church of England and nonconformists emerged as the English people began to think of themselves as a special people, "God's Chosen People," ordained by the Almighty to spread Christianity and British-style civilization to the rest of the world. Transplanted to America by immigrating Puritans, the idea of building a "city upon a hill" became part and parcel of the American psyche and was eventually secularized to fit the growing aspirations and political needs of an expansionist American nation. Almost all American presidents have included a secularized version of the Puritan vision of America as God's great hope for humankind as a part of their presidential rhetoric.[25]

In these and other ways, the English Reformation continues to impact the English-speaking world today. The Anabaptists, the subject of the following chapter, is another group that has made its mark on the modern world in a profound manner.

Notes

1. Patrick Collinson, *The Reformation* (New York: Modern Library, 2004), 125.

2. This section on the sixteenth-century Reformation is based on A. G. Dickens' magisterial volume *The English Reformation*, 2nd ed. (London: B. T. Batsford, 1989); and the revisionist work of Eamon Duffy, *The Stripping of the Altars: Traditional Religion in England, 1440–ca. 1580* (New Haven, CT: Yale University Press, 1992).

3. Geoffrey de C. Parmiter, *The King's Great Matter* (London: Longmans, 1967); and Hans Hillerbrand, *The World of the Reformation* (New York: Charles Scribner's Sons, 1973), 118–119.

4. "And if a man shall take his brother's wife, it is an unclean thing: he hath uncovered his brother's nakedness; they shall be childless." KJV.

5. Jasper Ridley, *Thomas Cranmer* (Oxford: Oxford University Press, 1962); Diarmaid MacCulloch, *Thomas Cranmer* (New Haven, CT: Yale University Press, 1996); G. R. Elton, *Policy and Police: The Enforcement of the Reformation in the Age of Thomas Cromwell* (Cambridge: Cambridge University Press, 1985); and Stanford Lehmberg, *The Reformation Parliament, 1529–1536* (Cambridge: Cambridge University Press, 1970).

6. Brian Moynahan, *God's Bestseller: William Tyndale, Thomas More, and the Writing of the English Bible* (New York: St. Martin's Press, 2002).

7. For details, see John Foxe, *The Acts and Monuments of John Foxe*, ed. by George Townsend, 8 vols. (New York: AMA Press, 1965). This work,

commonly known as Foxe's *Book of Martyrs*, has circulated in many different editions since its original publication in 1563.

8. Denis R. Janz, ed., *A Reformation Reader* (Minneapolis: Augsburg Fortress Press, 1999), 312–323.

9. Although Hooker's work did not become widely known until after his death, it provided the classic statement of what was later to become "Anglicanism." Richard Hooker, *Of the Laws of Ecclesiastical Polity*, ed. W. Speed Hill (Cambridge: Belknap Press, 1981), 3:330.

10. See Christine Peters, *Patterns of Piety: Women, Gender, and Religion in Late Medieval and Reformation England* (Cambridge: Cambridge University Press, 2003), 3–7 and 169.

11. Susan Doran, *Elizabeth I and Religion, 1558–1603* (London: Routledge, 1993), 66.

12. Patrick Collinson, *The Religion of Protestants: The Church in English Society, 1559–1625* (Oxford: Clarendon Press, 1982).

13. For Elizabethan Puritanism, see Patrick Collinson, *The Elizabethan Puritan Movement* (Oxford: Clarendon Press, 1990), the classic introduction to the subject.

14. Foxe, 1:vi–viii, 305–386, and passim; and William Haller, *Foxe's Book of Martyrs and the Elect Nation* (London: Jonathan Cape, 1963).

15. Collinson, *Elizabethan Puritan Movement*, 12–14.

16. Allen G. Chester, *Hugh Latimer: Apostle to the English* (Philadelphia: University of Pennsylvania Press, 1954), 16–22, 103–151, 187–188, 197–218.

17. Peter McCullough, *Sermons at Court: Politics and Religion in Elizabethan and Jacobean Preaching* (Cambridge: Cambridge University Press, 1998), 51–100.

18. Patrick Collinson, *Archbishop Grindal, 1519–1583: The Struggle for a Reformed Church* (Berkeley: University of California Press, 1979), 242.

19. For a useful overview of the Stuarts and seventeenth-century England, see Barry Coward, *The Stuart Age* (New York: Longman, 1980). The material for this section on the first half of the seventeenth century is taken mostly from this source, and from Robert Lockyer, *James VI and I* (London: Addison Wesley Longman, 1998); and L. J. Reeve, *Charles I and the Road to Personal Rule* (Cambridge: Cambridge University Press, 1989).

20. Alice Hogge, *God's Secret Agents: Queen Elizabeth's Forbidden Priests and the Hatching of the Gunpowder Plot* (London: Harper Collins, 2005). The plot inaugurated the celebration of Guy Fawkes Day on every November 5 among English-speaking Protestants, a practice that endured into the twentieth century.

21. Alan Simpson, *Puritanism in Old and New England* (Chicago: University of Chicago Press, 1955).

22. See Robert S. Paul, *The Lord Protector: Religion and Politics in the Life of Oliver Cromwell* (Grand Rapids, MI: Eerdmans, 1964).

23. For competing views on this matter, see Ann Hughes, *The Origins of the English Civil War*, 2nd ed. (New York: St. Martin's Press, 1998); Michael Finlayson, *Historians, Puritanism, and the English Revolution: The Religious Factor in English Politics Before and After the Interregnum* (Toronto: University of Toronto Press, 1983); and Conrad Russell, *The Causes of the English Civil War* (New York: Oxford University Press, 1990).

24. For Cromwell and his place in English history, see John Morrill, ed., *Oliver Cromwell and the English Revolution* (London: Longman, 1990); and Barry Coward, *Oliver Cromwell* (London: Longman, 1991). Paul is also valuable for understanding of Cromwell's religious beliefs and how they affected his political views.

25. Richard V. Pierard and Robert D. Linder, *Civil Religion and the Presidency* (Grand Rapids, MI: Zondervan, 1988), 45–64.

CHAPTER 5

THE ANABAPTISTS AND OTHER RADICALS

If John Calvin is the most misunderstood single individual of the Reformation Era, then the Anabaptists were the most misunderstood group. The Anabaptists were the largest single entity within a movement that historians have categorized as "the Radical Reformation." By radical, they mean that this cluster of believers wanted to get back to the roots or origins of Christianity and restore the primitive church of the first century. Therefore, they were "restorationists" rather than "reformers" like Luther, Calvin or the English Protestants. Whereas the mainline Protestants—Lutheran, Calvinist, Anglican—wanted to reform the old Church, the Radical Reformers wanted to discard it and go directly back to what they believed to be the New Testament norm.[1]

Unfortunately, most sixteenth-century Protestants and Catholics lumped all of the people who used the rhetoric of restoration into one group without distinguishing differences among them, and condemned them all as seditious and heretical. The Radical Reformers were considered seditious because it appeared to most Protestant and Catholic authorities that they were determined to overthrow the existing religious, political and social order. They were regarded as heretical because they rejected the established churches in the various territorial states, referred to themselves as "the true church," condemned Protestants and Catholics alike for having departed from New Testament Christianity, and advocated going back to the basics of the first-century Christian faith.

In reality, there were three strands to the Radical Reformation in addition to a number of free spirits who defied categorization. Although such distinctions were seldom made in the sixteenth century, modern historians now see Anabaptists, Spiritualists, and Antitrinitarians as the three main expressions of the Radical Reformation, with the Anabaptists far outnumbering the other two groups. No one knows how many there were because they were illegal nearly everywhere in Europe, and because they were often pursued relentlessly by the authorities with the intent to eliminate them as individuals and groups. Their numbers also fluctuated according to the ferocity of the persecution and the success of the authorities in destroying or exiling them. At their height, there were perhaps a half million in all of Europe, probably far fewer toward the end of the sixteenth century, but these are only crude estimates. In any case, whereas Lutheranism, Calvinism and Anglicanism all had geographical headquarters at Wittenberg, Geneva and Canterbury, respectively, no such place existed in the world of Anabaptism. Theirs was a highly decentralized movement. Moreover, almost nobody wanted them. Therefore, they became "Eternal Immigrants," wandering the face of Europe, seeking freedom, especially religious freedom.[2]

Anabaptist Origins

What were the origins of these peculiar people? This was once the subject of sharp debate. Some historians argued that they were really spiritual descendants of those believers who had somehow maintained biblical purity down through the ages, often at the peril of their very lives and often leaving a "trail of blood" in their wake. Others believed that they represented the remnants of medieval heresies that had long defied the Medieval Church and somehow escaped its clutches until the Reformation occurred and made it possible for them to come out into the open. Others claimed that they were simply biblical sects that had arisen in response to Christian humanism and the open Bible introduced by the first-generation Protestant reformers. In more recent time, social historians have established a revisionist school of Anabaptist historiography that insists that the Radical Reformation in general and the Anabaptist Movement in particular had a multiplicity of beginnings, now formalized by historians Klaus Deppermann, Werner Packull and James Stayer as the polygenesis theory.[3]

In any event, there is no need to speculate at length on origins because the nature of the movement is such that it could have risen spontaneously in several different areas at nearly the same time, as all of the various strands claimed to go back to the Bible for their basic beliefs. The common thread was not an institution, a hierarchy or even a kind of spiritual apostolic succession but a claim to re-embrace the original Christianity of the New Testament. In any event, most historians, including the polygenesists, usually point to the Swiss Brethren who appeared in and around Zurich in the 1520s and/or the radical Christians who followed Thomas Müntzer during the great German Peasants' War of 1524–1525 as the first Anabaptists.[4]

Why were they called Anabaptists? The term "Anabaptist" is a Latin derivative of the Greek word *anabaptismos*, meaning "to rebaptize." The German form was *Wiedertäufer*, which means "one who rebaptizes." Lutherans in Germany and Zwinglians in Zurich applied it in the beginning to those who separated themselves from the state churches. As for the radicals themselves, they resolutely rejected the name. They insisted that they did not "rebaptize" because infant baptism did not constitute a true biblical baptism and that they were not in reality rebaptizing anybody. They were only following Jesus and Paul who urged baptism following teaching and repentance. Their arguments, however, went unheeded. Further, the name Anabaptist proved so conveniently elastic that it came to be applied to all of those who defied the established state churches. As for the radicals themselves, they only wanted to be known as *Brüder* or *Täufer*, that is "Brethren" or "Baptists," or simply as Christians.[5]

However, the real reason that the word Anabaptist became popular with the authorities was because it afforded them an excuse to suppress the radicals with force. The enemies of the movement were insistent on the use of the term because the radical groups thereby became subject to the death penalty. Under the ancient Roman law against the fifth-century Donatists, who held views similar to the radicals, Anabaptists in the sixteenth century could be put to death. This ancient law against the Donatists, who had been declared heretics and subversives by the imperial government because they insisted on baptizing believers only and in general defied the ecclesiastical and imperial authority of Rome, had been preserved in the famed Justinian Code of the sixth century. The Code declared that rebaptism and denial of the Trinity in particular were capital crimes because they threatened to disrupt the political and social unity of the empire. Since most of Continental Europe in the sixteenth century was under Roman Law, this meant that the Code could be applied to the Anabaptists, who, by definition, were "rebaptizers." Thus, rebaptizing was a capital crime in Reformation Europe.

It is now obvious that the term "Anabaptist" was not one that was appropriate for this group of radical believers. It was really an epithet flung contemptuously at these people in order to pressure them into abandoning their beliefs or, failing that, to deal with them with finality. Unfortunately, the word has prevailed in the historical literature and is still used today even though terms like Swiss Brethren, Hutterite Brethren and Mennonites are far more appropriate and precise. In any case, the term Anabaptist only provides clues as to the identity of this group and not any kind of precise definition.

Perhaps the best path to a satisfactory definition lies in understanding how the Anabaptist viewed the nature of "the true church." According to historian R. J. Smithson, "The real issue between the Anabaptists and the other reformers was on the question of the type of Church which should take the place of the old Church.... The reformers aimed to reform the old Church by the Bible; the radicals attempted to build a new Church from the Bible."[6] In other words, the Anabaptists believed that the answer to worldly churches full of nominal Christians was to return to the New Testament emphasis on a local, gathered, disciplined congregation of self-confessed believers. Only those who had embraced Jesus as Savior and Lord and demonstrated a changed life and were baptized upon their confession of faith could be members of this local congregation.

This view of the church sharply separated Anabaptists from the old Roman Catholic Church and what historian George Williams called the Magisterial Protestants (the Lutherans, Calvinists and Anglicans who accepted the support of the magistrates in establishing the Reformation). The Catholics and Magisterial Protestants continued the medieval pattern in which the church encompassed the whole of society and in which the magistrates upheld the church. In contrast, the Anabaptists wanted a church separate from the state that allowed only mature believers as members. They intended to restore the New Testament understanding of the church as a local, gathered community, separate from the larger society, and known for adherents who could articulate their conversion to Christ.[7]

One last act further defined and set apart the Anabaptists from society at large. At the Imperial Diet of Speyer in April 1529, six German states and the delegations from 14 German free cities first took the name "Protestant" in order to designate themselves as stout followers of Luther's reforms. They, in fact, had risen "to protest" against imperial plans to bring Luther to heel. At the same meeting, an imperial law was published against the Anabaptists in which both Catholics and Protestants concurred. It was promulgated in the aftermath of the Peasants' War of 1524–1525, in which many of the peasants had been identified as Anabaptists or Anabaptist sympathizers. Therefore, on April 23, a decree of the Emperor Charles V gave specific instructions to imperial officials concerning how to deal with the Anabaptists. In this document, Anabaptism was defined as a terrible combination of sedition, schism and heresy. Therefore, there was only one course of action to take: exterminate them! After 1529, almost every segment of society stood ready to lend a hand in this task. They were prepared to take stern measures against these radical reformers who appeared to them to be both anarchists and anti-social, therefore a danger to church and state.

The Margins of the Movement

As indicated, Anabaptism had become identified with sedition and heresy in many parts of Europe. These charges had a certain validity on the margins of the movement where many individuals who rejected both the Roman Catholic Church and the various Protestant state churches had been branded as Anabaptists. Also, most of these individuals and groups speculated concerning the imminent return of Christ and held various millennial views. As noted, Thomas Müntzer was one such individual. Like Luther, Müntzer was born in Saxony into an economically respectable home and was also relatively well educated. Initially he and Luther were friendly. After ordination to the priesthood, Müntzer became pastor of several reformed churches in Saxony. He thought highly of himself, and both his mind and life were restless and erratic. It was not long before he broke with Luther and cultivated his own following, first at the small eastern Saxon city of Zwickau and later, after a period of wandering about, at Allstedt, another small Saxon town. In 1524, he wrote a tract in which he referred to Luther as "the unspiritual soft-living flesh in Wittenberg, whose robbery and distortion of Scripture has so grievously polluted our wretched Christian Church." In the same tract he called Luther "Father Pussyfoot," "Dr. Liar" and "the Pope of Wittenberg."[8] Müntzer's biting attacks and vivid epithets made the rounds. Thus, a "fellowship of discontent" was in the making in the 1520s.[9]

It was while at Allstedt in 1524 that Müntzer began to put some of his radical ideas into practice. He began to teach direct inspiration by the Holy Spirit, especially for himself, and to talk of Christ's imminent return. He stepped up his attacks on Luther. He preached before Duke John, the brother of the Elector Frederick of Saxony, and before John's son, John Frederick. He called for the princes to lead the way and to be prepared to use violence to establish the Kingdom of God on earth. In 1525, in a fiery appeal to Count Ernst von Mansfeld, whose territory abutted Allstedt, Müntzer tried to browbeat the count into supporting his plan to convert the world to his radical views. "I, Thomas Müntzer, admonish you," he raged.

"You have undertaken to destroy the Christians. Tell me, you miserable, shabby bag of worms, who has made you a ruler of the people whom God has redeemed with his precious blood? You are called upon to prove whether you are a Christian.... You will be prosecuted and exterminated."[10] Little wonder that he won few from among the rulers to his side.

The authorities and Luther became especially concerned about his growing radicalism when Müntzer created a paramilitary group of about 500 members, called the League of the Elect, which trashed a chapel near Allstedt that was dedicated to the Virgin Mary. Luther wrote to the Elector Frederick of Saxony urging him to take action against Müntzer. Expecting to be expelled, Müntzer fled Allstedt. Before leaving, he once again attacked Luther in a tract, indicating that he had become convinced that the Wittenberg Reformer was a tool of the established authorities and had acquiesced in the oppression of the peasants. He soon became pastor of a church in Muhlhausen where he came into contact with the peasant uprising that had broken out the previous year in southwestern Germany. In May of 1525, Müntzer traveled to Frankenhausen where about 9,000 peasants had gathered. He became their leader, convinced that he was God's prophet sent to inaugurate a new order. Consequently, when the peasants, armed mostly with farming tools, faced a professional army with cavalry and artillery, slaughter ensued. Both Müntzer and the peasants fled, Müntzer to a house in town where he hid under a bed. He soon was discovered, tortured, beheaded, and his head displayed on a lance in a field as a reminder of what happens to rebels. Since he had denounced Luther and his reformation for its failure to embrace the full implications of the gospel and had consorted with peasants who held Anabaptist views, Müntzer was himself widely assumed to be an Anabaptist. He may have rejected the main tenets of the Roman Catholic and Lutheran Churches but there is no evidence that he ever accepted believer's baptism. Nevertheless, in the eyes of the non-Anabaptist world, he had been a leader of the despised movement.[11]

A second and more deadly threat to Anabaptism at the margins was the Münster rebellion of 1534–1535.[12] From the beginning of the movement, there were many Anabaptists who emphasized the New Testament teaching of the Second Coming of Christ and believed that his return to set up his kingdom on earth was imminent. The troubles predicted in the New Testament seemed to have materialized, proving that the end time was near. By 1533, for example, a prominent Anabaptist leader named Melchior Hofmann became convinced that Christ would soon come to Strasbourg to set up his millennial kingdom. His followers were known as Melchiorites. A few, who were probably only hangers-on or Anabaptist sympathizers, claimed that they had been divinely commissioned to set up a theocratic kingdom in anticipation of Jesus' return. In this kingdom, true believers would gloriously reign and serve as the instruments of God in the destruction of the wicked. This was the kind of millenarian fanaticism that resulted in the infamous Münster uprising.

In any event, Hofmann languished in a Strasbourg prison as he awaited the glorious appearing. Meanwhile, as his imprisonment lengthened, his movement was hijacked by two unscrupulous Dutch opportunists named Jan Matthys and Jan van Leyden, who claimed to receive visions that revealed that Jesus was coming not to Strasbourg but Münster, an important cathedral city in Westphalia in northwestern Germany. Bernhard Rothman, the leading evangelical reformer in the city, had, after a considerable spiritual pilgrimage, become convinced that infant baptism was wrong. He also managed to install evangelical preachers in all of the city's churches except for the cathedral itself when Matthys and Van Leyden arrived. By this time, a majority of the adults in the city were evangelicals with a large number of Melchiorites among them. The charismatic Matthys and Van Leyden now seized the leadership of the city and declared that Münster was to be the New Jerusalem where Jesus would establish the capital of his millennial kingdom. Matthys claimed to be Enoch and Van Leyden declared he was King David. Under the leadership of the two Jans, Melchiorite Anabaptism was transformed into what became the holocaust of Münster.[13]

The Anabaptists gained control of the City Council on 23 February 1534, and with that Matthys became effective dictator of Münster. Catholics, Lutherans and Anabaptists alike now had to submit to his rule or leave. Communal ownership of property was introduced, all citizens who remained were baptized (except, apparently, for Matthys, Van Leyden and their immediate circle), and the call went out to Anabaptists everywhere to come to Münster. Horrified by reports of what was happening, the Catholic Bishop of Münster joined with Protestants to lay siege to the city. On 4 April 1534, Matthys was killed while leading a counterattack on the besieging army. Van Leyden took over and introduced even more radical measures. The City Council was dissolved and Van Leyden and 11 followers ruled, calling themselves the Twelve Elders of Israel. Compulsory polygamy was introduced in July 1534. After repulsing an attack by the besieging army in September 1534, Van Leyden had himself crowned King of Münster. His rule was short-lived. At the end of a period of acute famine and indescribable suffering, the city finally fell to the besieging army in June 1535. Those who survived the ordeal were massacred on the spot. Van Leyden and two of his associates were captured and publicly tortured to death with red-hot irons on a platform in the city center. Their bodies were then placed in iron cages and hung from the tower of St. Lambert's Church as a warning to all who might be tempted to do something similar in the future.

The successful suppression of the Münster uprising was the signal for nearly all of Europe to intensify the persecution of Anabaptists on the grounds that they, like the fanatics of Münster, were threats to law and order. The authorities in all parts of Europe, Protestant and Roman Catholic areas alike, executed thousands. It was a needless slaughter. Most Anabaptists were not in sympathy with the radical Münsterites or their ideals. But it was a convenient tool for discrediting the entire movement by pointing out the shocking aberrations of a small minority that was probably never a real part of Anabaptism at all. In any event, most of the millenarian fanatics perished in these attacks but tens of thousands of innocent people lost their lives as well. In the meantime, other Anabaptists were developing followings that eventually would comprise the mainstream of the radical movement for reform.[14]

Mainstream Anabaptism

At Strasbourg, for example, following the Peasants' War a large cluster of radicals of various persuasions adopted a policy of pragmatic survivalism that entailed dropping Hofmann's strident emphasis on millennialism and similar views.[15] In Zurich during the 1520s, Conrad Grebel, Felix Mantz and Georg Blaurock led a fledgling Anabaptist community that at first welcomed Zwingli's reformation but then opposed his state church. All three men were well educated and able to articulate their views with considerable eloquence. In particular, they objected to magisterial reform with its infant baptism and presumed nominalism and argued for believer's baptism and religious liberty. Their peaceful opposition to Zwingli came to naught as they suffered imprisonment and torture at the hands of the Zurich authorities. Grebel eventually fell victim to the plague in 1526, and Mantz and Blaurock were declared heretics and executed in 1527 and 1529, respectively. However, these three men were responsible for establishing a permanent Anabaptist community in the Zurich area and became the first of many martyrs for their cause.

Michael Sattler was another early Anabaptist martyr who exercised considerable influence in the fledgling movement in southern

Germany.[16] Sattler agreed with the Zurich Brethren who had advocated a gathered church, believer's baptism and religious liberty. He also taught that true Christians should avoid violence and oppose the use of force in all matters of religion. A former monk, he professed faith in Christ in an evangelical sense sometime in 1526 and soon became an Anabaptist leader. He wrote a number of tracts explaining the faith of those called Brethren and defending their cause against accusations of heresy. Sattler's most important achievement in the history of Anabaptism, however, was as the architect of what became known as The Schleitheim Confession of Faith of 1527. This document was not intended to be a doctrinal formulation but rather a church manual that dealt with order and discipline in Anabaptist congregations. It contained seven articles dealing with believer's baptism, excommunication (called the ban), the Lord's Supper (as a memorial, not a saving sacrament), separation from the world, the role of pastors, the restricted use of the sword by civil authorities, and the prohibition among believers to swear oaths in civil law. Even though not primarily a theological document, it contained an implied theology that embodied mainstream Anabaptist beliefs of the 1520s.

Sattler also exemplified the short life span of many Anabaptist leaders in this period. Most died before they reached the age of 40. Sattler managed to reach his 37th year. In any event, following his return from the Schleitheim gathering to his south German home in Horb, in 1527, local authorities arrested Sattler, his wife and many members of his congregation. Taken to Binsdorf near Rottenburg on the Nekar River, Austrian officials, who had jurisdiction in the area, interrogated and tortured Sattler and eventually condemned him as a heretic. His interrogation revealed a gross misunderstanding of Anabaptist teachings and no sympathy for the teachings that were understood. Moreover, it also revealed much about Anabaptist beliefs, including Sattler's assertion of the Anabaptist principle of peaceful nonresistance. In any case, Sattler's substantial defense of his views did him little good. He was condemned as a heretic on 18 May 1527, and executed two days later.

The fate of Sattler and his spouse became typical of Anabaptist martyrdom in the sixteenth century. The sentence was as much a ceremony as it was an act of criminal justice. Its fulfillment began with torture as a prelude to the execution itself. The preliminaries included cutting pieces of flesh from his troublesome tongue and from his miserable body with red-hot tongs. He was then forged to a cart and taken to the Rottenburg marketplace, the scene of the execution, and tortured again with the heated tongs along the way. In the marketplace itself, still able to speak, Sattler prayed for those who were about to put him to death. After he was bound to a ladder and pushed into the fire, he admonished the people and gathered public officials to repent and turn to Jesus. As soon as the ropes on his wrists burned, Sattler raised his forefingers, giving the promised signal to Brethren in the crowd that a martyr's death was bearable. His last reported words were: "Father I commend my spirit into your hands."[17] Three other condemned Anabaptist heretics were also executed on that day. Then, after repeated failed attempts to force Sattler's wife to recant, she was drowned eight days later in the Nekar River.

Dr. Balthasar Hubmaier was another major south German leader who became a martyr for the Anabaptist cause.[18] Hubmaier is interesting because he was, in many ways, a reluctant martyr who several times previously had recoiled from the role. Born in Friedberg near Augsburg around 1480, Hubmaier was the best educated of the Anabaptist reformers, having received a doctorate in theology at the University of Ingolstadt in 1512. He was a priest in the Regensburg Cathedral, and in Waldshut (twice in each place), and in Schaffhausen. He engaged in both friendly discussion and bitter debates with Zwingli in Zurich, and was imprisoned there in 1525–1526 for his theological insolence. He escaped with his life only by recanting.

Hubmaier wrote voluminously. In 1524, he issued his landmark booklet against the burning of heretics, *Concerning Heretics and Those Who Burn Them*. In 1525, he requested believer's baptism from Wilhelm Reublin, one of the Zurich community of Anabaptists. By this time he had broken with the Roman Church, as revealed by his abandonment of his vow of celibacy to marry Elisabeth Hügline.[19] At about this time he also wrote several powerful defenses of the baptism of believers only. His catechism for the instruction of new believers appeared in 1526, and the next year he published treatises on church discipline, baptism, the Lord's Supper and free will. In 1527, he broke with the Swiss and south German Anabaptists on the subject of nonresistance as set forth in his booklet *On the Sword*. According to Hubmaier, although Jesus enjoined nonviolence, believers could participate in politics and, on occasion, might be justified in resisting tyrannical magistrates.

There is no doubt that Hubmaier embraced the Anabaptist view that the New Testament was the sole authority for the Christian life and the church, and that he held most other Anabaptist beliefs. Moreover, his fervent evangelistic preaching resulted in thousands of converts to Christ and to the idea that baptized believers should gather in local congregations apart from a hierarchical Church. Perhaps in retrospect, Hubmaier's basic beliefs most resembled those of the Baptists, those spiritual descendants of the radical reformers of the sixteenth century.

Arrested for heresy in 1527, Austrian authorities imprisoned both Hubmaier and his wife in Vienna. He endured torture on the rack, but steadfastly refused to recant. He was burned at the stake on 10 March 1528. His wife was drowned in the Danube River several days later.

In the meantime, two large groups of Anabaptists were in the process of formation elsewhere in Europe. One of these eventually became known as Hutterites and the other as Mennonites. The Hutterites originated among those believers converted through Hubmaier's preaching in the Nicholsburg area of Moravia who came to reject his politicized Anabaptism.[20] Two hundred of them, influenced by Hans Hut, left Nicholsburg under the leadership of Jacob Wiedemann, agreed to share all of their possessions and settled in Austerlitz, also in Moravia. They organized as a communal farm called a Brüderhof. Others soon joined the group and a new settlement was started in nearby Auspitz. However, divisions soon developed within the groups because of Wiedemann's authoritarian leadership. At this point, Jacob Hutter arrived on the scene to salvage the movement and eventually give it his name, Hutterites. Hutter was originally a hatter, and he traveled extensively in the pursuit of his trade. During his travels, he came into contact with the Anabaptists and was converted to their beliefs and submitted to adult baptism. He became the leader of the Anabaptists in the Tyrol when Blaurock, whose missionary efforts contributed to the founding of the Anabaptists in the region, was executed. Severe persecution led the Tyrolese Brethren to flee to Moravia in 1533, where Hutter's sense of calling and leadership skills brought peace to the feuding Anabaptists. He was also responsible for transforming their unstructured communalism into a well-organized community, through a careful attention to *Ordnung* (corporate orderliness) with full economic sharing.

The Hutterites prospered for the next two years under Hutter's leadership until the impact of the Münster debacle resulted in a new wave of persecution. Ferdinand, the Habsburg ruler of the area, forced the reluctant nobles to expel the Hutterian Brethren in 1535, but they survived by living in caves and the forests. Hutter and his spouse were hunted down, however, and arrested. Hutter was tortured, immersed in freezing water, and burned at the stake in February 1536. In that same year, the persecution abated and the Hutterites again found refuge in Moravia, where they thrived despite sporadic persecution. During this period, the Hutterite lifestyle became standardized. They embraced Christian communalism; became famous for their rejection of the world with its swearing, drinking, betting and carousing; emphasized a basic education for all believers so that they could study the Bible for themselves; practiced a high level of sanitation; and became widely known for advanced medical practices and skilled physicians. Their physicians willingly treated non-Hutterites and thus built a measure of good will for the otherwise despised movement.[21]

As the Hutterites prospered, they came increasingly to the attention of the civil authorities. Severe persecution began again with the coming of the Thirty Years' War (1618–1648). Thousands were killed and some returned to the Roman Catholic Church. Finally, in 1622, all Hutterites were expelled officially from Moravia. There were at this time around 20,000 to 50,000 of them, estimates vary. They went first to neighboring Transylvania and Slovakia. There they became the targets of the Jesuits. Authorities declared them illegal and all pastors and other leaders were imprisoned. In 1767, the surviving Hutterites moved to Wallachia. By this time they numbered only a few thousand. In Wallachia, they were caught in the middle of the Russo-Turkish War of 1768. Both sides plundered and killed them at will. Finally, in 1770, Catherine II (the Great) of Russia invited them to settle in the Ukraine wilderness and develop it. The 123 surviving Hutterites accepted the offer, became Russian subjects and dwelled in that country in relative peace for the next hundred years.

During their Russian sojourn, the Hutterites enjoyed religious freedom and exemption from military service. However, in 1874, the government revoked their immunity from conscription and they decided once again to move. By this time they numbered around 800, and they decided to emigrate en masse to the United States where there was religious freedom and no military draft. They prospered there until the twentieth century when problems of military conscription once again troubled their existence.

Just as the Münster uprising caused grief and persecution for the Hutterites, so it did for those surviving Melchiorites and other Anabaptists in Germany and the Low Countries. The Münster tragedy set the stage for the appearance of the individual who became the conservator of the Anabaptist movement in Western and Central Europe: Menno Simons. He, too, would give his name to a branch of the Radical Reformation of which he was not the founder, namely, the Mennonites. Like Hutter, Menno rescued a movement that was persecuted, deeply divided and dangerously close to extinction.[22]

In any event, Menno later recorded in one of his autobiographical writings that he had first come into contact with the idea of believer's baptism in 1531, some seven years after he had become a Roman Catholic priest. He wrote: "Afterwards it happened, before I had ever heard of the existence of Brethren, that a God-fearing, pious hero named Sicke Snijder was beheaded at Leeuwarden for being rebaptized. It sounded very strange to me to hear of a second baptism. I examined the Scriptures diligently and pondered them earnestly, but could find no report of infant baptism."[23]

Menno was born in 1496 in Witmarsum, a village in West Friesland in the Netherlands. The fact that he lived until 1561 made him uniquely long-lived among Anabaptist leaders. In any event, he entered the Roman priesthood reasonably well educated. He knew Greek and Latin, and was familiar with the writings of the Church Fathers. However, he was not trained in biblical studies but later mastered the scriptures through his own efforts. He was ordained a priest in 1524, at age 28, and served in the nearby Pingjum parish before he returned to his home village in 1531. He began to hear of the work of Luther in Germany and read some of his pamphlets early in his priestly career. He soon came to doubt the doctrine of transubstantiation and, after considerable distress, finally began to search the Bible and the Church Fathers in order to find some answers to his growing doubts.

As a result of this study, he gave up the doctrine of the miraculous change of the bread and wine into the body and blood of Christ in the celebration of the Mass. Then, in 1531, he heard of the execution of Sicke Snijder at Leeuwarden for being rebaptized. This again led him to much soul-searching. He finally concluded that baptism should, in fact, follow an adult conversion to Christ, and that this was the key to ending the often nominal and lukewarm faith that had characterized European Christianity for centuries. He himself underwent some kind of conversion experience during this period from 1531–1534, and then came Münster.

In April 1535, he wrote a tract against the Münster disturbances. Then in June 1535, events connected with Münster caused him to break with his Roman Catholic past and join the Anabaptists. Prior to June, he had vacillated between the old and the new, between the Roman Church and the new reformation churches, troubled and perplexed by both. By a strange twist, it was his horror at the fanatical Münster outburst that finally led him to break with Rome. It was the very excesses of the Anabaptist movement in his area that in the end pulled him from his rectory to lead the frightened and bewildered Melchiorites in the Netherlands. Some 300 of these radical Anabaptists were en route to Münster when local authorities detected and attacked them. The radicals fled to a deserted monastery for refuge where they were besieged and overwhelmed. Most perished in the ensuing bloodshed, including a relative of Menno named Peter Simons. This senseless slaughter sickened Menno and plunged him into another period of intense soul-searching. Though he was opposed to the radicals' show of force and to what he deemed was their misunderstanding of biblical teaching, he was now moved to begin preaching evangelical reform from his Witmarsum pulpit and, eventually, to offer himself as a leader of what he regarded as these misguided but sincere people.

In January 1536, after attempting to reform his Witmarsum parish, Menno finally renounced his priestly living and quietly vanished from the public eye. He was fully aware of what he was doing. He was leaving personal and economic security at the very time when edicts against Anabaptists were ruthlessly enforced in the Low Countries, and when millenarian radicals were most hated by the authorities and most discredited by the actions of their devotees. Here was a respected priest making a break to join a group with which he had no fellowship before the Münsterite debacle and to whose radical ideas on the millennium he had always been opposed. Why did he give it all up to join such a disreputable group?

The answer to that question lies buried with Menno himself. However, it most likely was the result of a confluence of events: intense Bible study and the accompanying personal commitment to Christ, first-hand knowledge of those who were involved in the Anabaptist movement, the obvious need for reform in the Church, and a sensitive heart. All of these considerations led him to place his life in jeopardy for the Anabaptist cause.

During a year of hiding, Menno seems to have spent much time in meditation and Bible study. He also sought out one of the leaders of the local nonviolent Anabaptists, probably Obbe Philips, and was baptized at his hands. In addition, he married and settled down somewhere near Groningen. It was there that Menno was set aside as an elder (from the New Testament word "elder," the contemporary Dutch Anabaptist term for the leader of a congregation) and began his pastoral ministry. Because of his age, experience and education, he immediately became a leader of the peace wing of the Dutch Anabaptists. Always operating clandestinely and on the run, he ministered in the Netherlands from 1536–1543, in northwest Germany, mainly in the Rhineland from 1543–1546, and in Danish Holstein from 1541 until his death from natural causes in 1561. During his time as an Anabaptist leader, he was the most sought after heretic in

Western Europe, with the extraordinary price of 500 gold guilders on his head. In 1541, full pardon was offered to any Anabaptists then in confinement who would deliver Menno into their hands, but no Judas was forthcoming.

In any case, Menno somehow eluded capture and continued his ministry among the Brethren. As he ministered and traveled, he also wrote and published at least 25 books and smaller treatises. Menno's *Foundation of Christian Doctrine*, 1539, although shorter and less eloquent, was the Anabaptist equivalent of Calvin's *Institutes*. By the time he died, his followers, now called "Mennist" or "Mennonites," numbered in the tens of thousands. In 1570, the Dutch Republic granted religious toleration to all non-Catholics, and Menno's followers continued to thrive there. By the end of the sixteenth century, there may have been as many as 100,000 Mennonites in the Netherlands, a number second only to the established Reformed Church.

Menno's theological ideas became those of mainstream Anabaptism during his lifetime. Like Luther and Calvin, he was an evangelical who held to the major doctrines of the Protestant faith concerning authority and salvation. He talked more about the transforming power of the new birth than did many other reformers and defended believer's baptism over and against infant baptism. He also stressed that the Lord's Supper was not a saving sacrament but a memorial to the death of Jesus, and its celebration reflected the believer's faith in Christ's work of redemption and his promised return to establish his kingdom on earth.

As a true son of the Radical Reformation, Menno differed sharply from the Roman Church and the Magisterial Protestants in his teaching of nonviolence as the "way of Jesus" and in his belief that the New Testament indicated that the powers of the state are limited. He understood the biblical teaching to be that the state had no jurisdiction in the realm of the soul and spirit. Perhaps most significant of all, Menno and his followers believed and taught that all people should be allowed to have religious liberty. He argued that faith in Christ involved a personal commitment and that it had to be freely given in order to be meaningful, valid and biblical. Moreover, it is important to understand that he was not talking about toleration but full-blown religious liberty as a universal principle. Further, he developed as a corollary to his belief in religious liberty, his doctrine of the separation of church and state, because state interference in spiritual affairs was inimical to religious freedom and a free church. For the first time in human history, at least in embryonic form, a movement and its leader advocated the principle of a free people in a free church in a free society.[24]

Anabaptist Women: The "Steel Magnolias" of the Sixteenth Century

The Reformation Era produced some remarkable women, both Protestant and Catholic, but none tougher and more courageous than the Anabaptist women. These sixteenth-century "steel magnolias" played a central role in the emergence and persistence of this radical branch of the non–Roman Catholic Reformation. A number of Anabaptist women held the office of deacon in various congregations (in the New Testament sense of responsibility for the care of the physical, social and economic needs of believers), many taught and some even preached, although mostly to other women. But most impressive is how courageously they faced martyrdom and their contributions to Anabaptist hymn-writing, two areas apparently open to female participation among Anabaptists in this period.[25]

European civil authorities executed more than 5,000 men and women, most of them in a public forum and often in a gruesome manner, for refusing to abjure their religious convictions in the sixteenth and seventeenth centuries. The overwhelming majority of these were Anabaptists, and more than a third of those were women.[26] Many of these female martyrs are celebrated in the *Martyrs Mirror*, a seventeenth-century publication calculated to help the spiritual children of the Anabaptists to hold firm to their faith in a time when they were beginning to be accepted in European society. Among those Anabaptist women mentioned in the *Martyrs Mirror* is Elizabeth Dirks, who was apprehended in January 1549.

Dirks was an Anabaptist preacher, teacher and deacon. The authorities mistakenly believed that she was also Menno's wife, and, therefore, tortured her with relentless brutality in order to make her reveal her alleged husband's hiding place. Through it all, Dirks refused either to reveal anything about Menno (she was not his spouse) or her fellow believers. In the utmost pain from thumbscrews and shin screws, she not only refused to recant but also responded with alacrity to accusers during her cross examination, quoting scripture after scripture in answer to accusations of heresy. Finally, after a two-month ordeal, she was condemned as a heretic and, on 27 March 1549, placed in a bag and dropped in the nearest body of water to drown.[27]

Anneken Hendriks was another celebrated woman martyr. Betrayed by a neighbor in 1571 in Amsterdam, she was charged with heresy and with holding clandestine Anabaptist meetings in her home. She was subjected to repeated interrogation and torture but refused to recant. Finally, after several weeks of such treatment, she was pronounced guilty of heresy and condemned to death by fire. Hendriks was an uneducated women but she had memorized many sections of the Bible, which she recited to her tormentors while they sought her repentance. Finally, tired of her torrent of words, they stuffed her mouth with gunpowder and led her to the city center, tied her to a ladder and cast her into the fire to explode and burn.[28]

Many other Anabaptist women became prolific hymn writers. Many of their hymns celebrated the martyrdom in which many of them participated. One such hymn by an unknown Anabaptist woman captured the pathos of the Anabaptist experience:

> Sheep without shepherd running blind
> Are scattered into flight.
> Our house and home are left behind,
> Like birds we fly by night,
> And like the birds, naught overhead
> Save wind and rain and weather,
> In rocks and caves our bed.
>
> We creep for refuge under trees.
> They hunt us with the bloodhound.
> Like lambs they take us as they please
> And hold us roped and strong-bound.
> They show us off to everyone
> As if the peace we'd broken,
> As sheep for slaughter looked upon,
> As heretics bespoken.
>
> Some in heavy chains have lain
> And rotting there have stayed.
> Some upon the trees were slain,
> Choked and hacked and flayed.
> Drownings by stealth and drownings plain
> For matron and for maid.
> Fearlessly the truth they spoke
> And were not ashamed.
> Christ is the way and Christ the life
> Was the word proclaimed.
> Precious in Thy sight, O God,
> The dying of a saint.[29]

One of the best-known Anabaptist women hymn writers was Helene von Freyberg of the Tyrol. One of the very few members of the nobility who became an Anabaptist, she was drowned and then burned for her faith in 1529. Of the more than 130 Anabaptist hymn writers who can be identified by name, at least a dozen were women. Helene protected Anabaptists in her lands for several years before she herself had to go into hiding. During her years of Anabaptist patronage, she corresponded extensively with several radical leaders and with Habsburg authorities on behalf of her flock. Her means of death by drowning reflected the scorn the authorities had for her love of the baptismal waters and her deemed heretical beliefs. Her hymns were widely sung by various radical groups and most touched on the main Anabaptist themes of persecution, martyrdom, and holding firm to the true faith that was best reflected by love for both fellow believers and enemies. One such hymn ends with:

> Be comforted you Christians and rejoice,
> Through Jesus Christ forevermore,
> Who gives us love and faith.
> God comforts us through his Holy Word,
> On that we should rely.[30]

The Effect of the Radical Reformation

Historians often consider other smaller groups in addition to the Hutterites and Mennonites when they discuss the Radical Reformation. These other radicals include a number of disparate minimovements such as the Spiritualists (inspirationists), the Schwenkfelders (mystics), the Antitrinitarians (rationalists), various independent individuals and groups of what were deemed at the time as "fanatics," and, at the extreme left, a small number of Socianians (Unitarians).[31] Among these, however, the Mennonites and Hutterites, who emphasized a Christocentric theology and biblical authority, constituted the mainstream of the Radical Reformation.

The Hutterites have survived and today thrive in the United States and Canada. However, it was the Mennonites who ultimately made the greatest impact on those who followed, especially in the United States. The spiritual children of the Mennonites include all of those restorationists who followed in their train: Baptists, Quakers and Amish in the seventeenth century, the Church of the Brethren in the eighteenth century and the American Restoration Movement led by Alexander Campbell in the nineteenth century. Though they did not adopt Mennonite beliefs in their entirety, it would be hard to deny that much of Menno can be found in the thought of those aforementioned denominations and movements. This is especially true in terms of the Mennonite emphasis on freedom.

The civil authorities and the Magisterial Reformers considered the Anabaptists a radical threat because they applied the principles of the Reformation in an uncompromising way and drew conclusions that threatened the established order in both church and state. For example, they took the teaching of the priesthood of all believers literally, in contrast to the Magisterial Reformers, who became uneasy as they began to realize it could lead to a laity with little or no formal education challenging the clergy. In fact, the Mennonites and Hutterites, like their spiritual descendants, blurred the line between clergy and laity so that it was often difficult or impossible to locate. The fact that the Anabaptists refused to baptize infants threatened a principle at the heart of medieval society: the identification of the civic and religious communities.[32] The Magisterial Reformers never abandoned this concept as they, along with their Catholic opponents, found it difficult to imagine any other type of Christian society in which the state did not support the church, and vice versa. The Anabaptist rejection of infant baptism carried with it a conviction that individuals must make their own choice as to whether they wanted to be a part of the church, otherwise their faith would never be anything more than nominal. Therefore, their emphasis was on a free individual in a free church in a free society, and on a church that was a gathered community of self-confessed believers, separate from wider society, especially the state.

Further, the Anabaptists were Radical Reformers in the sense that they also applied literally the Reformation principle of *sola scriptura*. Once the Lutherans and Calvinists attacked the traditional sources of authority in the old Church, the doors were open to those who wanted to approach the Bible in a more literal way. Much of what the Magisterial Reformers taught about doctrines such as baptism and the Trinity depended partly on an interpretation of Scriptures based on the tradition and teaching of the Church. Having rejected that authority, the Radical Reformers questioned whether doctrines like infant baptism could actually be found in the Bible. They also wanted to introduce reforms immediately and to eliminate everything that they believed violated scriptural teaching, such as the Mass, clerical garb, images, liturgy and monasticism. In each case, the Magisterial Reformers were worried about the disruption that this would cause to society and to tender consciences, and they were not prepared to move as quickly. They believed that if the Anabaptist way were followed, society would be disrupted and all things would no longer be done decently and in order. Most of all, individual freedom and liberty of conscience would mean an end to the concept of officially supported state churches with all of the benefits obtaining thereto.

The Anabaptist beliefs in biblical authority alone, the necessity of a personal commitment to Christ followed by adult baptism, the ethical urge to embrace Christ's moral teachings as completely as possible, religious liberty, and separation of church and state were embraced in the main by their spiritual descendants: Baptists, Quakers, Amish, Brethren and Disciples of Christ. They, in turn, would make their mark on the future United States and its national ethos. It was left, however, to the courageous Mennonites and Hutterites, along with their Amish and Quaker cousins, to maintain the primary witness for nonviolence and peace in the modern world. Equally passionate in terms of defending and extending their way of life were those Catholics who attempted to stem the Protestant tide while at the same time reforming their traditional faith. These devout sons and daughters of the Old Church are the subject of the next chapter.

Notes

1. Roland Bainton called the movement "the left wing of the Reformation." However, historians now almost universally accept George H. Williams' term "the Radical Reformation," first introduced in 1962. See Roland H. Bainton, *The Reformation of the Sixteenth Century* (Boston: Beacon Press, 1952); and George H. Williams, *The Radical Reformation*, 3rd ed. (Kirksville, MO: Sixteenth Century Journal Publishers, 1992). Two other authoritative works on the Anabaptists in particular are Franklin H. Littell, *The Origins of Sectarian Protestantism: A Study of the Anabaptist View of the Church* (New York: Macmillan, 1964); and William R. Estep, *The Anabaptist Story*, 3rd ed. (Grand Rapids, MI: Eerdmans, 1996). Williams' magisterial work is regarded as the most thorough study of the Radical Reformation available.

2. Bainton, *Reformation of the Sixteenth Century*, 107–109.

3. Klaus Deppermann, Werner Packull, and James Stayer, "From Monogenesis to Polygenesis: The Historical Discussion of Anabaptist Origins," *Mennonite Quarterly Review*, 49 (Spring 1975):83–121. Polygenesists are those historians who believe that the Anabaptists originated from more than one historical source. This is in contradistinction to historians like George H. Williams who hold that the Swiss Brethren were the first Anabaptists of the era. See Williams, *Radical Reformation*, 212–245. Also see J. M. Carroll, *The Trail of Blood* (Lexington, KY: Ashland Avenue Baptist Church, 1931).

4. For three basic views of Anabaptist origins, see Fritz Blanke, *Brothers in Christ* (Scottdale, PA: Herald Press, 1961); James Stayer, *Anabaptists and the Sword* (Lawrence, KS: Coronado Press, 1972); and Estep, *Anabaptist Story*, 9–28.

5. Williams, *Radical Reformation*, 214–221.

6. R. J. Smithson, *The Anabaptists* (London: James Clarke, 1935), 14–15.

7. Williams, *Radical Reformation*, 300–303, 356–357, 387 and 1303.

8. Carter Lindberg, ed., *The European Reformations Sourcebook* (Oxford: Blackwell, 2000), 90.

9. Hans Hillerbrand, *A Fellowship of Discontent* (New York: Harper and Row, 1967), 1–30.

10. Thomas Müntzer to Count Ernst von Mansfeld, 12 May 1525, in Otto H. Brandt, *Thomas Müntzer* (Jena, Germany: E. Diederichs, 1933), 77–78.

11. Hillerbrand, *Fellowship of Discontent*, 28–30; and Abraham Friesen, *Thomas Muentzer: A Destroyer of the Godless* (Berkeley: University of California Press, 1990), 269–272.

12. For the Münster episode, see Williams, *Radical Reformation*, 553–582; Klaus Deppermann, *Melchior Hoffman* (Edinburgh: T. & T. Clark, 1987); and Ronnie Po-chia Hsia, *The German People and the Reformation* (Ithaca, NY: Cornell University Press, 1988).

13. The allusion to Enoch here comes from Jude 14–16, which refers to the Old Testament prophet who foretold the divine judgment of the ungodly that will occur upon the Second Coming of Christ. King David, of course, refers to Van Leyden's delusional messianic pretensions.

14. Among the best sources for understanding the Münster affair is Cornelius Krahn, *Dutch Anabaptism: Origin, Spread, Life and Thought, 1450–1600* (The Hague: Martinus Nijhoff, 1968), 80–164.

15. John D. Derksen, *From Radicals to Survivors: Strasbourg's Religious Nonconformists over Two Generations, 1525–1570* (Utrecht, The Netherlands: Hes and de Graaf, 2002).

16. For Sattler, see C. Arnold Snyder, *The Life and Thought of Michael Sattler* (Scottdale, PA: Herald Press, 1984).

17. Gustav Bossert, Jr., "Michael Sattler's Trial and Martyrdom in 1527," *The Mennonite Quarterly Review*, 25 (July 1951):216.

18. Torsten Bergsten is the leading authority on Hubmaier but his work is available only in German. His scholarship is incorporated into Estep, *Anabaptist Story*, 77–105.

19. Ibid., 83.

20. For the Hutterites, see John Horsch, *The Hutterian Brethren* (Goshen, IN: Mennonite Historical Society, 1931); and Leonard Gross, *The Golden Years of the Hutterites* (Scottdale, PA: Herald Press, 1980).

21. For example, they possessed advanced knowledge in the field of medical hygiene and in the cure of such diseases as scurvy. Gross, *Golden Years of the Hutterites*, 31 and 103.

22. For Menno and the Mennonites, see Krahn, *Dutch Anabaptism*, 170–262; and Estep, *Anabaptist Story*, 151–176.

23. Menno Simons, *Reply to Gellius Faber in The Complete Writings of Menno Simons*, ed. J. C. Wenger (Scottdale, PA: Herald Press, 1956), 668.

24. Estep, *Anabaptist Story*, 237–266.

25. For an introduction to the women of the Radical Reformation, see Joyce Irwin, *Womanhood in Radical Protestantism, 1525–1675* (New York: Edwin Mellen Press, 1979); and C. Arnold Snyder and Linda Huebert Hecht, eds., *Profiles of Anabaptist Women* (Waterloo, Canada: Wilfrid Laurier University Press, 1996).

26. "Women," in *The Mennonite Encyclopedia*, 5 vols. (Scottdale, PA: Herald Press, 1955–1990), 4:972–974 and 5:933–934.

27. T. J. van Braght, *The Bloody Theater, or, Martyr's Mirror of the Defenseless Christians*, 9th ed., trans. from the Dutch (Scottdale, PA: Herald Press, 1972), 481–483. Usually referred to as the *Martyrs Mirror*, this work contains 1141 pages of text and covers martyrdom from the first century to 1660. Historian Brad Gregory's magisterial study of martyrdom in Early Modern Europe attests to the fundamental reliability of the *Martyrs Mirror* as a historical source. Brad Gregory, *Salvation at Stake: Christian Martyrdom in Early Modern Europe* (Cambridge, MA: Harvard University Press, 1999), 199 and 243–249.

28. Van Braght, *Martyrs Mirror*, 872–874.

29. Bainton, *Reformation of the Sixteenth Century*, 104.

30. Linda Huebert Hecht, "An Extraordinary Lay Leader: The Life and Work of Helene of Freyberg, Sixteenth-Century Noblewoman and Anabaptist from the Tirol," *Mennonite Quarterly Review*, 66 (July 1992):312–341.

31. For a sophisticated discussion of these various radical subgroups, see Leonard Verduin, *The Reformers and Their Stepchildren* (Grand Rapids, MI: Baker Book House, 1964).

32. Sixteenth-century society still embraced the medieval dictum "one king, one law, one faith." With few exceptions, European rulers believed in a unitary political arrangement in which the state, the law and the faith mutually supported each other. Therefore, baptism was not only a means of dealing with original sin and making the baptized individual a member of the church but also of the society at large. In short, rulers believed that loyalty to the Medieval Church was synonymous with loyalty to the state. Any threat to what was regarded as this indispensable condition of public order was not tolerated. The Anabaptists, with their insistence on a free church and adult baptism was a threat to this system. James Westfall Thompson, *The Wars of Religion in France, 1559–1576* (Chicago: University of Chicago Press, 1909), 10–11; John T. McNeill, "John Calvin on Civil Government," *Journal of Presbyterian History*, 42, no. 2 (June 1964):71–91; and Estep, *Anabaptist Story*, 68–69 and 258–259.

CHAPTER 6

THE CATHOLIC REFORMATION

Ironically, the Catholic Reformation began at about the same time that Luther nailed his Ninety-Five Theses to the church door in Wittenberg in 1517. Unfortunately for the Old Church, it was too little, too late. Like Luther and Calvin and a host of other Catholics who became Protestants during the sixteenth century, there were many Christian believers who recognized that the Church of Rome badly needed reform. However, unlike Luther, they chose to remain and try to change things from within. One such reformer, already mentioned, was Desiderius Erasmus, the great humanist scholar who was a critical lover and a loving critic of his church. There were many others.

Therefore, the Catholic Reformation began as a reform-minded movement to restore genuine piety and spirituality to the Roman Church. Early Catholic reformers were much like a spring of renewal gushing of its own accord out of the rock of the Church. However, in the 1540s, the mainly positive Catholic Reformation turned with considerable intensity into a movement chiefly concerned with counter-reform and repression. The burning question for the Church of Rome after it became apparent that Luther and the Protestants would not go away was: What can be done with "the wild boars in God's vineyard"?[1] Even though historians now prefer to use the term Catholic Reformation rather than Counter Reformation, both elements were clearly present and both will be discussed in this chapter.[2]

Early Concern for Reform and Conciliation

The first stirrings of genuine reform came in 1517, the same year that Luther nailed his theses to the door of the Castle Church

in Wittenberg. It was in that year that a branch of the Oratory of
Divine Love was established in Rome. On the eve of the Protestant
Reformation, many Christian humanists, and a number of theologians, pious monks and concerned lay people had been trying to
renew spiritual life by promoting piety and ethics and by establishing
confraternities and oratories. Under the inspiration of St. Catherine
of Genoa, for example, the Oratory of Divine Love was founded in
Genoa in 1497 and brought to Rome during the pontificate of Leo X.
This informal organization of about 50 laymen and clergy emphasized the harmonization of faith and learning and advocated reform
through personal piety, prayer, frequent confession and performing
works of charity and service.

Among those attracted to the Roman Oratory were such eager
and highly placed reformers as Gaetano da Thiene (later St. Cajetan,
founder of the Theatine Order of Clerics Regular in 1524), Gian Pietro Carafa (later Pope Paul IV, 1555–1559) and Jacopo Sadoleto (the
humanist Bishop of Carpentras in southeastern France). The group
was soon joined by the most conciliatory figure of the Catholic Reformation, Gasparo Contarini (Cardinal Contarini from 1535). The
Theatines attracted to their ranks Reginald Pole, the English reforming cardinal and cousin of Queen Mary I. Spiritual regeneration on
the upper levels of the Church hierarchy was the goal of the Oratory
and later of the Theatines as well.[3]

Other examples of early sixteenth-century concern for renewal
included the report of a commission appointed by Pope Paul III
(1534–1549) to investigate the spiritual condition of the Church and
to make recommendations for reform. It read, in part:

> Concerning ordination: no care is taken. Whoever they are
> (uneducated, of appalling morals, under age), they are routinely
> admitted to the holy order from which came so many scandals
> and a contempt for the church.... Concerning Rome: honest
> manners should flourish in this city and church, mother and
> teacher of other churches ... [yet] whores perambulate like
> matrons or ride on mule-back, with whom noblemen, cardinals
> and priests consort in broad daylight.[4]

The commission's report was published in 1537, and its findings
were so embarrassing that Protestants eagerly cited them as evidence
that they were right in what they had said about the Church. Nevertheless, the pope and the leading cardinals who served on the commission were committed to reform, and the publication of their
findings provided a major impetus for what was to become a wide-
ranging reform movement in the Roman Church.

There were also in the period Catholic scholars who agreed with the essence of Luther's theology of salvation. For example, the Benedictine monk Benedetto da Mantova preached justification by faith in Christ as the way of salvation as early as the 1530s. In 1543, he published his little book in Venice with the title *A Most Useful Treatise on the Merits of Jesus Christ Crucified for Christians.*[5] The theology of this work was very similar to that of Protestantism. Benedetto's work was at first well received. However, it was later placed on the Index of Prohibited Books and so successfully repressed by the Roman Inquisition that of the many thousands of copies of the Italian edition that were in existence only one is known to survive, discovered in the library of a Cambridge University college in the nineteenth century. That sort of successful repression was a part of the Counter Reformation that took hold after 1542.[6]

However, before major efforts at repression began, dedicated reformers like Contarini energetically tried to find common ground with the Protestants.[7] Contarini was from a distinguished Venetian family and in the course of his career in the secular world had held a number of important posts in the government of his native city-state, including ambassador to Emperor Charles V from 1521–1525. Earlier, in 1511, he had experienced a spiritual crisis similar to that of Luther and, like Luther, eventually found peace through faith in Christ's suffering and death rather than through works. However, Contarini never challenged the Church's sacramental theology and, therefore, never followed Luther in openly questioning papal power. Rather, he repeatedly tried to reconcile his unwavering personal belief in justifying faith with Church teaching. In any case, Contarini and others of a like mind within the Old Church reached out to the Protestants in the hope of reconciliation. Pope Paul III made Contarini a cardinal in 1535, after which he took up residence in Rome and became one of the pope's closest advisors.[8]

For his part, the pope, although he was guilty of the very abuses the report of his 1537 reform commission severely criticized, played a central role in placing the papacy at the head of the Catholic Reformation. In his younger days, Paul had a mistress who bore him at least four children, but he changed his ways after he became a bishop in 1509. Moreover, once the Protestant Reformation began, he identified himself with the reform party in the Papal Curia. Upon the death of Clement VII in 1534, Paul was unanimously elected pope. Although he was 67 years old at the time, he lived 15 more years and led the way to serious reform. He not only created the aforementioned reform commission but also appointed Contarini and a number of other reform-minded individuals as cardinals, recognized several new monastic orders that would play important roles in the Catholic Reformation, including the Jesuits, and convened the long-delayed church council (Trent) in 1545 to deal with Protestant complaints.

Contarini became Pope Paul III's point man in dealing with the Protestants. Contarini and other reform cardinals were committed to finding a way to reconcile the straying brethren to Rome, while more conservative reformers like Carafa believed that suppression was the only way to treat heretics. An opportunity for Contarini to achieve reconciliation came when Emperor Charles V, who desperately needed internal peace within his empire so he could cope with the threat of Turkish invasion, encouraged conversations between Catholics and Protestants in 1540–1541. In April 1541, the two sides met in Regensburg, where an imperial diet was in session. Calvin, Melanchthon and Bucer attended the Colloquy of Regensburg, where the two sides used as their basis for discussion the *Regensburg Book,* which had been composed by Johann Gropper, a Catholic humanist, and modified by Bucer.

The most surprising achievement of the colloquy was that the participants reached an agreement on the doctrine of justification by faith. The article dealing with that doctrine was worded in such a way that it took into consideration the major concerns of both sides. The final formula seemed to satisfy all concerned in that justification was not only attributed to the imputation of Christ's righteousness but also stated that justifying faith must result in works of righteousness. Contarini, who served as papal legate to the colloquy, understood and sympathized with the Protestant position and considered the agreement a major breakthrough. Others were not so sure. Luther grumbled that it was a patchwork affair and Carafa viewed it as a threat to Catholic teaching on works and purgatory.[9]

In any case, after agreeing on four articles, the conference stumbled over the fifth and came to an abrupt end because of differences over the Eucharist. Nine days of debate resulted in stalemate over the real presence in communion and in a number of areas as well. Failure was difficult for Contarini to accept, but he no doubt hoped the long-delayed general council might continue the work of reconciliation begun at Regensburg. He did not live to see the council that was convened four years later because he died in 1542. Even before his death, hard-liners in the Curia, led by Carafa, urged suppression rather than dialogue as the realistic way to stop the Protestants. Carafa, who had become acquainted with the Spanish Inquisition while serving as papal nuncio in Spain, proposed establishing a similar institution in Italy, and in 1542, Pope Paul III bestowed on him the power to do so. One of the supporters of Cara-fa's proposal to establish the Inquisition in Italy was a Spaniard living in Rome who was to play a major role in the next stage of the Catholic Reformation. His name was Ignatius de Loyola.

The Society of Jesus: God's Special Forces

As historian Hans Hillerbrand has pointed out, "The incarnation of the Catholic Reformation, as well as the Counter Reformation, was a Spanish nobleman named Inigo de Onez y de Loyola."[10] St. Ignatius, as he was to become in 1622 following his canonization by the Church, was by all measures an extraordinary man. On the basis of his background, it seemed unlikely that he would become one of the great figures of the sixteenth century. Loyola was born in Basque country in northern Spain, probably in 1491, into a family that belonged to the lesser nobility. He seems to have aspired to become a Spanish grandee, of the sort who in his generation conquered America. Moreover, he apparently realized this ambition to a certain extent by 1521, but in Spain and not America.[11]

Loyola became a knight and entered military service in 1517. In the next few years, he proved himself a formidable warrior, both on the battlefield and in the bed of certain ladies at court. In 1521, his king assigned him to defend the northern Spanish fortress of Pamplona against the advance of a French army. He did this with considerable ability and courage. However, on 20 May he was badly wounded by a cannonball that shattered one leg and badly broke the other. Despite several painful operations in a day before anesthetics, the legs could not be completely repaired and the once active young soldier found himself at age 30 a cripple for life.

While convalescing at the Castle of Loyola, he found none of the tales of chivalry that he loved to read. In desperation he turned to the only literature at hand—some legends of saints and a life of Christ. They led him to speculate about the possibility of fashioning his own life after the saints and of imitating their deeds, cast by him into the mode of the chivalric heroes with whom he was so familiar. If he could not continue his quest for heroism and fame as a soldier of the king, then perhaps he could achieve positive recognition through saintliness and zeal for the Church.

Therefore, he took the Madonna as his lady and determined to become a soldier of Christ. As soon as he had recovered sufficiently, Loyola made a pilgrimage to Seville and Manresa. At Manresa he dedicated his weapons and armor to the Madonna in imitation of the medieval knights about whom he had read. This was followed by a general confession of sin and a long period of fasting, meditation and self-flagellation. While performing these strenuous religious exercises, he was stricken with a period of doubt and spiritual anguish that has sometimes been compared with that of Luther. However, Loyola was a man of limited education and religious experience and he had to find his way without the help of biblical scholarship or learned insights. Instead, he pushed ahead on his own, seeking counsel from local clergy and discovering St. Thomas à Kempis's medieval devotional classic, *The Imitation of Christ*, a book that made a lasting impression on him. He also experienced some impressive internal enlightenments that often took the form of extraordinarily vivid visions that he believed were from God. It was also during this time that he discovered his calling and began to sketch the essential elements of what became his great book, *The Spiritual Exercises*.

If one reckons the importance of a piece of literature by its influence over the human mind rather than the beauty of its style or the profundity of its thought, then *The Spiritual Exercises* was a great book. The main outlines of this work took shape during the 1520s even though it was not published in its entirety until 1548. It was a kind of simplified distillation of his own meditations and experiences and of his reading of St. Thomas à Kempis framed in such a way as to be useful to others in serving the Church with single-minded devotion. In many ways it was "spiritual aerobics," designed to keep one in good shape for spiritual warfare. Further, the book revealed the blending of soldier, mystic and monk into one mind.

"The purpose of these Exercises," according to Loyola, was "to help the exercitant to conquer himself, and to regulate his life so that he will not be influenced in his decisions by any inordinate attachment."[12] In order to accomplish this, the volume outlined specially designed exercises that take place over a period of 30 days. The reader is called upon to use his imagination in the process. The first week is devoted to a consideration of sin, which is followed by three weeks of meditations on Christ's life, concluding with his passion, resurrection and ascension. Throughout the book there are instructions on prayer, suggestions for the ascetic life, and ways to evaluate motives and impulses.

The end of all these exercises and the discipline that they instilled was to be the complete subjection of the man to the Church. Nothing illustrated this better than the section titled "Rules for Thinking With the Church," which begins with the words: "In order to have the proper attitude of mind in the Church Militant, we should observe the following rules." There follows 18 rules, of which number 13 is particularly potent.

> If we wish to be sure that we are right in all things, we should always be ready to accept this principle: I will believe that the white that I see is black, if the hierarchical Church so defines it. For, I believe that between the Bridegroom, Christ our Lord, and the Bride, His Church, there is but one spirit, which governs and directs us for the salvation of our souls, for the same Spirit and Lord, who gave us the Ten Commandments, guides and governs our Holy Mother Church.[13]

The *Exercises* proved to be extremely effective in grooming future Jesuits to be agents of the Catholic Reformation.

In the meantime, Loyola began his work by going on a pilgrimage to Jerusalem in September 1523, in order to visit the holy sites and preach to the Muslims. However, he was turned back by the Franciscan vicar of the Church of Jerusalem, who told the zealous but ignorant ex-soldier that if he wanted to serve Christ, he needed an education. Therefore, on returning to Spain in 1524, Loyola went to Barcelona where he started to learn Latin with a class of small boys. He did this because his training as a gentleman had included only a rudimentary knowledge of Spanish. Latin was necessary in order to enter a university in the sixteenth century. After mastering Latin, he went to the University of Alcalá where he soon won a group of disciples. However, he appeared suspicious and, therefore, was reported to the Holy Office of the Inquisition. Inquisitors detained him for six weeks, and then released him with a warning to cease holding religious meetings. Practically the same thing happened at the University of Salamanca, where he was imprisoned by the Inquisition for 22 days and again prohibited from holding meetings.

Sensing that his destiny did not lie in Spain, Loyola journeyed to Paris in 1528 in order to enroll at the University of Paris. There he was free from the Inquisition but not all authority. He was once publicly whipped as a dangerous fanatic. Nevertheless, at Paris he won his first permanent disciples, who would become future Jesuit Hall of Famers, including Peter Faber from Savoy, Francis Xavier from Portugal, and Diego Lainez and Alfonso Salmerón from Castile. They were tall, handsome, young and brave. In contrast, Loyola was short, balding with sparse red hair, deformed and 37 years old. But he won these younger men to himself and his cause by his enthusiasm, his sense of mission and his charismatic personality. *The Spiritual Exercises* soon molded them into a spiritual unit of considerable power.

Loyola and his student followers agreed to form themselves into a body henceforth to be known as the *Societas Jesu*, the Society of Jesus, commonly known as the Jesuits. It was a military designation, with the Latin *socii* connoting followers of a chief in arms. They took vows to live in poverty and chastity and to make a pilgrimage to Jerusalem. However, they were obstructed in their desire to go to the Holy Land by a war then raging between Spain and the Turks. Therefore, they turned to Rome and requested papal approval for their enterprise. With the help of Cardinal Contarini, they secured official recognition of their new monastic order from Pope Paul III on 27 September 1540. One innovation was added to the Jesuit constitution: the Society was to report directly to the pope rather than be subject to the jurisdiction of a bishop in the diocese in which they were working. To nobody's surprise, Loyola was chosen as the first superior general of the fledgling order, a post that he held until his death in 1556.[14]

The Jesuits were not only a tightly disciplined organization but also an elitist order that sought out only the brightest and most committed men. Before becoming a full member, the aspirant underwent 12 years of rigorous training, which included a year of general studies, three years of philosophical studies, and four years of theological studies. Training also included preaching, practical theology and the mastery of *The Spiritual Exercises*. The dominant trait of the Society was complete submission to hierarchical authority. They also were willing to do almost anything for the Church, no matter how distasteful the mission. Their flexibility—especially their willingness to embrace dissimulation, equivocation, casuistry and probabilism—was legendary, and has led some observers to suggest that they were the Machiavellians of the spiritual world.[15]

Whatever the case, because of their dedication, iron discipline and spirited self-assurance, Jesuit growth was extraordinarily rapid. By the time Loyola died, they numbered 1,500, and Jesuits were present, either openly or secretly, in nearly every European country. They also could be found in faraway places like Brazil, Ethiopia, the Congo and Japan. Many had reached responsible positions in the Church and in the universities of Europe. Two served as papal nuncios, to Ireland and Poland. They were especially active in education, counter-reform and foreign missions.

They specialized in the education of the young and used quality education as a tool of evangelism. Jesuit schools at all levels soon became famous for their excellence. They also were successful in winning back large areas of Europe to Catholicism. In so doing, they showed the most devotion and met with the least success in England. They were moderately successful in France where they faced both religious and secular opposition. But even there they eventually were able to persuade French King Louis XIV in 1685 to revoke the Edict of Nantes, a royal decree that had provided limited toleration of the French Huguenots for nearly three generations. They were most successful in central and eastern Europe where they helped save Bavaria and where they were instrumental in recovering much of Austria, Hungary and Poland for the Church. They also were notable for their deeds in the lands beyond the European heartland where they served as some of the most courageous and successful Catholic missionaries of all time. The most remarkable of a number of Jesuit foreign missionaries was St. Francis Xavier who took the Gospel to India, Ceylon, Vietnam, the islands of Asia and Japan.[16] The zeal and devotion of the Jesuits were so suited to the problems that the Roman Church was facing that something would have been missing in the Catholic Reformation had there been no Jesuit Order. As far as the papacy was concerned, these soldiers of the cross were in a very real sense God's Special Forces.

The Council of Trent, 1545–1563

Roman Catholic renewal and reaction found its formal and definitive expression in the Council of Trent, which met intermittently in three distinct phases for almost two decades between 1545–1563 (1545–1547, 1551–1552, 1562–1563).[17] As in the past, the concept of a general council that corrected the abuses within the Church when the papacy seemed unable to do so had gained momentum in the early sixteenth century. Reform-minded Catholics, including Luther, expressed a widespread hope that a council was the way forward in terms of Church reform. However, despite these sentiments, it was not until the fourth decade of the century that a council finally was convened at Trent, in northern Italy. The delay must be attributed in part to the reluctance of the papacy, which feared that a council might mean the resurgence of the conciliar idea that had caused the fifteenth-century popes so many headaches. The delay, however, was not caused entirely by papal failings. As a matter of fact, Pope Paul III had in 1536 summoned a council to meet the following year. The machinations of the Emperor Charles V, who had his own ideas concerning how the German religious conflict should be settled, were one cause of delay. His perennial conflict with France was another major obstacle.

The initial meeting of the council finally convened at Trent in December 1545. Only 31 bishops and 42 theologians, the vast majority of them Italians, were present—a meager representation for what was supposed to be a gathering of the Universal Church. In any event, both Lainez and Salmerón were present at all three phases of the council as theological advisors, a position from which they exercised considerable influence.[18] Since most of the delegates were from Italy and voting took place according to heads rather than nations, as had been the case at earlier councils, a papal majority was assured on all questions from the very beginning. In any case, the initial accomplishments of the council were impressive and incredibly important. A number of doctrinal pronouncements defined the position of the Roman Church in regard to some of the contested positions. After heated debates, the Protestant positions were repudiated in each instance.

For example, a decree on authority in April 1546 rejected the Protestant teaching that the Bible was the sole source of authority in the church. Moreover, the primacy of the Latin Vulgate translation was affirmed along with the exclusive right of Holy Mother Church to interpret it. But the council's pronouncement on justification in January 1547 was particularly significant. The upshot of a long and sophisticated treatment of the subject was that a combination of faith in Christ and works of merit justified the individual. As historian N. S. Davidson pointed out, it "completed the separation of Protestants and Catholics from the shared theological inheritance of the Middle Ages and created a new Catholic doctrinal orthodoxy."[19] Shortly after this decree was promulgated, the first phase of the council came to an end.

The next meetings of the council depended upon the reforming inclinations of the man sitting on the papal throne. Paul III died in 1549 and was succeeded the next year by Julius III (1550–1555). Julius was a typical, pleasure-loving Renaissance churchman who was devoted to providing privileges for his relatives. However, he was not opposed to reform as long as it did not diminish papal power. Therefore, under considerable pressure from Emperor Charles V, he reconvened Trent in May 1551. Although it met for less than a year, this session produced important decrees reasserting the doctrine of transubstantiation and condemning the various Protestant teachings on the Eucharist. The sacrament of penance was also discussed and reaffirmed. At the insistence of the emperor, the council allowed a delegation of German Lutherans to join the proceedings. However, when they arrived in January 1552, they discovered that all of the essential questions had already been decided. They asked for a reconsideration of the doctrines that had already been promulgated, their request was denied, and Protestant participation in the Council of Trent came to an end. Meanwhile, the political situation in Germany deteriorated as the emperor defended himself against the armies of the Christian king of France in the west and an invasion by the Muslim Turks in the east. Moreover, the emperor also was faced with Protestant resistance to his sporadic attempts to end internal religious divisions by force. Shifting alliances based on both religion and princely self-interests brought a series of Protestant victories, and with them fear that a Protestant army only a few hours' march from Trent might swoop down on the council. This brought another adjournment in April 1552. The council did not meet again for almost a decade.

One principal reason that the council was not reconvened sooner was the election of Gian Pietro Carafa as Pope Paul IV in May 1555. Carafa was 79 years old when he became pope, but the passing of the years had not mellowed him. He was a hardliner as a younger man and he was a hardliner in old age. He was totally opposed to councils, considering them at best theological debating societies and at worst dangerous to the power of the papacy. He was a reformer who resisted compromise and advocated harsh measures in dealing with the Protestant heretics on the one hand and corrupt Church officials on the other. Consequently, his brief but important papal reign was devoted to suppression and counter-reform.

Pope Pius IV (1559–1565) differed radically from his predecessor in that he was open and worldly rather than ascetic and despotic. Further, he returned to the Renaissance practice of nepotism as he made his 21-year-old nephew, Charles Borromeo, a cardinal and archbishop of Milan. Borromeo proved to be a good choice, however, and became one of the important leaders of the Catholic Reformation. Moreover, Pius IV did not share Paul IV's attitude toward councils and reconvened the Council of Trent in January 1562.

Two hundred bishops attended this session, and they were more representative of the Church outside of Italy than in the two previous meetings. Spanish and French bishops, who were present in larger numbers, were determined to protect the independence of their national churches from papal dominance. Serious inner-Catholic tensions concerning the duties of the bishops to reside in their dioceses and the primacy of the papacy prolonged the proceedings. Some of the sessions became so stormy that the delegates threw punches and denounced each other as heretics. Meanwhile their lay supporters fought each other in the streets of Trent. In the end, compromises were reached and decrees stated that bishops were the successors of the apostles and that the Holy Spirit instituted them to rule the church, without specifically defining the limits, if any, of papal power. Although the council did not resolve questions of papal authority, it continued the process of clarifying doctrine and issued a series of reforming decrees. Among those beliefs reaffirmed and clarified were the sacrificial Mass and purgatory. In general, the council made certain that the future theological orientation of the Roman Catholic Church would be Thomistic, that is, it would follow the teachings of the great medieval theologian St. Thomas Aquinas. Moreover, new provisions for clerical training were enacted and such practices as clerical concubinage prohibited. Certain tasks, such as the revision of the Missal, the Breviary and the Index, were delegated to the pope, who confirmed the acts of the council in January 1564. The council even restored a note of unity as the delegates broke out in spontaneous cheering for Pius IV on the final day.[20]

It is difficult to overestimate the importance of the Council of Trent in the story of the Catholic Reformation. First, it marked the official repudiation of Protestantism by the Church of Rome. To be fair, by the time the council first met in 1545, it was almost too late to heal the breech between the two sides. The tensions between them were by this time too pronounced and too firmly established to afford much chance of conciliation. The course of events both at the council and in the outside world between 1545 and 1563 confirmed this fact. Second, Trent was a milestone in church history as it affirmed the ties of the Roman Church with its rich medieval Catholic heritage, and created the outward face of the modern Roman Catholic Church from the time of Trent in the mid-sixteenth century until Vatican Council II (1962–1965) in the mid-twentieth century.[21]

The Spanish Mystics

The Spanish Mystics, especially Santa Teresa de Avila and her follower, San Juan de la Cruz, demonstrated that true spirituality and devotion never ceased to be a part of the heartbeat of Catholicism during the sixteenth century. As the reformers dealt with widespread ecclesiastical corruption, this spirituality became more prominent and distinct. Stimulated in part by the Protestant Reformation and in part by a renewed sense of devotion to the best of medieval piety, the mystics emphasized personal religion and thereby countered Protestant individualism and channeled strength into the Church.

Santa Teresa is an example of a woman who experienced criticism when she stepped out of the boundaries of what was considered acceptable for a woman in that day. Nevertheless, when she set her mind to do something for God, it was difficult to deter her. Born in 1515 into a wealthy and noble family in Avila, Teresa de Cepeda y Ahumada was a charming, vivacious and winsome young woman. Her paternal grandparents were Jewish converts to Christianity (*conversos*), and her father retained a lifelong fear of being exposed as not genuine Christian nobility. As she moved toward adulthood, her choices were limited to marriage or becoming a nun. The Carmelite Order's Convent of the Incarnation, just outside Avila, was one where the sisters could have their own rooms, receive visitors and read. These freedoms appealed to Teresa who, against the wishes of her father who expected her to marry and to marry well, joined the Carmelites as a novice in 1533, taking her vows two years later.[22]

With her sharp mind and social skills, Teresa might have risen in time to become Mother Superior, and otherwise lead an unremarkable life. However, as she pursued her devotions, she began to have raptures and visions, mystical experiences that turned her into something of a holy celebrity. Teresa's claims that her raptures allowed her to converse directly with God bypassed the authority of the Church. Spain at the time was in the grip of the Inquisition, therefore, she had to be careful. Some accused her of deviation, perhaps even heresy. Teresa turned to confessors, learned men who had the authority to diagnose her states as real or imaginary. Their probing led to a consensus that her experiences were a genuine gift from God.

In 1562, she left the convent where she had lived for almost 30 years to found, in a small house in Avila, the Convent of St. Joseph. She also worked to reform the Carmelite Order toward stricter observance, and established 17 new convents and two monasteries. These activities are chronicled in her popular and influential *Life*.[23] Most important, Teresa's personal example and her writings influenced thousands of Catholic believers who were seeking genuine spirituality in the midst of a time of religious turmoil. She attracted people by the intensity of her longing for God. She wanted to lose herself completely in God. As historian Pierre Janelle has observed:

> Her account of her soul's journey, her minute psychological analysis of the successive phases of prayer, her practical advice to those who wished to follow in the same tracks, are the main points of interest in her written works, the story of her *Life*, the *Foundations*, the *Way to Perfection*, the *Interior Castle*. These books make no claim to literary excellence, but they derive great beauty from the genuineness of her emotions, and the freshness of her poetical imagery. Indeed, it is difficult for St. Teresa to convey to her readers a concrete notion of spiritual states, which

were before all a matter of personal experience. Hence her use
of beautiful similes to describe the soul's ascent on the mystical
ladder.[24]

The Interior Castle of 1571 is her masterpiece. The book is a
description of the stages of her soul's growth, and was originally
intended for the eyes of the Carmelite sisters only, so that they might
feel less alone in their spiritual trials. Teresa's inspiration lay in her
ability to imagine the soul as a castle made of a single diamond or of
a very clear crystal, in which there are many rooms, just as in heaven
there are many mansions.[25]

Santa Teresa the mystic was also Teresa the powerful figure who
did not suffer fools gladly. Contemporaries admired her and
described her as single-minded, even brash. She was a good negotia-
tor for her order and had learned something of finance and law. She
enjoyed conversations about good books, knew many people in the
community beyond the confines of her convent, and liked having a
good meal and a laugh. She is reputed to have said, "There is a time
for penance and a time for partridge." At the same time, she committed her total essence to God and lived a life of the spirit that many
wanted to follow. She was, indeed, a teacher of her generation and of
many generations that followed. As such, she helped to make certain
that the Spanish-speaking world of the day remained securely within
the Catholic fold.

Teresa died in 1582 at the convent of Alba. Her body was
exhumed a few months later and its total lack of decomposition indicated to the faithful that she was a saint. Her body parts then were
given away to various convents as holy relics. It was said that her
unearthed body emitted the "odor of sanctity." She was canonized in
1622, and in 1970 was the first woman to attain the Vatican's distinction as a Doctor of the Church.[26]

The Iron Fist: The Roman Inquisition and the Index of Prohibited Books

During the 1530s prospects for religious reunion appeared to
be good. The pope made plans for the upcoming general council to
promote reform and renewal in the Church that surely would please
the Protestants. However, plans to convene the council stalled and
the Church continued to grant questionable dispensations and
licenses and to permit the sale of indulgences in order to meet its financial needs. Both the pope and the emperor assumed that all that

was necessary to bring Protestants back to the fold was for Holy Mother Church to put its own moral house in order. Neither the pope nor the emperor understood the complex nature of the Protestant movement or of the spiritual forces it had unleashed.

Therefore, as tensions between Catholics and Protestants heightened during the 1540s and prospects for reunion faded, hardliners gained the upper hand in the quest for reform. The result was more emphasis on countermeasures against the growing Protestant threat rather than on positive internal reform and attempts at conciliation with the Protestant dissidents. Jesuit counter-reform activities became increasingly numerous and intense after the order's authorization in 1540. The initial meeting of the Council of Trent in 1545–1547 also signaled a new hard line against Protestant doctrine and practices. Cardinal Carafa, who had never conceded the need for doctrinal accommodation with the Protestants, began to warn against talking to the enemy and increased his lobbying of the Vatican for a Catholic counterattack. He finally persuaded Pope Paul III to introduce a new Inquisition to help crush the growing plague of heresy and to strengthen the Church's powers.

The papacy had established a medieval Inquisition to combat witchcraft and other heresies. The Spanish Inquisition was authorized in 1478 primarily to ferret out those Jews and Muslims who had feigned conversion to the Catholic faith but who had secretly retained their old beliefs. However, it quickly had become an organ of the Spanish government over which the Roman Church had little control. The new Holy Office of the Inquisition, usually called the Roman Inquisition, was created on the Spanish model but aimed at heresy throughout Europe, especially the Protestant variety. It was endorsed by the papal bull *Licet ab Initio* in July 1542. The pope appointed Cardinal Carafa as Inquisitor-General and six other cardinals as Inquisitors. They had the power to try heresy cases originating in Rome and to function as a court of appeals from subordinate bodies established throughout Italy and elsewhere as secular rulers permitted. Like the Spanish Inquisitors, their Roman counterparts were authorized to imprison suspects, confiscate property, and employ the secular authorities to extort confessions, by torture if necessary, and to carry out punishment. Stories of excesses and atrocities committed by the Holy Office, many based on fact, became legendary in the Protestant world. The Inquisition, with the help of civil authorities, succeeded in almost completely eradicating all traces of Protestantism in Italy and Spain.[27]

Hand in hand with the Inquisition the papacy authorized a close supervision of all printed matter called the Index of Prohibited

Books. Since the invention of printing in the previous century, there had been local and fragmentary lists of books that the faithful were not supposed to read. The flood of Protestant writings created an even greater sense of urgency in this regard. At mid-century the papacy began to list prohibited books. Then, in 1559, Pope Paul IV issued a general *Index Librorum Prohibitorum*, a list of officially prohibited books applicable to all Catholics everywhere. It became a basic Roman Catholic institution. In the sixteenth century, the Index proved to be a powerful weapon in Catholic countries, where the dissemination of heretical books and ideas became virtually impossible. Among the vast number of books prohibited were all vernacular translations of the Bible that were not specifically authorized by the Church, all books by Protestant leaders such as Luther, Calvin, Zwingli, Cranmer, Knox and those of many second echelon Protestant authors, the books of many humanists, including several writings of the great Erasmus, and certain other dangerous works like *The Prince* and the Koran. Not even Catholic scholars or high Church officials were allowed to read prohibited books unless they obtained special permission from the pope. In certain areas and under certain circumstances, the iron fist of suppression worked very well.[28]

The Results of the Catholic Reformation

By 1550, the Roman Church seemed to be in full retreat and Protestantism seemed about to engulf all of Europe. By 1600, the Roman Church had renewed and reformed itself in many ways, and not only checked the Protestant advance but also won back large areas in central and eastern Europe. In addition, by 1600, the dividing lines between Protestant lands and Roman Catholic countries were set largely as they would remain for the next 400 years. England, Scotland, the Netherlands, the Scandinavian countries and most of Germany were firmly Protestant. Spain, Portugal, Italy, the Austrian lands and most of Eastern Europe were solidly Catholic. Large numbers of Protestants still remained in places like France and Hungary, and Catholics still prevailed in Ireland. And so it would remain for centuries. In any event, "the wild boars in God's vineyard" had been fenced off and contained.[29]

Catholic historian Pierre Janelle believed that, taken as a whole, the results obtained by the Catholic Reformation were monumental. He regarded it "as a second birth of the Church." Janelle admitted that it was a Church that was greatly reduced in size and from which all abuses had not been weeded out, but a Church, nevertheless, purified and strengthened, concentrated, more sinewy, more capable of endurance and of expanding in the mission field, and a Church with its dogma more clearly defined and firmly settled and fit to serve as a rallying point.[30]

The Council of Trent did, indeed, reform and recast the Church of Rome into the Roman Catholic Church as it would be for the next 400 years: theologically, politically and socially conservative and opposed to the Protestant churches wherever they were found. It also suppressed most of the abuses that had helped to bring on the Reformation in the first place. A reformed papacy played a major role in the implementation of the Tridentine legislation. Slowly but surely, the popes of the last half of the sixteenth century systematically implemented the decisions of Trent.

The Catholic Reformation also benefited from a substantial increase in the number of reforming bishops, among whom was Charles Borromeo, already mentioned. These bishops, in turn, appointed and trained able parish priests who not only lifted the level of religious understanding among their parishioners but also helped to win back areas from Protestants because they were now better educated and thus better able to challenge Protestants to public debates. They established quality schools for Catholic children and young people and even infiltrated schools in hostile Protestant environments.

The 1550s saw momentous changes that switched the Roman Church from defense to offense, and from conciliatory to tough measures. Beginning with the establishment of the Society of Jesus in 1540 to the climax of the Council of Trent in 1563, the Roman Church took the offensive. The stepped-up efforts of the Roman Inquisition during the 1550s and the establishment of the Papal Index of Prohibited Books in 1559 all added to the new Catholic counterattack mode. Further, the work of the Spanish mystics and renewed piety among the masses in Catholic lands helped to shore up Holy Mother Church. Pope Paul IV never seriously contemplated reopening the Council of Trent but he not only issued many reform regulations for the Roman Curia and the Church in the Papal States but also rigidly enforced them.

The year 1559, in which Paul IV died, marked one of the watersheds in the history of European religion as well as politics. The great political figures of the first half of the sixteenth century had passed from the scene: the Emperor Charles V, Francis I of France and Henry VIII of England were all gone. Further, the long struggle between France and Spain had been brought to an end by the Treaty of Cateau-Cambrésis in April 1559. The new rulers of Europe, whose lands had been exhausted by wars, were now disposed to maintain the peace and to devote their attention to internal affairs.

What of the Catholics and Protestants? Although the Catholic Reformation was directed toward problems raised by Protestantism and many of its manifestations were anti-Protestant, ironically it also had much in common with the Protestant Reformation. Both Reformations sought to christianize a European population that was often Christian in name only. Both the Catholic and Protestant Reformations launched a frontal attack on nominalism and popular religion—a form of Christianity that the Medieval Church had tolerated and even in some respects promoted. Both movements produced an educated clergy that had been to a great degree absent in the Medieval Church. Both movements also stressed the importance of educating the laity, and both Protestants and Roman Catholics produced catechisms and homilies for this purpose. Unfortunately, the two movements, which had so many objectives in common, found it impossible to reconcile the areas where they differed. Perhaps by the mid-sixteenth century things had simply gone too far. In any event, the result was religious hostility, intermittent fighting, and permanent schism in the Christian Church.

Notes

1. Luther was the original "wild boar" in the vineyard. He was soon joined by many others. See chap. 2; and Roland Bainton, *Here I Stand: A Life of Martin Luther* (New York: Abingdon Press, 1950), 147.

2. Among the best works on the Catholic Reformation are Pierre Janelle, *The Catholic Reformation* (Milwaukee, WI: Bruce Publishing Company, 1963); Marvin O'Connell, *The Counter Reformation, 1559–1610* (New York: Harper and Row, 1974); Louis Chatellier, *The Europe of the Devout: The Catholic Reformation and the Formation of a New Society* (New York: Cambridge University Press, 1989); and John C. Olin, *Catholic Reform: From Cardinal Ximenes to the Council of Trent, 1495–1563* (New York: Fordham University Press, 1990).

3. See Introduction, William V. Hudon, ed., *Theatine Spirituality* (Ann Arbor, MI: Paulist Press, 1999); and Janelle, *Catholic Reformation*, 92–103.

4. Denis R. Janz, ed., *A Reformation Reader* (Minneapolis, MN: Fortress Press, 1999), 346–347.

5. *Trattato utilissimo del beneficio di Gesù Christo crocifisso i cristiani* (Venice: n. p., 1543).

6. Patrick Collinson, *The Reformation* (New York: Modern Library, 2004), 105–106.

7. An up-to-date biographical account of Contarini is found in Elizabeth Gleason, *Gasparo Contarini: Venice, Rome, and Reform* (Berkeley: University of California Press, 1993).

8. Peter Matheson, *Cardinal Contarini at Regensburg* (Oxford: Clarendon Press, 1972), 36–52.

9. Ibid., 97–144; and V. H. H. Green, *Luther and the Reformation* (New York: Capricorn Books, 1964), 165–168.

10. Hans Hillerbrand, *The Reformation* (New York: Harper and Row, 1964), 418.

11. This section on Loyola and the Jesuits is based on John Patrick Donnelly, "For the Greater Glory of God: St. Ignatius Loyola," in Richard DeMolen, ed., *Leaders of the Reformation* (Selinsgrove, PA: Susquehanna University Press, 1984), 153–177; A. Lynn Martin, *The Jesuit Mind: The Mentality of an Elite in Early Modern France* (Ithaca, NY: Cornell University Press, 1988); John O'Malley, *The First Jesuits* (Cambridge, MA: Harvard University Press, 1993); and Jonathan Wright, *God's Soldiers: A History of the Jesuits* (New York: Doubleday, 2004).

12. Ignatius de Loyola, *The Spiritual Exercises of St. Ignatius*, trans. Anthony Mottola (Garden City, NY: Image Books, 1964), 47.

13. Ibid., 140–141.

14. O'Malley, *First Jesuits*, 34–35.

15. Niccolò Machiavelli in his book *The Prince*, 1517, coined the phrase "the end justifies the means." Some scholars see this as the signature principle of the Jesuits. For example, see René Fülöp-Miller, *The Power and Secret of the Jesuits* (New York: George Braziller, 1956), 152–154 and 478–479; and Malachi Martin, *The Jesuits* (New York: Simon and Schuster, 1987), 186–187.

16. For Francis Xavier, see Georg Schurhammer's monumental *Francis Xavier: His Life, His Times*, trans., M. J. Costelloe, 4 vols. (Rome: Jesuit Historical Institute, 1973–1982).

17. This discussion of the Council of Trent is based on Herbert Jedin, *History of the Council of Trent*, trans. Ernest Graf, 2 vols. (St. Louis, MO: Herder, 1957–1961). Also see John O'Malley, *Trent and All That* (Cambridge, MA: Harvard University Press, 2002).

18. O'Malley, *First Jesuits*, 324–326.

19. N. S. Davidson, *The Counter-Reformation* (Oxford: Blackwell, 1987), 11–12.

20. A. G. Dickens, *The Counter Reformation* (New York: Harcourt Brace, 1969), 118.

21. For a sampling of the decrees and canons of Trent, see Janz, *Reformation Reader*, 348–365.

22. This section on Santa Teresa de Avila is based on Margaret Rees, ed., *Teresa de Jesus and Her World* (Leeds: Trinity and All Saints' College, 1981); and Stephen Clissold, *St. Teresa of Avila* (New York: Seabury Press, 1982).

23. *The Life of Teresa of Jesus*, trans. and ed. E. Allison Peers (Garden City, NY: Doubleday Image Books, 1960).

24. Janelle, *Catholic Reformation*, 191.

25. Helmut Hartzfeld, *Santa Teresa de Avila* (New York: Twayne Publishers, 1969), 42–61.

26. Victoria Lincoln, *Teresa: A Woman* (Albany, NY: State University of New York Press, 1984), 419–424.

27. See Gustav Henningsen and John Tedeschi, eds., *The Inquisition in Early Modern Europe: Studies in Sources and Methods* (DeKalb: Northern Illinois University Press, 1986); and Edward Peters, *Inquisition* (Berkeley: University of California Press, 1988).

28. Francis Betten, *The Roman Index of Forbidden Books* (Chicago: Loyola University Press, 1935); and Paul Grendler, *Culture and Censorship in Late Renaissance Italy and France* (London: Variorum Reprints, 1981).

29. O'Connell, *Counter Reformation*, 267–306.

30. Janelle, *Catholic Reformation*, 303–304.

CHAPTER 7

CONCLUSION: THREE CENTURIES OF CREATIVE TENSION

The Reformation Era may be regarded as lasting from 1517 to 1660, but its influence would continue to reverberate for at least three centuries. The era's boundaries extend from the posting of Luther's Ninety-Five Theses to the restoration of the monarchy in England in 1660. Of course, as pointed out previously, stirrings of reform began in the fifteenth century and many concerned Christians, including Luther, began to think in terms of widespread renewal before the German reformer locked horns with Tetzel over the doctrine of indulgences in 1517. Likewise, reform and counter-reform faded gradually in different parts of Europe at various rates of speed over the years following 1600, until the lines of demarcation between the two expressions of Christianity, Roman Catholic and Protestant, hardened by the middle years of the seventeenth century.

The final throes of reform came amidst political unrest and war. The Thirty Years' War (1618–1648) convulsed central Europe beginning in 1618. It began as a primarily religious conflict with political overtones and ended as a primarily political struggle with religious overtones. During the 30 years of intermittent warfare, the various European states shifted sides and goals until, during the last stage of the war, Catholic France was an ally of several Protestant states. Meanwhile in England, civil war erupted between Parliament and the Crown beginning in 1642 and continued until 1649, when the English shocked the European world by removing their Sovereign King Charles I's head and declaring a republic. Most Puritans, including the great cavalry commander Oliver Cromwell, enthusiastically supported the parliamentary forces. After the failure of the republic and Cromwell's protectorate (benevolent dictatorship, according to many historians), the monarchy was restored, the Puritan Movement collapsed and the Reformation Era in England came to a close. In France, conflict between the various religious and political interests came to a formal end with the Edict of Nantes in 1598. King Henry IV's royal decree, in effect, partitioned France between the Catholics, who controlled approximately nine-tenths of the country, and the Protestants, who were given approximately one-tenth of the land. However, the compromise thus established proved unsustainable and Protestant rights and privileges came to an end when the revocation of the Edict of Nantes by King Louis XIV sent thousands of Huguenots scurrying out of the country. Many of these religious refugees were bankers, lawyers and skilled artisans, thus depriving France of their talent. Most fled to the Protestant lands of the Netherlands, Prussia, England and British North America.

Thus, the Reformation Era that began with a monk's hammer came to an end amidst blood, thunder and compromise. By 1660, the major upheavals triggered by the outbreak of the Protestant Reformation were over. Europe was now a significantly different place than it had been in 1517. Northern Europe, including most of Germany, was now Protestant while southern Europe and much of eastern Europe remained Roman Catholic. Three centuries of tension between Catholics and Protestants followed.

Historians began to ponder what it meant and what it accomplished almost the minute the last polemic was written and the last musket cooled. Most important was the question of what it meant in terms of change and progress. Did the Modern Era begin with the Reformation? Most Protestant historians answered in the affirmative but Catholic scholars were not so certain. More recently revisionist historians have questioned Protestant assumptions that the Reformation introduced modernity to Western civilization. Others, like the distinguished cultural historian Jacques Barzun, himself no religious partisan, have reiterated the belief that the Protestant Reformation constituted nothing less than a major shift in Western thinking and habits.

According to Barzun:

> The Modern Era begins, characteristically, with a revolution. It is commonly called the Protestant Reformation, but the train of events starting early in the 16th century and ending—if indeed it has ended—more than a century later has all the features of a revolution. I take these to be: the violent transfer of power and property in the name of an idea.

But it did much besides. It posed the issue of diversity of opinion as well as of faith. It fostered new feelings of nationhood. It raised the status of the vernacular languages. It changed attitudes toward work, art, and human failing. It deprived the West of its ancestral sense of unity and common descent. Lastly but less immediately, by emigration to the new world overseas, it brought an extraordinary enlargement of the meaning of West and the power of its civilization.[1]

How accurate is Barzun's assessment?

Divided Authority

As Barzun noted, the Reformation "posed the issue of diversity of opinion as well as of faith." These differences of judgment concerning the fundamental beliefs of Christianity introduced a division of authority among the faithful that would last until the twenty-first century. In the process, the contestants raised the question of what constituted the final authority for faith and practice among Christians: the Church or the Bible? Further, if the authority of the Roman Church could be questioned, then perhaps that of the Bible might also be. Moreover, if religious authority could be questioned, then perhaps that of the monarch might be also, especially if he or she were of a different faith. Of course, neither Catholics nor Protestants proposed to allow authority to be abandoned. Catholics still insisted on fidelity to the Church and Protestants to the Scriptures. However, diversity of belief had been established, and the door of doubt that had been opened a crack by the Protestant reformers would be kicked in by the intellectuals of the Enlightenment. Therefore, the questioning of established authority in the sixteenth century laid the groundwork for even more daring explorations of new ideas in the centuries that followed.

Religion and the Rise of the Nation-States

Barzun also claimed that the Reformation "fostered new feelings of nationhood." This was certainly true in the case of England, Spain and France, and to a lesser extent in the Scandinavian countries. The Church of England with its latitudinarian stance allowed for nearly all English people to embrace it to the extent that for most it came to be the accepted view that to be English was to be Anglican, that is, to belong to the Anglican Church. Moreover, the sonorous tones of the Book of Common Prayer and the Authorized Version of the English Bible of 1611, commonly known as the King James Version, helped to tie a nation together. In France and Spain, the Roman Catholic Church reasserted itself as the national church, a church to which loyal French and Spanish subjects would adhere. "The Most Catholic Kings of Spain," as they were denominated, were especially insistent that to be a true Spaniard was to be a good Catholic. Although not as pronounced, membership in the established Protestant churches of the various Scandinavian countries was considered essential to loyalty to king and country.

In Germany, the reverse was true. The religious divisions introduced by the Reformation worked against German unification in this period because of the Emperor Charles V's staunch adherence to the Catholic faith. The Emperor stubbornly clung to his Catholicism while the majority of his imperial subjects became Protestants. The French Emperor Napoleon I, as he contemplated his own nineteenth-century interests, once remarked that had he been Charles, he would have become a Protestant in an instant in order to unify the empire.[2] But this was not to be and German unification would have to wait until the nineteenth century.

The Reformation and the Use of the Vernacular

Barzun further asserted that the Reformation "raised the status of the vernacular languages." It is true that the Protestant churches destroyed the linguistic unity of Latin as they provided the Bible in the various national tongues so that all might read and understand that it was necessary that they personally trust Jesus for salvation. This conviction stimulated not only the translation of the Scriptures into native languages but also the push for literacy among the masses, both male and female.

For example, Luther's translation of the Bible into German greatly affected the development of the German language. Immediately after his appearance at Worms in 1521, when he refused to recant what the Church considered to be his heretical views, Luther was spirited away to the Wartburg Castle of the Elector Frederick of Saxony for protection against seizure by Emperor Charles V. Luther remained at the Wartburg until he returned to Wittenberg in March 1522. While at the Wartburg, he translated the Greek New Testament into German, which took him from December 1521 to the end of February 1522. Later he and his university colleagues translated the

Old Testament from the Hebrew, completing the project in 1534. It was a linguistic milestone important for its direct religious impact, for its formative power in the development of New High German as the standard language of the people and of literature, and for its influence on translations of the Bible into other vernacular languages, including English.

The English Reformation stimulated a wave of Bible translations into the native language. Encouraged by Luther's precedent, William Tyndale produced a fresh English version of the New Testament from the original Greek in 1526. He also translated portions of the Old Testament before his untimely death in 1536. Miles Coverdale followed with a complete English Bible in 1535, largely based on Tyndale's translation. These versions were superseded by the Great Bible of 1539, published by royal authority to be made available in every parish church in England. The Geneva Bible of 1560, produced by the community of Protestant exiles in Geneva during the reign of Queen Mary I, was the first English version translated throughout from the original text. The Geneva translation became the household Bible of English-speaking Protestants until well into the seventeenth century when the Authorized Version of 1611 gradually replaced it. Commonly called the King James Version because King James I authorized it, this new translation set a standard of "Bible English" that exercised a profound literary influence on the English language for the next 300 years.[3]

The Impact of the Reformation on Economics, Art, Music and Literature

Similarly, as Barzun noted, the Reformation "changed attitudes toward work, art and human failings." The impact of the Reformation on economics and attitudes toward work has been the subject of extensive controversy. In the early years of the twentieth century the German sociologist Max Weber proposed an intriguing theory that linked the growth of capitalism to Calvinism. In a classic essay titled "The Protestant Ethic and the Spirit of Capitalism," Weber argued that the new type of commercial capitalism that appeared in the post–Reformation era in large part stemmed from a Calvinistic ethic.[4] The new capitalism, carried on by self-disciplined Calvinist types, was characterized by the relentless pursuit of profit and limitations on consumption that resulted in the accumulation of surplus capital that could be reinvested to produce further economic growth. The Calvinist ethic of hard work, thrift, self-discipline and a sense of vocation, combined with an understanding of the doctrine of election that encouraged reassurance by adhering to the ethic and being blessed by economic success, helped to stimulate this type of capitalism. The fact that commercial capitalism flourished in areas such as England and the Netherlands and later in British North America, where Calvinism was strongest, tended to offer support for the theory.

Those who have questioned Weber's thesis point out that capitalism existed well before the Reformation and contend that many of the connections between the Calvinist ethic and capitalism made by Weber and his followers are based on a misunderstanding of the Protestant ethic.[5] For example, both Calvin and Luther opposed many of the practices associated with the growth of capitalism and would have been horrified to have their names associated with a system that made the pursuit of profit the main motive of economic activity. They both were especially opposed to an unfettered capitalism that flouted economic justice.[6] On the other hand, some Protestant beliefs, such as the concept of vocation that raised the status of ordinary occupations, had an economic impact, as did their changing views of usury. Calvin, especially, implied that it was all right for an individual to become rich if it were done "for the glory of God" and provided that profits were shared with God via the church. Moreover, the Protestant work ethic became standard fare in the Protestant countries of Europe during this period and remained strong for many years. Further, by instilling into the laboring classes a view of life that raised work from drudgery to a source of self-respect, Protestantism and especially Calvinism helped to build up a group of productive and reliable people that became a solid base for a capitalist society. Therefore, latter-day Calvinists could find much in Protestant thought to support both a capitalist society and those progressive critics of such a society who tried to limit its abuses.

Likewise, the Reformation influenced artistic development, especially in its Lutheran, Anglican, and Catholic expressions. Zwingli, Calvin, and the Anabaptists were suspicious of what they regarded as idolatry in art and had a mixed reaction to the use of music in worship, with the Calvinists using psalmody and the Anabaptists certain types of hymns and spiritual songs. The Lutherans and Anglicans considered art and music beneficial to worship. In any case, visual presentations of various kinds were combined with music and preaching to propagate the doctrines of the Protestant Reformation. Historian Peter Matheson, who has studied the popular presentation of Reformation teaching, observes that "poet, artist, musician, painter and pamphleteer allied with preacher so that in

Luther's words the Gospel was not only preached, but painted, sung, and—we might add—rhymed."[7]

The Catholic Reformation also had a significant impact on art, especially painting. Although the Council of Trent said little about the visual arts, it made it clear that paintings and church decorations must not corrupt faith or morals. For instance, depictions of Mary breast-feeding the baby Jesus were discouraged in order to avoid an overemphasis on the humanity of Christ at the expense of his divinity. The new papal moral rigor resulted in a "breeches painter" being hired to paint clothing on the nude figures in Michelangelo's *Last Judgment* on the walls of the Sistine Chapel. According to historian A. D. Wright, paintings also reaffirmed visually Catholic doctrines that Protestants denied, such as "the holy souls in purgatory, and associated with them, the holy guardian angels," and "the doctrine of the Eucharistic Real Presence was asserted by the adoption of the scene of the breaking of the bread at the Last Supper,"[8] resulting in a great run of paintings of this particular holy event. The negative results of these new attitudes were more than balanced by a great outpouring of artistic expression inspired by the Catholic Reformation, some of it under the direct supervision of papal commissions, such as the painting and sculpture used to decorate the interior of St. Peter's in Rome. Much of the art inspired by the Catholic Reformation was produced in Spain. Three great painters who spent their careers working in Spain provide examples of the diversity and depth of painting in that kingdom: El Greco, Bartolomé Murillo, and Francisco de Zurbarán. The cult of the Virgin Mary, which had become especially popular in the Catholic Reformation, helped to inspire Murillo in particular.

The artistic style that gave the most characteristic expression to the religious revival of the Catholic Church was the baroque. After it became apparent in the last half of the sixteenth century that the Roman Church would not be able to regain the half of Europe lost to Protestantism, the papacy undertook to celebrate the glories of Catholicism in those areas where the people had remained steadfast, especially Rome itself. Therefore, Pope Sixtus V (1585–1590) began the process of beautifying Rome as a proud capital of a resurgent Church. He enlarged the Vatican, built the Vatican Library and saw the dome of St. Peter's completed at last. Significantly, the great colonnades around the magnificent piazza, the beautiful canopy over the altar and much of the church's interior were the creations of Giovanni Bernini, the greatest artist of the baroque. In Rome, baroque artists and architects executed grand designs, and baroque buildings and piazzas were made as large as the funds available allowed. In so doing, order was superimposed upon the turbulence of Renaissance art and the themes were now mainly derived from the special emphases of Catholic Reformation theology, such as the assumption of the Virgin, Mary as queen of heaven and regnant pontiffs holding the keys of St. Peter. The prototype of baroque churches was the Gesù, the central church of the Jesuits in Rome, which features a wide tunnel-vaulted nave, a modest-sized dome from which light streams down into the church interior, the use of light through oval apertures and a series of small side chapels instead of the aisles that normally run along each side—all of which became models for churches throughout Catholic Europe in the centuries that followed. The Escorial, the great monastery-palace of King Philip II of Spain (1556–1598), and the Louvre in Paris are but two of the architectural monuments erected during the baroque age.

Bernini's work illustrates the impact of the Catholic Reformation upon art. For example, his *The Ecstasy of St. Teresa* portrays the Spanish mystic as a young woman swooning at the moment when the arrow of divine love pierces her breast. For another, his shrine for the chair of St. Peter in the Vatican Cathedral shows a mighty throne enclosing a wooden stool, which allegedly had once been St. Peter's own. The shrine is constructed with magnificent grandeur, including a scene on the back of the chair in which Christ presents the keys of the kingdom to St. Peter, and at the very top the Holy Spirit hovers in the form of a dove. This whole creation gives powerful expression to that sense of triumph that characterized Catholicism in the seventeenth century.[9]

Similarly, the Reformation played a significant role in the development of music in the period. For example, Luther was himself a talented musician. He revived the ancient Christian tradition of congregational singing, a lead followed by most Protestants, and composed at least eight original hymns, the most famous of which, "A Mighty Fortress is Our God," became the anthem of Protestantism in the centuries that followed. Calvin favored the singing of the Psalms, and in 1562, the first complete edition of the French Psalter was published with Calvin's blessing. Musical innovation flourished in the Low Countries as such Flemish musical luminaries as Jean d'Okeghem and Josquin Des Prez developed new techniques. The Italian Catholic Giovanni da Palestrina was perhaps the most famous composer of the sixteenth century. He employed all the advances made by Flemish composers and his style was the exemplar of their contrapuntal techniques. His music embodied the loftiest impulses of the Catholic Reformation. He served various churches in Rome for over 40 years and became the official composer for the papal choir.

The Council of Trent sanctioned his work as the official model for all composers in the service of the Church.

The Reformation also had an enormous impact on literature as it promoted theological, devotional and polemical writing, helped to inspire writing in the vernacular, which, in turn, contributed to the development of national languages, and commented on the human condition. This was especially true in England where it was the era of Edmund Spenser, William Shakespeare, John Bunyan and John Milton. The works of Spenser and Shakespeare reflect the indirect influence of the Reformers while those of Milton and Bunyan were directly affected. In any event, both Milton's *Paradise Lost* (1667), one of the great epics of Western writing, and Bunyan's *The Pilgrim's Progress* (1678), one of the most influential allegories of Western literature, addressed the shortcomings of humanity. In France, the Reformation influenced some outstanding writers who criticized the failings of the Roman Catholic Church from within. Included in this number were François Rabelais, Michel de Montaigne, René Descartes and Blaise Pascal.[10]

The End of Christendom

Furthermore, Barzun noted that the Reformation destroyed the West's "sense of unity and common descent." Europe had, in fact, entered the sixteenth century at least nominally unified by the Church of Rome. It emerged from the Reformation in the next century with a variety of evangelical communities competing with the old Church and with each other for the faith and devotion of the European masses. At the outset Europe still conceived of itself as Christendom, a body of believers with common goals to match their common faith. By the end of the era, it openly acknowledged the special interests of the new monarchies and territorial principalities, and witnessed the bursting of its long-established boundaries by colonial expansion into all parts of the world. At the beginning of the century, Europe had a lively but geographically limited capitalist economy on a broad agrarian base. At the end of the period, its capitalism had vastly expanded and its mercantile enterprises circled the globe. Europe came to the Reformation epoch with a certain uniformity of ecclesiastical culture and still aglow with the artistic and literary triumphs of the Italian Renaissance. At the close of the Reformation, it was moving rapidly toward new secular cultural foundations and the world of modern science. Even though it is no longer acceptable to refer to the Reformation, as did the nineteenth-century historian James Froude, as "the hinge on which all modern history turns,"[11] its tremendous importance in the shaping of modern Europe must still be acknowledged. Integral to an understanding of the modern world is the concept of the new Europe as a congeries of highly competitive states with enormous vitality that carried European culture into new geographical and intellectual worlds.[12]

The Reformation as a Stimulus to European Expansion

Finally, Barzun notes that the Reformation impacted the modern world by spurring "emigration to the new world overseas." It is also true, of course, that economic opportunities and adventurism induced many Europeans to leave home in the years following the Reformation. Religion was not the only motivating factor. However, it was a major part of the emigration equation.

Many Protestants sought new homes overseas in response to discrimination and persecution in the homeland. This was certainly the case of the Puritans who fled to British North America in the early seventeenth century to escape persecution in England. Large numbers of Baptists and Quakers followed. The French Huguenots departed France in substantial numbers after the Revocation of the Edict of Nantes in 1685, relocating in several different Protestant countries, most notably in North America. Many of their descendants, such as John Jay, Elias Boudinot and Paul Revere, later became important figures in the founding of the United States in 1776. Likewise, many Lutheran and Reformed Christians left the European Continent for various and sundry reasons, many of them religious.[13]

Roman Catholics also journeyed to British North America in search of religious peace and quiet, most notably in Maryland, a colony originally intended as a haven for English Catholics. More important and impressive were the numerous Catholic missionaries who traveled to all parts of the globe during and in the wake of the Reformation to seek new citizens of the Kingdom of God on behalf of their Church. Chief among them were the Jesuits who scoured the Americas, Africa, India and the shores of Asia in search of converts. As noted previously, among the bravest of their number was St. Francis Xavier who died while trying to enter China. In any event, the French, the Spanish and the Portuguese took part in and supported such ventures in the sixteenth, seventeenth and eighteenth centuries, all eventually sponsoring settlements of the faithful ranging from Quebec to the Philippine Islands. These efforts to establish overseas empires often were motivated by religion as well as politics, economics and demographic pressures.[14]

The Reformation and Politics

Barzun did not spotlight politics, except for his allusion to the Reformation as a stimulant of national identity, in his analysis of the impact of the Reformation on the modern world. This omission needs to be addressed because the political impact of the Reformation was substantial and important. For example, it is evident that the Reformation had a direct effect on the development of resistance theory, a concept important to modern revolutionary and democratic thought. Although both Luther and Calvin, based on Romans 13, taught their followers routinely to obey those in power, their followers found ways to justify resistance to magistrates who sought to suppress their faith.[15] Lutherans first justified resistance to the emperor when the latter threatened to eliminate Protestantism by force. The establishment of the Schmalkaldic League in 1531 was based on the contention that the constitution of the Holy Roman Empire gave "inferior magistrates" the right to resist a tyrannical emperor. After Charles V defeated the Lutheran princes in 1547, Lutherans in the city of Magdeburg defended the right to resist the religious settlement imposed by the emperor based on the same argument. Calvinists found these arguments useful when they faced government persecution in France. French-speaking Protestant leaders, like Theodore Beza, Pierre Viret and François Hotman, argued that when "The Powers That Be" were misled by evil advisors or did not produce "the good" upon which Romans 13 was predicated, then legitimately constituted lesser magistrates could lead believers in defending the faithful against a tyrannical ruler. In England, John Ponet, one of the Protestant Marian Exiles, even sanctioned tyrannicide if a prince tried to suppress "the true faith." A few Catholic writers, like the Jesuit Juan de Marina, also maintained that royal authority was based on a social contract and justified the right of deposition, and even tyrannicide, if a ruler violated the fundamental laws of the kingdom.[16]

It is important to note that the Reformers and the resistance theorists would have recoiled at the suggestion that their theories might be used to argue for "democracy," since they associated democracy with anarchy and radicals such as the leaders of the Peasants' Revolt. However, the Reformers' attacks on church privilege and their doctrine of the priesthood of all believers suggested a basic

equality of rights and interests that would one day aid the development of a political system that in their day was considered anathema
by responsible individuals. Political theorists would later draw on
the resistance theories first articulated during the Reformation to justify eighteenth-century revolutions.

In addition, many historians would contend that the Reformation played a major role in the creation of the modern state, which
is characterized by "independent councils, written constitutions,
complex bureaucracies, standardized legal codes and university-edu-
cated ministers of government,"[17] maintaining that "the modern state
had its beginning not in its monopoly of taxation and the military,
but in its monopolizing of religion."[18]

Finally, and most important of all in the political realm, was the
contribution of the Anabaptists and Baptists to the expansion of freedom. Menno Simons, Jacob Hutter and, later, Thomas Helwys and
his Baptist colleagues preached and dreamed of a free people in a
free church in a free state. The Anabaptists argued that New Testament Christianity taught that in order to have a congregation of truly
committed Christians, all believers had to make their decision to follow Jesus freely and without state interference. In other words, in
order to be valid, faith had to be freely chosen. Therefore, it was im-
perative that the state allow religious freedom and that church and
state be separate. Of course, they realized their ideals nowhere in the
sixteenth and seventeenth centuries. However, several places in the
Protestant World during that period introduced toleration, a right to
hold religious views different from the established ones as long as
minorities behaved with discretion and assented to certain political
disabilities. Among them was limited toleration of non-Catholics in
the Dutch Republic beginning in 1579 and toleration of all Protestants in England in 1689. However, full-blown religious freedom for
all people, Christian and non-Christian, and separation of church
and state would not become a reality anywhere until 1791, when the
fledgling United States initiated its great experiment in republican
liberty. Strongly supported by Baptists, Presbyterians and other Protestants, the first clause of the First Amendment to the U. S. Constitution established the practice of religious freedom that became a
beacon to the entire world.[19]

Conclusion

In any event, from the mid-seventeenth century down to the
mid-twentieth century, the two communities of faith, Catholic and

Protestant, lived apart and together in creative, dynamic tension. In some countries, those of the alternative faith were not permitted, while in certain other places Christians of a different persuasion suffered stigma and disabilities. In still other countries, like the United States, they sometimes even lived in relative harmony at the local level. Meanwhile, nations continued to struggle for supremacy on the world stage: Spain, France, England, Germany and eventually the United States, each informed in part by its dominant national faith. These rivalries often brought economic and cultural rivalry and sometimes war. However, these contests also often yielded advancements in the political, economic and social realms as well. As usual, competition was a mixed blessing.

The overwhelming majority of Catholics and Protestants no longer wish each other ill. Serious issues still divide these two major expressions of Christianity, the most important being the role of the papacy in the Church and the place of the Virgin Mary in Christian worship. However, with the convocation of Vatican Council II (1962–1965), with the rise of the Charismatic Movement among the churches and with Evangelical and Catholic Christians in dialogue in the last half of the twentieth century there has come a measure of peace and harmony among believers worldwide. The often creative and sometimes harmful tension that marked three centuries of Western religious history following the Protestant Reformation is at last beginning to subside.

Notes

1. Jacques Barzun, *From Dawn to Decadence: 1500 to the Present, 500 Years of Western Cultural Life* (New York: HarperCollins, 2000), 3–4.

2. Robert Ergang, *Europe: From the Renaissance to Waterloo* (Boston: D. C. Heath, 1954), 161.

3. A. G. Dickens, *The English Reformation*, 2nd ed. (London: B. T. Batsford, 1989), 151–160, 212–216, 343–344.

4. Max Weber, *The Protestant Ethic and the Spirit of Capitalism*, intro Anthony Giddens (Gloucester, MA: Peter Smith, 1988).

5. For more information on Weber and his critics, see Gordon Marshall, *In Search of the Spirit of Capitalism* (New York: Columbia University Press, 1982); and Hartmut Lehmann and Gunther Roth, eds., *Weber's "Protestant Ethic": Origins, Evidence, Contexts* (Cambridge: Cambridge University Press, 1993).

6. Both Luther and Calvin placed limits on the taking of interest based on Christian principles, but later theorists such as Hugo Grotius and

Claudius Salmasius justified usury on economic grounds alone without reference to religious principles. E. G. Schwiebert, *Luther and His Times* (St. Louis, MO: Concordia Publishing House, 1950), 443–466; and André Biéler, *The Social Humanism of Calvin* (Richmond, VA: John Knox Press, 1964).

7. Peter Matheson, *The Imaginative World of the Reformation* (Minneapolis: Fortress Press, 2001), 67. See also Andrew Pettegree, ed., *The Reformation World* (London: Routledge, 2000), especially the articles by Pettegree and Francis Higman on "Art" and "Music," respectively.

8. A. D. Wright, *The Counter-Reformation: Catholic Europe and the Non-Christian World* (New York: St. Martin's, 1982), 235.

9. John Sewall, *A History of Western Art* (New York: Holt, 1961), 678–687.

10. Colin Brown, *Christianity and Western Thought: A History of Philosophers, Ideas and Movements,* 2 vols. (Downers Grove, IL: IV Press, 1990–1998), see volume 1, *passim.*

11. James A. Froude, *Lectures on the Council of Trent* (New York: Scribner's, 1899), 1.

12. Lewis W. Spitz, *The Renaissance and Reformation Movements* (Chicago, IL: Rand McNally, 1971), 301–327.

13. Sydney Ahlstrom, *A Religious History of the American People* (New Haven, CT: Yale University Press, 1972), 124–259; and David L. Holmes, *The Faiths of the Founding Fathers* (New York: Oxford University Press, 2006), 143–160.

14. A classic example was the duel for empire between Britain and France in the eighteenth century that led to a British victory followed immediately by a large influx of Protestant missionaries into India in the early nineteenth century. Brian Stanley, *The Bible and the Flag: Protestant Missions and British Imperialism in the Nineteenth and Twentieth Centuries* (Leicester: Apollos, 1990).

15. Quentin Skinner, *The Foundations of Modern Political Thought,* 2 vols. (Cambridge: Cambridge University Press, 1978), 2:12–19 and 191–194. Some scholars argue that Calvin allowed for resistance to "The Powers That Be" in certain highly qualified instances. See, for example, John T. McNeill, "The Democratic Element in Calvin's Thought," *Church History,* 18 (September 1949):153–171.

16. Skinner, *Foundations of Modern Political Thought,* 2:189–358.

17. C. Scott Dixon, "The Princely Reformation in Germany," in Pettegree, *Reformation World,* 158–159.

18. Richard van Dulmen, "The Reformation and the Modern Age," in C. Scott Dixon, ed., *The Reformation in Germany* (Oxford: Blackwell, 2002), 206.

19. William R. Estep, *Revolution Within the Revolution: The First Amendment in Historical Context, 1612–1789* (Grand Rapids, MI: Eerdmans, 1990).

Although not a patron saint of animals and birds like St. Francis of Assisi, Luther loved cats and dogs. Here he sits during his period of protective custody in the Wartburg Castle in 1521–1522 as he works on his translation of the New Testament into German, with his beloved companions at his side. Courtesy of the Archives of the Evangelical Lutheran Church in America, Chicago, Illinois.

A nervous ex-brother Martin Luther takes the hand of a confident ex-nun Katharina von Bora in marriage in the former Augustinian Monastery at Wittenberg, 13 June 1525. Courtesy of the Archives of the Evangelical Lutheran Church in America, Chicago, Illinois.

Students through the ages doodle. A pen drawing of Professor Dr. John Calvin as he lectures at the Academy of Geneva (now the University of Geneva) some time between 1559 and 1563. Snark/Art Resource New York.

The English Reformers "burned well," remarked historian Hurrell Froude. So they did, especially the elderly Archbishop Thomas Cranmer, recently stripped of his insignia of office and convicted of heresy. After recanting his recantation of his Protestant faith, he died bravely in the great ditch in the Broad Street opposite Balliol College, Oxford on 21 March 1556. From John Foxe's *Book of Martyrs*, 1563.

MENNO   SIMONS, WT FRIESLANT

On the Road Again: Menno Simons, leader of the Dutch and north German Anabaptists, and the "most wanted man" in the Netherlands from 1536–1561, as he appeared crippled and in old age. Note that his Bible is open to his motto, I Corinthians 3:11: "No other foundation can anyone lay than that which is laid, which is Jesus Christ." Courtesy of the Mennonite Library and Archives, North Newton, Kansas.

Anneken Hendriks, an Anabaptist woman of Amsterdam who refused to renounce her faith, was burned at the stake in 1571, her mouth stuffed with gunpowder to silence her allegedly heretical tongue. Courtesy of the Mennonite Library and Archives, North Newton, Kansas.

St. Ignatius de Loyola, from the anonymous *Vita Ignatii*, 1600. Loyola was not only a "soldier of Christ" and a man of action but also a mystic and a man of prayer.

"Mercy, oh Lord, for all eternity I will continually repeat." Santa Teresa de Avila at prayer, the only known contemporary portrait of the Spanish saint painted by Lay Brother Juan de la Miseria when she was 55 years old.

BIOGRAPHIES

Teresa de Avila (1515–1582)

Also known as Teresa of Jesus, she was born in 1515 in Avila, Spain. Teresa was a major figure of the Roman Catholic Reformation, a prominent Spanish mystic, a writer, and a Carmelite monastic reformer. Her family on her father's side were *Conversos*, that is, descendants of converted Jews. Her transformation from a pampered rich child to a humble nun was a gradual one, which occurred over a period of nearly 20 years. In contrast to her former life, Teresa stressed strict poverty and strict enclosure in her monastic houses, refusing even to accept the *rentas*, or fixed incomes, that most religious institutions received as financial support.

Teresa is one of only three females to be recognized by the Roman Catholic Church as a Doctor of the Church. In 1534, at the age of 20, Teresa entered the convent of the Incarnation of the Carmelite nuns at Avila, where she experienced periods of spiritual ecstasy through prayer and the use of the devotional book, *Becedario Espiritual*, which consisted of directions for tests of conscience and for spiritual self-concentration and inner contemplation.

When around 1556, various people suggested that her newfound knowledge was diabolical, not divine, she inflicted various mortifications on herself. However, Father Francisco Borgia, to whom she made confession, reassured her of the divine inspiration of her thoughts.

During the last 17 years of her life, she composed four major works: *The Book of Her Life, The Way of Perfection, The Interior Castle*, and *The Book of Her Foundations*, as well as several other works, and some 500 letters. These books, as well as her activities as the reformer of the Carmilite Order and as a mystic, allowed her to make a major impact on the lives of ordinary Catholic believers and on her monastic colleagues alike. Further, her ideals continued through the teachings and influence of her main disciple, San Juan de la Cruz. She died 4 October 1582 at Alba de Tormes in the arms of her secretary and close friend Anne of St. Bartholomew.

Theodore Beza (1516–1605)

French Reformed scholar and theologian and John Calvin's successor as Chief Pastor of the Geneva Church, Beza was born Théodore de Bèze, a member of the lesser nobility on 24 June 1516 in Vézelay, France. Also a trained humanist, Beza served as Calvin's main lieutenant during the Geneva reformer's last years and then provided stable leadership for Reformed Protestantism from 1563 until his own death in 1605.

When nine years old, Beza's father sent him to Orléans to study law. There, young Beza encountered the humanist Melchior Wolmar, one of Calvin's old professors, from whom he learned to write elegant Latin and Greek and to love poetry. Wolmar also introduced Beza to the Protestant Reformation. Following his graduation in law, Beza traveled to Paris to practice his profession and to continue his study of the humanities.

While in Paris, his family suggested that he be ordained and seek advancement in the Church. However, the fact that he had recently secretly married Claude Desnoz complicated the situation. After a severe illness in 1548, he then suffered an equally profound spiritual crisis that led to his evangelical conversion and renunciation of Catholicism. He then embraced Protestantism and went to Geneva where he publicly married Claude. The years that followed included teaching at the Academy of Lausanne and a spate of polemical and theological publications. Upon the invitation of Calvin, Beza went to Geneva in 1557 to become a professor of Greek in the newly established Academy of Geneva. In 1559, he was named rector and eventually taught theology at the Academy. From 1561–1563, he carried out several important diplomatic missions in France on behalf of the Reformed Church. He returned to Geneva in 1563, and upon Calvin's death succeeded him as leader of the Geneva Church.

Beza continued his activities on behalf of the Huguenot Movement in France by serving as an advisor. After the St. Bartholomew's Day Massacre in 1572, he published *Du droit des Magistrats sur leurs subjets* (*Concerning the Rights of Magistrates on Behalf of Their Subjects*) in which he argued that all authority, including that of the French king, comes from God through election by the people. Kings remain responsible to their people, and if they abuse their authority, the people may resist under the leadership of duly constituted lesser magistrates. But the great body of writing left by Beza is theological, in what could be described as the Calvinist tradition. His primary role throughout his long career in Geneva was as a professor at the Academy that trained most of the French Protestant pastors as well as students from all of the Reformed areas of Europe, including England, Scotland, the Netherlands, Poland, Hungary, and Germany. Beza died peacefully in Geneva at age 89 on 7 October 1605.

John Calvin (1509–1564)

Along with Martin Luther, Calvin was one of the two leading Protestant Reformers as well as the greatest systematic theologian of the era. Calvin was the preeminent figure in second-generation Protestantism who eventually became the leader of an international Calvinist Movement.

Born in Noyon in Picardy in the Kingdom of France on 10 July 1509, Jean Cauvin (Latinized to Johannes Calvinis and Anglicized to John Calvin) became one of the most loved, hated and feared of Protestant thinkers. Of solid middle-class stock, his father Gérard was a notary public and a trustee for the cathedral chapter in Noyon, and his mother, Jeanne Le Franc, was the pious daughter of a prosperous innkeeper. Young Calvin studied at the University of Paris from 1523 until 1527, when he left Paris to pursue law at the University of Orléans. After he completed his doctorate in law, he returned to the University of Paris to continue his study of the classics. In April 1532, the budding humanist scholar published his first book, a commentary on Seneca's *De Clementia*.

During the course of his university studies, Calvin came into contact with reform ideas and a number of Protestants. This culminated in his personal conversion to Christ and a decision to join the Protestants at some point around 1534. This life-changing decision led Calvin to a community of believers who were spreading Reformation doctrines in the Paris area. Following an attempt to introduce New Testament ideas into the university, riots ensued and Calvin and his friends fled for their lives. Calvin spent the next seven years as a religious refugee before he finally settled in Geneva in 1541.

During this interlude, in March 1536, Calvin published, in Basel, the first of many editions of his important work of theology, the *Institutes of the Christian Religion*. This first edition earned him the reputation as a theologian in the Protestant community. However, it grew from an outline of faith in 1536 to the systematic treatise of

1559, and eventually appeared not only in Latin but also in French, English, German and Spanish. In its final form, it contained Calvin's mature reflection on matters of faith and served as a powerful defense of the new evangelical faith.

After a false start as a Reformer and Bible lecturer in Geneva in 1536–1538, the City Council expelled Calvin and his colleagues for overzealousness in the application of church discipline, only to invite Calvin to return in 1541, as the city-state descended into ecclesiastical anarchy following his departure. During the interim, he settled in Strasbourg where he worked on several books and married a widow named Idelette de Bure. When Calvin came back to Geneva, he did so on his own terms, which included the adoption of the *Ecclesiastical Ordinances*, a document setting forth a new church order, and a promise that the civil government would support reform but not interfere in the internal affairs of the church. Calvin was named as Chief Pastor, the only office he held in Geneva to the end of his life.

After a long struggle with papal and secular elements in the city, Calvin's supporters finally won a majority of seats on the City Council in the 1555 elections. From that time forward, he had a free hand in reforming both church and state, making the city of around 20,000 people a virtual "biblical commonwealth." After 1555, Geneva became the center of an international Calvinist Movement, with Calvin as its chief figure.

On the international scene, Calvin's influence was spread by his Academy of Geneva (established in 1559), the missionary pastors he sent forth from the academy to France and elsewhere, his establishment of Geneva as a center for Protestant refugees from several countries, his many books and pamphlets, his prolific correspondence with people from every walk of life in many different countries, the example of his city of Geneva, and his personal touch that provided many a follower in other lands with a mentor and model.

As a theologian, Calvin exerted a universal and lasting influence, especially in the English-speaking world, not only in the ecclesiastical realm but also in the social and cultural arenas. His support of republicanism, his tacit approval of the right of political resistance, and his advocacy of what became known as the "protestant work ethic" were especially important. Further, he became the dominant figure of the Protestant Reformation by the middle of the sixteenth century. In any event, he drove himself relentlessly, especially following the death of his wife in 1549, working intensively up to the time of his death on 27 May 1564.

Charles V (1500–1558)

King Charles I of Spain (1516–1556) and Holy Roman Emperor Charles V (1519–1556), Charles of Habsburg was born in Ghent in Flanders. He inherited from his grandparents Ferdinand of Aragon and Isabella of Castile the recently united country of Spain and its vast empire. He inherited from his grandparents Emperor Maximilian I and Mary of Burgundy the Low Countries, the Habsburg family lands in central Europe and the right to become Holy Roman Emperor. He would spend his adult life trying to manage these far-flung holdings amidst enormous religious upheaval, most historians would judge unsuccessfully.

After securing his election as Holy Roman Emperor in 1519 by means of the usual bribes, Charles set about trying to resolve the three great problems that would plague his reign: the Protestant break with Rome, the Turkish threat from the East, and the continuing struggle with France for European hegemony. Like all sixteenth-century rulers, Charles believed that in order to rule effectively, his lands had to be united religiously. Therefore, he expended enormous energy trying first to bring conciliation between his Protestant and Catholic subjects, and then attempting to coerce the Protestants back into the Roman fold. Neither worked.

However, Charles succeeded in securing Protestant aid in meeting the invasion of the Muslim Turks. The emperor's armies battled the Turks intermittently over the years, and were able to push them back after their unsuccessful siege of Vienna in 1529. Charles gained the upper hand over Francis I of France in two Italian wars—his army sacked Rome in 1527—and in 1530 was the last emperor to be crowned by the pope. In any case, he was able to hold French ambitions in check during his lifetime.

Tired and bewildered, Charles divided his possessions between his son Philip II of Spain (Spain, the Netherlands, Sicily and the overseas empire) and his brother Ferdinand I (Habsburg hereditary lands in central Europe and the imperial title), and retired. A genuinely devout man, Charles spent his last two years in prayer and contemplation at the Monastery of San Yuste in Spain.

Gasparo Contarini (1483–1542)

Italian diplomat, statesman, cardinal, and papal legate to the colloquy between Roman Catholic and Protestant theologians at Regensburg, Germany, in 1541, Contarini was born 16 October 1483, into a noble family in Venice. He studied Greek, mathematics, philosophy and theology from 1501 to 1509 at the University of Padua, Italy. In 1535, Pope Paul III made Contarini a cardinal. However, unlike many cardinals of his time, Contarini actually became a priest and celebrated his first Mass in June 1537.

Contarini used his influence with the pope to abolish abuses in the papal government and to secure honest men for ecclesiastical appointment. In 1536, Contarini was the president of a papal commission charged with submitting plans for a reform of the Roman Curia. It was largely due to Contarini that early in 1537, the commission presented the *Consilium de Emendanda Ecclesia* that targeted abuses and recommended needed changes in the Church. Contarini also encouraged his friends among the bishops to take appropriate measures for discipline and good order in their dioceses. Contarini also appeared to sympathize with Protestant views on several points of doctrine.

At the Colloquy of Regensburg, Protestant theologians such as Philip Melanchthon and Martin Bucer, faced Catholic scholars led by Contarini in an attempt to resolve issues between the two camps. Despite a conciliatory attitude on the part of Contarini and the Protestant leaders, doctrinal differences could not be settled, and the conference ended in failure on 22 May 1541. A few months after Contarini was appointed cardinal legate at Bologna, he died on 24 August 1542.

Thomas Cranmer (1489–1556)

Thomas Cranmer was King Henry VIII's chief supporter in his pursuit of an end to his marriage to Queen Catherine of Aragon and at the same time the first Archbishop of Canterbury with genuinely Protestant convictions. He led the Church of England at a time when it was buffeted by every wind of political and religious change and, in the end, gave his life for the Protestant cause.

Cranmer was born in Nottinghamshire in 1489, and educated at Jesus College, Cambridge. He became a fellow there in 1510, and took holy orders in 1513. A scholar by temperament and profession, Cranmer became a member of a Cambridge circle that met regularly at a local inn to discuss Luther's books and other evangelical writings. He soon became one of those who promoted Protestantism in England. He also rose steadily in royal favor during the 1520s, and in 1533 was consecrated Archbishop of Canterbury.

It was Cranmer who first proposed that the marriage issue be resolved by canvassing the learned opinion of the Continent, and he himself was sent abroad by the king to present Henry's case to the universities. Cranmer was sympathetic to the king's cause and increasingly disenchanted with papal authority. Moreover, he was a prelate who could be counted on to follow the king's command and at the same time persuade others in the English Church that the king's wishes were right. Following his elevation to archbishop, Cranmer pronounced Henry's marriage to Catherine void, and four months later married the king to Anne Boleyn.

In the last years of Henry's reign, Cranmer began the task of revising the liturgy of the Church of England. He made it more Protestant and created the first vernacular services. Under Edward VI he had even greater freedoms to reform the liturgy and theology along Lutheran lines. He produced the first Book of Common Prayer in English in 1549 that made the Church of England more Protestant while retaining the Mass, and a second Book of Common Prayer in 1552 that broke with the Mass entirely. Liturgically and linguistically, the second prayer book has been hailed as a masterpiece.

When Mary I came to the throne in 1553 and returned the Church of England to Rome, Cranmer was condemned to death for treason, but the sentence was not carried out. Following the renewed heresy laws of 1555, he was tried at Oxford, convicted of treason and stripped of his ecclesiastical titles. He was forced to watch the burning of his friends, Bishops Hugh Latimer and John Ridley, after which he was pressured to sign a recantation of his Protestant views. Cranmer acquiesced because of his loyalty to the royal supremacy and his fear of suffering. On the eve of his execution, however, his courage returned and he renounced his recantations. He went to the stake on 21 March 1556, denying his recantations and dying for his faith.

Elizabeth I (1532–1603)

Queen of England from 1558 to 1603, the daughter of Henry VIII and Anne Boleyn was declared illegitimate just before the execution of her mother in 1536. However, in 1544, Parliament reestablished her in the line of succession after her half brother, Edward, and her half sister, Mary.

When Elizabeth succeeded to the throne in 1558, she was faced with religious strife, a huge government debt, and failures in a war with France that had drained England's treasury. However, through cunning and by appointing able counselors and taking their advice, at her death England had passed through one of the greatest periods of its history, an age in which English literature, commerce and industry prospered and English colonization was begun.

The so-called Elizabethan Settlement in religion attempted to create a Church of England in which the overwhelming majority of her subjects felt at home. This approach became known as the *via media*, or the "middle way" between reactionary Roman Catholicism and strident Protestantism. The Settlement gained only partial success as a few Catholics continued to resist the new regime and growing numbers of Puritans called for a more thoroughgoing reform of the English Church. As long as she lived, Elizabeth, a moderate Protestant herself, managed to keep these factions under control.

After the defeat of the Spanish Armada in 1588 and the threat of invasion diminished, Parliament became less responsive to her wishes. Nevertheless, she remained enormously popular with the common people who saw her as the symbol of growing English power. A veteran of many romances but of no marriages, Elizabeth died without children. Before her demise, however, she arranged for Parliament to pass an act of succession that provided for her nearest living male Protestant relative, James Stuart of Scotland, to become the next English ruler. On 24 March 1603, the last of the Tudor monarchs passed quietly away in London.

Desiderius Erasmus (c. 1466–1536)

The illegitimate son of a Dutch priest and a local woman, Erasmus was born Gerrit Gerritszoon, in Rotterdam, the Netherlands. A precocious child, he became the most celebrated Christian humanist of the sixteenth century.

Educated by the Brethren of the Common Life, 1475–1484, he became an Augustinian monk. In 1491, he was able to leave the monastery. He was ordained a priest in 1492, and the next year became the private secretary of the Bishop of Cambria. He was then sent to Paris, where he studied and taught at the university. In 1498, he became professor of divinity and Greek at Cambridge University in England. While there he began a lifelong friendship with Thomas More, and in 1509, wrote *The Praise of Folly*, a satirical attack on the traditions of the Roman Catholic Church and popular superstitions, which he dedicated to More.

After 1514, Erasmus lived alternately in Basel on the Continent and in England, then in Louvain in the Low Countries from 1517 to 1521. In 1516, he issued a new critical edition of the Greek New Testament based on the most reliable Greek manuscripts. He also published numerous other books, including satirical attacks on papal abuses, criticisms of Luther, and various works of biblical scholarship. In all of this, his main aim was to reform the Church through humanist scholarship, the study of the New Testament and the Church Fathers, and an emphasis on the teachings of Christ.

Even though many of his works were openly critical of the Church, he always considered himself a loyal son and not a Protestant heretic. In any case, he lived a life of controversy and fame as he became the first best-selling author in the history of printing. He died on 12 July 1536 in Basel.

John Foxe (1516–1587)

Protestant historian and martyrologist, John Foxe was born at Boston, Lincolnshire, England, and is the author of the influential *Book of Martyrs*. Foxe attended Magdalen College, Oxford, where he completed his B.A. degree in 1537 and his M.A. in 1543. Some controversy surrounds Foxe's reasons for leaving Magdalen in 1545, after becoming a fellow in 1539. However, according to the records, Foxe left of his own volition because he disagreed with the college's rules for regular attendance at Mass, and because he objected to the policy of enforced celibacy of fellows, along with the obligation of fellows to take holy orders within seven years of election.

Instead of taking holy orders in 1545, Foxe became a Protestant, and when Mary Tudor became queen in 1553, he fled to Strasbourg on the Continent. At Strasbourg in 1554, he published the first part of his history of the persecution of Protestant reformers. Foxe then moved to Basel where in 1559, he published the first complete edition, in Latin, of his history. After Elizabeth I's accession to the throne in 1558, he returned to his native land and issued an expanded English edition of his book in 1563, titled *The Actes and Monuments of These Latter and Perilous Dayes*. The work, commonly known as *Foxe's Book of Martyrs*, traced the history of Christian martyrdom from the first century down through the reign of Mary I (1553–1558). Almost every English-speaking Protestant home owned and read a copy of this book from the sixteenth well into the twentieth century.

Foxe spent his last years in London where he died peacefully on 8 April 1587, and was buried at St. Giles', Cripplegate Church.

Henry VIII (1491–1547)

King of England from 1509 to 1547, and educated in the new Renaissance learning, Henry Tudor developed great skill in music and sports. In 1503, following the death of his older brother Arthur, heir apparent to the throne, Henry received a papal dispensation to marry Arthur's widow, Catharine of Aragon, in order to preserve close diplomatic ties between England and Spain.

After several failed attempts to produce a male heir with Catherine, Henry determined to dissolve his marriage with her and to marry Anne Boleyn. Beginning in 1527, Henry appealed to Pope Clement VII, arguing that the original papal dispensation that authorized his marriage to Catherine had violated biblical and canon law and was, therefore, invalid. It so happened that at the time the pope was at the mercy of Catharine's nephew, the Emperor Charles V, whose army currently occupied Rome. Therefore, Henry's request for an annulment was denied.

By 1533, matters reached a critical stage when Anne became pregnant and Henry still had no male heir. He thus authorized Thomas Cranmer, his newly appointed Protestant Archbishop of Canterbury, to take jurisdiction in the matter. Cranmer, in consultation with university scholars and theologians, granted Henry his annulment. In retaliation, the pope excommunicated the English king.

This, in turn, led to the formal breach with the Church of Rome. Parliament enacted a series of laws that severed England's ties with Rome, the most important of which was the Act of Supremacy of 1534, which made the king rather than the pope the Head of the Church of England. Henry's motives for this break were personal and political but there was growing sentiment in the country for religious change that helped to make Henry's move against Rome possible.

Religious turmoil continued for the remainder of Henry's reign. When he died in 1547, the Church of England was in many ways still basically a Catholic Church without a pope. However, religious change was in the air and the English Church would become distinctly Protestant by the end of the century.

Jacob Hutter (1500–1536)

Jacob Hutter was a layman who gave his name to a significant segment of the Anabaptist Movement. Like Menno Simons in the Netherlands, Hutter was not the founder of the Hutterite Anabaptists, nor the formulator of their distinctive doctrines. However, he became the conservator of the southern European Anabaptists in a brief period of leadership in the early 1530s.

Born in Moos in the Puster Valley of the Tyrol, Hutter left his native land at an early age to travel to Prague to learn the hatter's trade. Though the facts are uncertain, Hutter most likely was converted to Christ and received believer's baptism at the hands of Georg Blaurock. By 1528, Hutter had become the chief pastor of the Tyrolese Anabaptists. In order to escape fierce persecution, he led his flock on a perilous trek to Moravia where he had heard of the existence of the large congregation of Balthasar Hübmaier and other clusters of Anabaptists. Once there, he found Hübmaier dead and the Anabaptists of the region in disarray. He immediately asserted his apostolic calling and was elected their chief elder. Steeped in the ideas of the New Testament, the Moravian Anabaptists had already embraced the notion of Christian communalism. Hutter accepted this principle and reorganized the Moravian believers into tight-knit congregations with common ownership of all goods, based on the practice of the apostolic church, as reported in Acts 5 in the New Testament. Under his charismatic leadership, the Hutterites, as their enemies now called them, emerged as an economically viable, socially cohesive, and religiously vital community. Missionaries were sent out into all parts of Europe to preach Christ, baptize new believers, and encourage converts to gather in Moravia.

After news of the Münster uprising reached Moravia, the authorities began the systematic suppression of the Hutterites for fear that they, too, would try to establish a Münster-like kingdom. It was wholly unnecessary because the Hutterites were apolitical and nonviolent. In any event, severe persecution followed, thousands were killed, and Hutter was arrested and burned at the stake on 15 February 1536.

Hutter was important because he was a fearless, effective leader and because he established the Hutterite colonies on the basis of the Schleitheim Confession, a classic Anabaptist statement of faith. In any case, his followers succeeded in maintaining their identity and became one of the strongest and most successful survivors of sixteenth-century Anabaptism. In the nineteenth century, the entire Hutterite community emigrated to North America, always maintaining their close-knit communally organized Christianity.

John Knox (1513–1572)

John Knox was the principal leader of the Scottish Reformation and the man most responsible for the shape of Protestantism in Scotland. It was he more than any other individual reformer or politician who made the Kirk of Scotland "Presbyterian and Reformed," meaning presbyterian in church polity and Calvinist in theology. Fiercely opposed to the Church of Rome, Knox helped make the name Scots synonymous with Presbyterianism.

Historians have given Knox's year of birth as anywhere between 1505 and 1514, illustrating his obscure peasant origins. A native of Haddington in East Lothian, he studied at St. Andrew's University and subsequently became a country lawyer, a private tutor and, sometime around 1536, a priest. Knox's conversion to Christ in an evangelical sense came at some point in the 1540s when Protestantism began to spread in Scottish intellectual circles. The decisive moment when he decided to make a final break with Rome most likely came when he witnessed the execution of the Protestant scholar George Wishart at the stake for heresy (that is, for being a Protestant) at St. Andrews in 1546. After Wishart's death, Knox renounced his clerical vows and joined the band of Scottish Protestants who called themselves the Lords of the Congregation. Captured by the French in 1547, he was condemned to the galleys, where he survived mistreatment and starvation until rescued by the English in 1549. In the England of Edward VI, Knox became a popular preacher of considerable power and influence. However, when Catholic Queen Mary I ascended the throne in 1553, he was forced to flee to the Continent to escape arrest and almost certain death. There he came under the influence of John Calvin.

In Geneva, he was pastor of the English-speaking exiles and became imbued with Calvin's spirit and theology. Most important, he determined that if he ever were allowed to return to England, he would make it into a godly commonwealth on the Geneva model. That opportunity to return to England never came, however, because of a book he rashly published in 1556 in anticipation of his return from exile. The book, titled *The First Blast of the Trumpet Against the Monstrous Regiment of Women*, was aimed at the Catholic Mary I of England and the French Catholic political regent of Scotland, Mary Guise, the widow of King James V. Unfortunately for Knox, his book appeared shortly before both women died and, in England, just before Elizabeth I ascended to the throne. The book was a forceful attack on women rulers in general and Catholic women rulers in particular. It made Elizabeth reluctant to allow Knox to return to England, so he traveled to his native Scotland instead.

Therefore, in 1559, Knox was back in Edinburgh, ready to resume the reform of the Church of Scotland. Led by his passionate and uncompromising preaching, nobles joined with commoners to oppose the established order and eject the queen-regent from power. The death of the regent in 1560 resulted in the Treaty of Edinburgh and left the field open to Knox and his followers. The government was reorganized, a parliament summoned, a Scottish Confession of Faith proclaimed and a complete Calvinist-style ecclesiastical overhaul accomplished. By the end of August 1560, the Mass had been abolished, papal supremacy overthrown and the Roman Church replaced by the Reformed Kirk of Scotland, with a directing board of presbyters and a national consistory. A Book of Discipline was drafted by Knox and five others and adopted as the official ecclesiastical handbook of the new Kirk.

There followed a clash with Mary, Queen of Scots, who returned from France following the death of her husband King Francis II in 1561 to reclaim her Scottish throne. She was as determined to restore the Roman Catholic Church as Knox was to keep it Protestant. In a face-to-face confrontation with Mary in August 1561, Knox affirmed that when princes exceed their bounds, meaning attempted to restore what he deemed false religion, then the magistrates and the people could resist with force, if necessary.

After six stormy years, Knox and his noble allies forced Mary to abdicate and flee to England for sanctuary. Her son became James VI and was reared as a Presbyterian. Knox remained as the guiding light for the Kirk, drafting and revising various official books and documents and writing his somewhat self-serving *History of the Reformation of Religion Within the Realm of Scotland*, the first complete edition of which was published in 1644. Knox died on 24 November 1572, and was buried in the churchyard of St. Giles Cathedral, the so-called High Kirk of the Kirk of Scotland.

Pope Leo X (1475–1521)

Born Giovanni de' Medici, Leo was pope from 1513 to 1521, a critical time in Reformation history. A member of the powerful Medici family of Florence, he is known chiefly for his failure to act quickly and decisively following Martin Luther's attack on indulgences abuses and papal power in 1517, and for his papal bull of excommunication against Luther issued in 1520.

Leo was elected pope largely because of his peace-loving qualities as opposed to the warlike tendencies of his immediate predecessor Julius II. Leo was one of the Renaissance popes who personified Renaissance culture: he loved art, music and the theater, and patronized many humanists. Moreover, he enjoyed the good life and spent lavishly on his cultural projects. Unfortunately, he was not greatly interested in church reform and did not seem to be even aware of the many abuses then rampant among his spiritual charges.

At first only amused by the theological questions raised by Luther in Germany, Leo finally realized the seriousness of the situation in 1519 and 1520 when he heard first-hand reports that Germany was aflame with support for Luther and for what appeared to be from the papal point of view his heretical ideas. By then, it was too late.

One of Leo's last acts was to commend King Henry VIII of England for his book against Luther, titled *In Defense of the Seven Sacraments*, published in 1521. For this act of piety, Leo conferred on Henry the appellation "Defender of the Faith," a designation still cherished by British monarchs.

Leo contracted malaria and died on 1 December 1521, so suddenly that last rites could not be administered. He was buried in the Church of Santa Maria Sopra Minerva in Rome.

Ignatius de Loyola (1491–1556)

Born Iñigo de Oñez y de Loyola in 1491 at the Castle of Loyola in the Basque province of Guipúzcoa, Spain, Loyola was the founder of the Society of Jesus and a Roman Catholic saint. As such, he was perhaps the most important single figure in the success of the Catholic Reformation and in the rejuvenation of the Catholic Church in the last half of the sixteenth century.

Loyola was a professional soldier, born and reared among the hardiest and most willing fighters of Spain, whose training and valor at arms appeared to destine him for a life of military exploits and glory, like many of the conquistadores of his generation. However, his military career was cut short in 1521 while commanding the garrison at Pamplona on the northern border when a French cannonball ripped through his leg, shattering tendons and bones and leaving him a cripple for the remainder of his life. It seemed that his soldiering days were over. While recuperating, he happened to read a biography of Jesus and some lives of saints that inspired him to new heights of glory in the service of the Church instead of his king. He now decided to become a soldier of Christ, vowing lifelong chastity and obedience to the Church. He retreated to the monastery at Manresa where he spent nearly a year in ascetic practices, experienced many mystical visions and completed the essence of his influential manual of spiritual warfare later known as *The Spiritual Exercises*. After a pilgrimage to Jerusalem in 1523, he began his formal preparation for the priesthood, starting with learning Latin with children and culminating with the M.A. degree at the University of Paris in 1535.

At Paris, he gathered around him a band of associates who worked through *The Spiritual Exercises* (finally published in 1548) and who embraced Loyola's ideal of unstinting and unquestioning obedience in the service of the Church. *The Exercises* were not an exposition of doctrine but a detailed program, in outline form, for a month of prayer, fasting and reflection on one's life and the central mysteries of Christianity. It gave the first effective codification to what became known as the religious retreat in its most rigorous form. The book is based on the presupposition that God speaks directly to the individual in ways registered through feelings of consolation and desolation experienced by the novice. Perhaps the best-known section of *The Exercises* is its "Rules for Thinking With the Church."

In any event, Loyola and his six companions at the St. Mary's Church in Montmartre in Paris on 12 May 1534 vowed to live a life of poverty, chastity, and to follow a career of service in the Holy Land, or failing that, of unreserved service to the pope. They met the following year in Venice, found their way to Jerusalem blocked by war, and finally journeyed to Rome where they won a favorable response from Pope Paul III, leading to their approval as an order of the Church in 1540. Officially the Society of Jesus, they became popularly known as the Jesuits.

Early in 1548, the pope chose Loyola as the "general" of the society. He, in turn, provided for the organization of the order according to the Constitutions, which outlined a paramilitary structure with obedience, discipline and efficiency as the key ideas. Education and a determination to do whatever was necessary to save and serve Holy Mother Church were also stressed. Based on these ideals, the Jesuits took the lead in the Catholic Reformation, attacking Protestantism with ideas, persuasion, deception, threats, innuendo and whatever was necessary to advance the cause of the Church, so much so that many, including Catholics, regarded them as Machiavellians of the spiritual world. In any case, through counter-evangelism, education and missions, they greatly aided in the recovery and revitalization of the Roman Church in the last half of the sixteenth century and after. As for Loyola, he was beatified in 1609 and canonized in 1622.

Katharina von Bora Luther (1499–1552)

Martin Luther's spouse and model of the Protestant pastor's wife, Katharina von Bora also helped define Protestant family life, making her one of the most important women of the Reformation. In addition, her unstinting support and wise counsel were undoubtedly major reasons that Luther was able to cope with his stressful existence as a Protestant reformer in a dangerous world.

"My Lord Katie," as Luther often fondly called her, was born of an impoverished Saxon noble family in Lippendorf near Leipzig on 29 January 1499. After her mother's death, she was first raised at the Benedictine convent of Brehna near Halle, and later at the Cistercian convent of Nimbschen near Grimma in the Duchy of Saxony. In 1515, she became a nun at Nimbschen, and in 1523, was one of 12 sisters whose escape from the convent Luther himself had organized. Katharina's fate after she left the convent illustrates how difficult it was to provide for such women. She considered and turned down several suitors, indicating something of her independence and strong will. She wanted Nikolaus von Amsdorf or Luther himself. However, the latter was not considering marriage, much less to Katharina.

When the wedding of the two took place on 13 June 1525, it came as a surprise even to some of Luther's friends. For centuries the marriage of a monk and nun had encountered by far the harshest criticism and fostered vile gossip in Catholic religious circles. By contrast, within Protestantism this union was held up as a model for the clergy. In any case, it became a successful marriage of two strong partners who had to come to terms with each other. Luther cherished his Katie and said that he would not give her up for anything, but he also sometimes chaffed under her driving energy. For her part, Katie was fully aware of her husband's greatness, and even their last letters express their mutual and warm affection. Her education was sufficient to enable her to follow Luther's ideas and innovations, and she continued to study the Bible until her dying day.

The marriage produced three boys and three girls, one of whom died early. Another child, Magdalena, expired at age 13 and was deeply mourned by her parents. Katharina managed the growing household in the former Augustinian monastery with great acumen and energy. This was not easy since neither she nor Luther had any wealth and his professorial salary was not sufficient to cover all expenses, strained by the large number of guests and Luther's sometimes-reckless generosity. Consequently, Katharina took in student boarders, managed a small farm and maintained a strict budget.

After Luther's death, she suffered economic hardship but survived. As a result of a plague in Wittenberg, she planned to migrate to Torgau in 1552 but in the process had an accident and died. She is buried in Torgau.

Martin Luther (1483–1546)

When the "Great Man Theory of History" was still in vogue, Martin Luther was always a prime example. Often called "The Father of the Reformation," he was the primary formulator of Protestant orthodoxy and, along with John Calvin, one of the two leading reformers and theologians of the era. All Protestants regard Luther in some measure as the progenitor of their faith.

Born in Eisleben, Germany, on 10 November 1483, Luther spent his childhood in neighboring Mansfeld. After preparatory schooling, according to his father's wish for him to become a lawyer, Luther enrolled at the University of Erfurt in 1501, where he completed his B.A. and M.A. degrees, and began legal studies. While on a trip home in the summer of 1505, he was struck down by a bolt of lightening. Long troubled by questions of the meaning of life and the fear of death, Luther during this moment of terror vowed to become a monk. Thus, much against the will of his father, he shortly thereafter joined the monastery of the Observant Augustinian friars in Erfurt. By 1507, he had completed a program of theological studies and been ordained a priest.

In 1508, Luther transferred to the newly founded University of Wittenberg where he eventually earned his Th.D. (Doctor of Theology) degree in 1512, and immediately following was named to a professorship in Bible. Two years later, he was appointed to the important position of preacher in the city church of Wittenberg, a responsibility he fulfilled for the remainder of his life.

During the period from 1505 through 1517, first as a young monk and then as a young professor, Luther continued to undergo periodic spiritual crises as he searched for peace with God. As he prepared lectures on several biblical books, including the important letter of St. Paul to the Romans, Luther eventually reached a solution to his spiritual quest. Influenced by Erasmus, he gradually abandoned standard medieval hermeneutics and embraced the historical-grammatical method of biblical interpretation in order to find the core meaning of the text. This, in turn, led to his discovery, or as he would have put it, his recovery, of St. Paul's teaching of justification through grace by faith in Jesus Christ alone. It was not works of merit but faith in Christ alone that saved sinners like himself from the penalty and power of sin. This milestone in Luther's spiritual pilgrimage occurred sometime during the winter of 1515–1516.

The critical event in the beginning of the Reformation Era occurred in 1517 when a new indulgences campaign initiated by

Pope Leo X and the Archbishop of Mainz aroused Luther's ire. Luther repudiated the practice because it undermined the seriousness of penance and contradicted the Pauline idea that an individual was saved by faith and not by works. Since the doctrine of indulgences was still under discussion in academic circles, Luther had the right to challenge the now corrupt practice of selling indulgences in script, and on 31 October 1517, nailed his Ninety-Five Theses questioning the entire penitential system of the Church on the door of the Castle Church for debate by the University of Wittenberg faculty.

Although meant for academic disputation, these theses were soon translated into German and circulated throughout Germany. Thanks to the recently invented printing press, this could be done with speed and dispatch. After a series of disputations and interrogations by papal officials, and after Luther published numerous books defending his position, the German Reformer was finally declared an intransigent heretic and excommunicated from the Church of Rome in 1520. In a final attempt to rescue Luther from his heresies and to force him to renounce his writings, he was summoned to Worms in 1521, to answer to the recently elected Emperor Charles V. Luther reluctantly answered the summons but did not retract his works. Therefore, he was by imperial edict declared both a heretic and an outlaw.

Ordinarily this meant that Luther would be seized and burned at the stake. However, immediately following the Worms confrontation, he was spirited away by troops of Frederick III, the Elector of Saxony, and hidden at the Wartburg Castle near Erfurt for a year until his safety at Wittenberg could be guaranteed. Returning to Wittenberg in 1522, Luther devoted the remainder of his life to the Reformation that he had begun.

Two highlights of Luther's post-1522 career included his marriage to the ex-nun Katharina von Bora in 1525 and his completion of the translation of the entire Bible into German in 1534. The former produced six biological children and the latter millions of spiritual descendants. Tired and worn out, Luther died 18 February 1546, at Eisleben.

Philip Melanchthon (1497–1560)

German humanist and reformer and Martin Luther's successor as leader of the Lutheran Reformation, Philip Melanchthon was born Philip Schwartzerdt on 16 February 1497 in Bretten, a city in the Palatinate near present-day Karlsruhe, Germany. Melanchthon, his humanist name, was known as the gentle reformer because of his conciliatory nature.

A precocious student, Melanchthon eventually graduated from the Universities of Heidelberg, Tübingen and Wittenberg. The great humanist scholar Johann Reuchlin recommended him to the Elector Frederick of Saxony as professor of Greek and Hebrew at the University of Wittenberg in 1518. There, at age 21, he met Luther and became his loyal supporter and almost constant companion. Luther immediately offered to teach Melanchthon the Gospel of Christ if he would teach Luther Greek. The exchange was mutually beneficial. Luther's character and strong spiritual convictions helped determine the subsequent direction of Melanchthon's intellectual pursuits, while the latter's sharp mind and moderating personality was a leavening influence on Luther. Some of the value of this partnership can be seen in Melanchthon's *Loci Communes* (*Commonplaces*), published in 1521, the first and most important systematic discussion of Luther's theology. It was immediately recognized as a masterful exposition, which Luther himself pronounced worthy of immortality. This work was only one of countless services that Melanchthon rendered to the evangelical cause.

Much of Melanchthon's work involved trying to reconcile various Lutheran factions, especially following Luther's death, and even to find common ground with the Roman Catholic Church. For example, he was instrumental in the drafting of the important Augsburg Confession of 1530, a summary of the evangelical faith presented to the Emperor Charles V. Moreover, he participated widely in negotiations between the Lutherans and Catholics, notably the Ratisbon Colloquy of 1541 that foundered on such points as the doctrines of justification by faith and the church. It eventually was rejected by both Rome and Wittenberg.

Melanchthon was the foremost humanist among the Lutheran reformers. His historical significance may be seen chiefly in his recognition of the problem of the relation between humanism and the Protestant Reformation, that is, between the Greco-Roman and biblical heritage of the West, his coming to terms with the problem, and his introduction of the results of his solution to the thought and organization of both ecclesiastical and educational reform in Germany. In so doing, he avoided the twin dangers that either the fledgling reform movement would get sidetracked into an anti-intellectual spiritualism or, at the other extreme, philosophy would be imposed upon theology, knowledge upon faith, and reason upon revelation. Because Melanchthon allowed both poles to retain their own characteristic, he was able to bring about a fruitful joining of the two. Together with Luther and several others, he created a Christian and humanist educational system that continued to be influential through the Enlightenment and into the twentieth century.

On a journey to Leipzig in March 1560, Melanchthon contracted a severe cold, followed by a fever that consumed his strength. Weakened by many previous illnesses, he died on 19 April 1560.

Thomas More (1478–1535)

A martyr and saint of the Church to Roman Catholics, a persecutor of the godly to Protestants, and the foremost early Tudor exponent of humanism to many historians, Thomas More was a layman and trained lawyer who eventually attained the highest political office in the realm, next to the king. More, immortalized as "a man for all seasons" in Robert Bolt's 1960 play and in a 1966 movie by the same name, was, indeed, a well-rounded individual. He was a barrister, statesman, scholar, author, observant Catholic and bon vivant who was knighted in 1521, beatified in 1886, and canonized in 1935.

Son of a prosperous lawyer, More was born in London on 7 February 1478 and given the best educational opportunities available, including study of the humanities at Oxford University and law at the Inns of Court. During his lifetime, he earned a reputation as a leading humanist scholar and occupied many public offices, including that of Lord Chancellor from 1529 to 1532. More coined the word "utopia," a name he gave to an ideal, imaginary island nation whose political and social system he described in a book by the same name published in 1516.

As a devout Catholic, he fiercely persecuted Protestants and Protestant sympathizers as Lord Chancellor. This was especially true of his relentless pursuit of the Protestant scholar and Bible translator William Tyndale who was finally apprehended and executed on the Continent with the help of More's English agents. However, he is chiefly remembered for his principled refusal to take the oath attached to the Act of Supremacy of 1534, which demanded not only the acceptance of King Henry VIII's annulment of his marriage to Queen Catherine of Aragon but also the king's claim to be Supreme Head of the Church of England. This decision ended his political career and led to his execution in London for treason on 6 July 1535.

Thomas Müntzer (1489–1525)

An early sixteenth-century pastor and a rebel leader during the Peasants' War (1524–1525), Thomas Müntzer was born in Stolberg in the Hartz Mountains of Germany. He studied for the priesthood, earned his M.A. degree and then completed advanced studies in theology. He was well versed in Greek, Hebrew and Latin. After his ordination in 1513, he became a priest at St. Michael's Church in Braunschweig in May 1514.

Müntzer lived in Wittenberg from 1517–1519, and while there was influenced by Martin Luther. He came to agree with Luther's opposition to the Roman Catholic Church's sale of indulgences and the abusive use of power by the clergy. However, Müntzer eventually disagreed with Luther on several key points. For example, Müntzer believed in and taught the "living word of God," by which he meant continuing revelation and the gift of prophecy, that infant baptism was wrong, and that the wine and bread of the Eucharist were only symbols of Jesus Christ's sacrifice. Luther rejected all of these doctrines. Müntzer is sometimes associated with the Anabaptist Movement because of his position on infant baptism. However, there is no evidence that he was ever baptized as an adult.

Influenced by a radical group called the Zwickau Prophets, Müntzer took the side of the peasants against the landed aristocracy during the peasants' uprising. Increasingly erratic in thought and behavior, he turned against Luther, insulted members of the German aristocracy, and stirred up the peasants against their overlords.

Müntzer's end came in 1525 when he led an army of about 8,000 peasants at the Battle of Frankenhausen, convinced that God would intervene on their side because their grievances were just. Utterly defeated, captured, imprisoned, and tortured, Müntzer recanted and asked to be restored to his original Roman Catholic faith. He was then beheaded at Mühlhausen on 27 May 1525, and his remains displayed as a warning to any other would-be rebels against the established order.

Pope Paul IV (1476–1559)

Known as the Father of the Roman Inquisition and the most anti-Protestant of the Reformation pontiffs, Paul IV was born Giovanni Pietro Carafa of a noble Neapolitan family and reigned as pope from 1555 to 1559. He was known for his stern character and his zeal to achieve reform in the Church.

Paul was well educated and experienced in papal government and diplomacy before he became pope. Always active in reform movements within the Church, Carafa was a member of the Oratory of Divine Love from 1520 to 1527 and a co-founder of the Theatines in 1524. He was made a cardinal and Archbishop of Naples in 1536 and remained a hard-liner in opposition to Protestants everywhere. He was 79 years of age when he came to the papal throne and set in his ways. One of his first acts as pope in 1559 was to establish the Index of Prohibited Books, a list of books that are forbidden reading for members of the Roman Catholic Church. One of the tasks of the Inquisition was to compile a catalog of forbidden books and, with papal approval, to publish it. All of the books of Protestant leaders, those of many Catholics, such as Erasmus, and all Italian and German translations of the Bible were banned.

Further, Paul was a strong supporter of the Inquisition, especially against those suspected of heresy who held high office in the Church. During his administration, the Inquisition was reorganized in order to make it more efficient and less compromising. In his attempt to apply medieval concepts of papal power to sixteenth-century politics, he was unable to stem the tide of Protestantism in northern Europe.

Paul IV died on 18 August 1559 at age 83 amidst general rejoicing and was buried in St. Peter's Basilica.

Menno Simons (1496–1561)

Menno Simons, a former Roman Catholic priest, gave his name to the Mennonites, the most numerous and enduring of the various Anabaptist groups of the Reformation Era. Menno faithfully led the Anabaptists of the Netherlands and north Germany through the crucial years 1536–1561, and in so doing set the tone of the evangelical Mennonite nonviolent lifestyle.

Born Menno Simonszoon (Simon's son) in Witmarsum in Friesland in the Netherlands in 1496, very little is known of his peasant parents or his childhood. He studied for the priesthood and was ordained at Utrecht in 1524. His first assignment was Pingjum where his father had originated. During his years as a parish priest, he heard rumblings of the Protestant Reformation and began to discuss it with his priestly colleagues. In 1526, troubled by some Lutheran pamphlets that fell into his hands, Menno began to question the doctrine of transubstantiation. An intense study of the Bible led him to conclulde that the Mass and many other Roman Catholic doctrines were unscriptural. Then in 1531, he was stirred by news of the beheading of Sicke Snijder, the first Anabaptist martyr in the Netherlands. This caused him to examine the reason for Snijder's execution: "rebaptism." Snijder (real name Freerks) had suffered capital punishment for renouncing his infant baptism and asking for the rite following his adult confession of faith in Christ. This seemed so strange to Menno that it led him once again to the Bible for answers. A renewed search of the scriptures convinced him that the concept of infant baptism was not in the Bible. He discussed this and other related issues with his fellow priests, searched the Church Fathers and read the works of Martin Luther for answers to his increasingly numerous questions. It was at about this time that he was transferred to his home parish of Witmarsum.

The Münster episode of 1534–1535 caused Menno even greater soul-searching because he saw among the Münsterites righteous souls who had been led astray by wicked leaders. He regarded the misled as poor straying sheep and tried to correct them by exhortations, but to no avail. When the desperate city finally collapsed and its inhabitants were massacred, Menno felt the full impact of his own dilemma. The massacre brought him face to face with himself, and forced him to make the long-avoided decision. The breaking point apparently came when some of Menno's acquaintances, among whom was most likely his cousin Peter Simons, were slaughtered by local authorities as they made their way to Münster to re-enforce their beleaguered co-religionists. They were Melchiorites, as the Anabaptists in the area were called, followers of the millennial enthusiast Melchior Hofmann who had introduced the Anabaptist message publicly in the Netherlands.

This combination of events, the depredations of Münster and the senseless killing of several score Melchiorites, led Menno to renounce his traditional faith and to preach evangelical doctrines from his Witmarsum pulpit. After nine desperate months of impassioned preaching with few results, on 30 January 1536, he finally laid down his priestly office and vanished from the public eye. In so doing, he was fully aware that he was leaving social and economic security for the perils of evangelical preacherhood in a land that was still largely Roman Catholic and where edicts against Anabaptism were ruthlessly enforced. Moreover, he made this break at precisely that moment when Anabaptism was most hated by the authorities and most discredited by its devotees. Menno, however, believed that he had an obligation to guide the survivors of the Münsterite upheaval as well as those more peaceful Anabaptists who had no part in Münster in their quest for normative New Testament Christianity. This was an unusual case of a respected priest deciding to join a group with which he had had no fellowship before the Münsterite debacle and whose radical ideas on the millennium he had opposed.

Sometime during 1536, Menno requested and received believer's baptism at the hands of an Anabaptist leader, most likely Obbe Philips. From that time on, because of his education, experience and commitment to the cause, Menno was the popular leader of the Dutch Anabaptists. He devoted the remainder of his life to the cause of peaceful, evangelical Anabaptism. By 1544, the authorities routinely referred to the Dutch Anabaptists as "Mennonites." However, as he became the dominant leader of the movement, he also became increasingly a target of the authorities. He soon became the "most wanted man" in the Low Countries, with a large reward offered for his capture. Thanks to his steadfast friends and followers and to his own agility, Menno was able to elude his pursuers and live to old age, dying in seclusion in 1561.

William Tyndale (1492–1536)

Sometimes spelled Tindal, or Tindale, he was an English Bible translator and Protestant martyr, who was probably ordained in the Church of England around 1521. Born in western England, probably in 1492, he was educated at Magdalen Hall, Oxford, and afterward at Cambridge University where he most likely became a Protestant believer.

As one of England's earliest Protestants, Tyndale was determined to translate the New Testament into English, and moved from Gloucestershire, England, to London to accomplish this. Thwarted by the authorities there, he traveled to Hamburg in Germany in 1524, and later visited Martin Luther at Wittenberg. At Cologne in 1525, Tyndale began the publication of an English New Testament. Halted by an injunction, he had the edition completed at Worms. When copies of his new translated scriptures entered England in 1526, they were seized and most copies burned. Cardinal Thomas Wolsey asked German authorities to arrest Tyndale but he eluded capture. While living in concealment, Tyndale pursued his translation of the remainder of the Bible, issuing the Pentateuch in 1530, and the Book of Jonah in 1536. His work later became a basis of the King James Version of the Bible of 1611. Thomas More, the Lord Chancellor, denounced his tracts in defense of the principles of the English Reformation, namely, his *The Obedience of a Christian Man* and *The Parable of the Wicked Mammon*, both published in 1528. *The Practice of Prelates* in 1530, which condemned the divorce of Henry VIII, drew the king's wrath. Hounded by More's English agents, Tyndale finally was seized in 1535, in Antwerp. His trial ended in condemnation for heresy. Consequently, he was strangled and then burned at the stake on 6 October 1536.

Ulrich (Huldrych) Zwingli (1484–1531)

Zwingli was the reformer of Zurich, Switzerland, who is often regarded as the founder of the Reformed tradition. A contemporary of Luther, the two men shared similar socio-economic backgrounds. However, they developed different Protestant theologies, largely because of their different educational backgrounds and the different environments in which they worked.

Following an excellent university humanist education, Zwingli was ordained in 1506, and assigned to a parish in Glarus. While there, he lived the pleasant life of a rural clergyman that included at least one dalliance with a local maiden. In any case, by 1516, he had embraced the Erasmian principle that Christian belief and worship should be based on the Bible itself.

Moving to Einsiedeln in 1516, Zwingli saw Church corruption there first-hand. He also intensified his study of New Testament Greek, especially the words of St. Paul, and became widely known as a superb preacher. His growing reputation as a scholar-pastor and eloquent speaker soon earned him promotion to the prestigious position of People's Priest in Zurich's Great Minster in December 1518. He used this powerful pulpit to introduce the Reformation into Zurich.

Zwingli's reformation was different from that of Luther and the Anabaptists. His meeting with Luther at Marburg in 1529 revealed that the two men had different views of communion, and the Anabaptist minority in Zurich sharply disagreed with Zwingli's corporate view of society that did not distinguish between church and state. Moreover, Zwingli repeatedly clashed with Catholic authorities over his introduction of reform into the Zurich Church. He also had to contend with elements of the City Council who feared that he sometimes went too far, too fast. Even though marriage in 1522 brought him a measure of comfort and stability, his life after 1525 was one of increasing stress as he engaged his opponents on many fronts. Nevertheless when he died, he left behind a city and canton that was thoroughly reformed and strongly Protestant.

Zwingli's end came while in full military gear at the Battle of Kappel on 11 October 1531, as he accompanied Zurich troops into the fray against an army from the Catholic Swiss cantons. Badly wounded on the battlefield, his death came at the hands of his captors. The Zurich Reformation eventually was absorbed by Calvinism and became part of the Reformed Church of Switzerland. In the process, however, much that was foundational to the Calvinist Movement received its first expression in Zwingli's theology, thus making it possible to consider the Zurich Reformer the father of the Reformed tradition.

PRIMARY DOCUMENTS

Document 1: Desiderius Erasmus, Excerpt from his classic satire *The Praise of Folly*, 1511

Desiderius Erasmus (c. 1466–1536) was the greatest scholar and Christian humanist of the Reformation Era. As a humanist, he read the New Testament and the Church Fathers and noted that the Church of his day fell short of the Ancient Church in terms of following the teachings of Christ and the Apostles. Many of his works were, therefore, critical of contemporary Christianity. *The Praise of Folly*, written in 1509 and published in 1511, was one of these works. After introducing "Folly," a woman, as the symbol of all of the good things of life, he proceeds to severely criticize those things that he believes are most responsible for the ills of humanity, including the universities and the Church. In this section, he comments on the Church, especially its leadership. The fact that he remained to the end of his life a loyal Roman Catholic shows that critical thought did not necessarily mean becoming a Protestant. Erasmus longed for reform but not at the price of disunity.

> Our popes, cardinals, and bishops have, for a long while now, diligently followed the example of the state and the practices of the princes, and have come near to beating these noblemen at their own game. If our bishops would but stop and consider what their white albs signify—namely, sincerity and a pure life in every way untainted; what is signified by their two-horned miter, the peaks of which are joined by a common knot—a perfect knowledge and understanding of the Old and New Testaments; what is meant by their wearing of gloves—the immaculate administration of the sacraments, untainted by any selfishness or self-concern, what their crozier symbolizes—their diligent and protective watch of the flock that they are charged with; and what is signified by the cross that is carried before them in procession—the victory of spiritual charity over carnal affections.

If they would but contemplate these and other virtues, I am sure that it would be safe to say that they would not lead such troubled and shameful lives. But as it is they are kept too busy feeding themselves to think on these things; as for the care of their sheep, they delegate this duty to one of their subordinates (suffragans, as they call them) or to Christ Himself. Nor have they stopped to contemplate the title that they bear or to examine its meaning; bishop, meaning labor, diligence, and solicitude. Yet when it comes to pecuniary matters they truly act the part of a bishop to the hilt overseeing everything—and overlooking nothing.

If, in a similar manner, the cardinals would stop and consider the fact of their succession of the Apostles, they would realize that the same good deeds are expected of them as were expected of their predecessors; that they are stewards, not lords of spiritual affairs; and that soon they will be held accountable for all those things in which they should firmly trust and believe. It would do them a great deal of good, also, to consider the significance of their vestments and to ask themselves these questions. Does not the whiteness of the upper garment symbolize the purity and stainlessness of the heart and of the disjunction of the wearer from human wants and selfishness? Is not the scarlet or crimson color of the lower garments an emblem of a burning love and desire of God? What is the significance of the outer robe of his Exalted Reverence? Do not its abundant folds serve another purpose than just to cover the mule of his worship, although they could just as easily cover a camel? Is it not a symbol of a charity sufficient enough to receive all men by its helpfulness through teaching, encouraging, chastising, cautioning, settling wars, defying evil sovereigns, and freely spending blood—not money alone—for the advancement of the fold of Christ? And finally, "What need do I, a needy apostle, have for all this ill-gotten money?" It is my belief that if they would stop and consider these questions, then they would not clamor after the bishopric, or, if they did get the office, they would lead a weary and pious life of the sort lived by the ancient Apostles.

As to the Supreme Pontiffs, if they would recall that they take the place of Christ and would attempt to imitate His poverty, tasks, doctrines, crosses, and disregard of safety; if they were to contemplate the meaning of the name Pope—that is, Father—or of the title of Most Holy, then they would become the most humble and mortified of men. How many would then be willing to spend all their wealth and efforts in order to procure this position? If someone were foolish enough to procure it in this manner, would they further be willing to defend their position by the shedding of blood, by the use of poison, or by any other necessary means? Oh, how wisdom would upset their nefarious plans if it were to inflict them! Wisdom, did I say?

Nay! Even a grain of salt, that salt spoken of by Christ, would be sufficient to upset their plans. It would lose them all their wealth, their honor, their belongings, their powers won by victories, their offices, dispensations, tributes, and indulgences. They would lose a great many horses, mules, and carts. And finally, they would lose a great many pleasures. (See how I have comprehended in a few words many marketsful, a great harvest, a wide ocean, of goods.) These forfeitures would be replaced by vigils, fasts, sorrows, prayers, sermons, education, weariness, and a thousand other bothersome tasks of the sort. We should also mention that a great many copyists, notaries, lobbyists, promoters, secretaries, muleteers, grooms, bankers, and pimps—I was about to add something more tender, though rougher on the ears, I am afraid—would be out of jobs. In other words, that large group of men that burdens—I beg your pardon, I meant to say adorns—the Holy Roman See would be done away with and would have to, as a result, resort to begging as a means of making a living. Those who are even the worse, those very princes of the Church and guiding lights of the world, would become nothing more than a staff and a wallet. However, this action would be barbarous and abhorred.

Under the present system what work need be done is handed over to Peter or Paul to do at their leisure, while pomp and pleasure are personally taken care of by the Popes. They believe themselves to be readily acceptable by Christ with a mystical and almost theatrical finery. Thus, they proceed with pomp and with such titles as Beatitude, Reverence, and Holiness—between blessings and curses—to execute this role of a bishop. Miracles are considered to be antiquated and old-fashioned; to educate the people is irritating; to pray is a waste of time; to interpret Sacred Scripture is a mere formality; to weep is distressing and womanish; to live in poverty is ignominious; to be beaten in war is dishonorable and not worthy of one who insists that kings, no matter how great, bend and kiss His sacred foot; and to die is unpleasant, death on the cross—dishonor.

The only remaining powers invested with the pontiffs are the sacred benedictions of which Paul speaks. The popes are certainly liberal enough with these interdictions; excommunications; re-excommunications; anathemas; edicts, vivaciously depicting damnation; and the terrific lightning bolt of the bull, which by merely flickering submerges the souls of men below the floor of hell. And these powers are launched against no one with more vigor than against those who, under the devil's tutorship, dispute and deny the heritage of Peter's throne. Although Peter has been recorded as saying in the gospels, "We have left all and followed Thee," the popes of our time still insist on profanely attaching Peter's name to territories, cities, taxes, wages, and all money. These are the things they fight to uphold with fire, sword, and blood—inflamed by a zeal for Christ, of course.

Having thus fought, they believe themselves to be justly called defenders of Christ, bragging that they have routed the enemies of the Church—as if the Church had any greater enemies than these charlatan popes who encourage the disregard of Christ, who depict Him as mercenary, who corrupt His teachings by forced interpretations, and who scandalize Him by their infamous lives.

Now the Christian Church was founded on blood, built on blood, and strengthened on blood, and yet the belief that one should defend one's own property by one's own means has been abandoned. Instead of defending the Church in the way that is necessary, the popes, neglecting all their other functions, make war their only duty. War! Because of its barbarity, it is befitting of beasts, not men; it is so violent that many scholars say that it is sent with evil purposes by the Furies. It is referred to as pestilent because it is accompanied by a general disregard of morals; as iniquitous because the worst bandits usually are its leaders; and as hypocritical because of its discord with Christ's teachings and principles. In these wars even old and feeble men receive a great deal of pleasure and satisfaction by upsetting the established laws, religion, and peace—so much so, in fact, that they assume the vitality of youth and are not troubled by the waste of countless numbers of lives in the war or exhausted by the work involved. There are many learned sycophants who refer to this obvious madness as zeal, piety, or fortitude, thus making it legal for a man to draw his sword, kill his brother with it, and still be considered to be of the greatest charity—charity, which, according to Christ, is due every man by his neighbor. I find it hard to decide at this point whether certain German bishops set or followed the example of these popes. Because these bishops, putting aside their robes and forgetting about benedictions and other such formalities, personally acted as the heads of armies; as if they considered the battlefield the only place where they could do repentance for their blackened souls without shame and with a suitable amount of pomp and decorum.

The priests feel that it is sacrilegious to be in a lesser state of holiness than their prelates, so that they too go to war in the best military manner—with swords, spears, stones, and other weapons. They use their right to tax as an excuse in entering these wars. How ingenious these men are to interpret from the writings of the ancients an article by which they convince their appalled audience that they owe more than their just tithes! They never stop to consider those many teachings in Scripture by which they are indebted to perform certain duties for the people. Nor do they recall that their shaven heads are symbols of a priestly disinterest in worldly desires and a devoted interest in spiritual matters. On the contrary, these men insist that they have carried out their responsibilities when they have recited those little prayers. These, however, make me doubt whether even God hears or understands them, since they are barely audible to the priests themselves, who are still not able to understand them even though they repeat them constantly. The priests may also be paralleled with the ill-reputed in this way: they both anticipate profiteering and both remain up to date concerning the laws and restrictions on the subject. If there is any responsibility to be borne, they assign it to the shoulders of someone else, just as men toss a ball to one another. Or just as princes transmit to their ministers the ruling of some part of their realm, and these ministers, in turn, to one of their subordinates, so also do priests leave to the people the pursuit of piety. These common people then pass it back to those that they call the "ecclesiastics," as if they bore no moral responsibilities by merit of their baptismal vows in the pursuit of this virtue. The "ecclesiastics," who prefer to be called secular, as if dedicated to the world instead of to Christ, then delegate their burden to the regulars; the regulars to the monks; the more eminent monks to the less eminent ones; and both of these to the mendicants; and lastly the mendicants put it off to the Carthusians, among whom piety is such a hidden virtue that it is next to impossible to detect it in any degree. In this same manner proceeds the Apostolic responsibilities of the Pope, whose time is entirely engulfed in his personal pecuniary harvests, to the bishops, who in turn relegate them to the pastors, and thence to the vicars, from which they are laid upon the mendicant friars. These friars, however, return them to the shepherds of the fold, or to those who rob their people under the pretense of sanctity.

Source: John P. Dolan, ed., *The Essential Erasmus*, selected and translated with an introduction and commentary by John P. Dolan (New York: Meridian, 1983), 156–160.

Document 2: Disputation of Doctor Martin Luther on the Power and Efficacy of Indulgences by Dr. Martin Luther, 1517

When Martin Luther (1483–1546) posted these "Ninety-Five Theses" for debate on the door of the Castle Church at Wittenberg on 31 October 1517, he was following a long-established medieval academic tradition. This series of propositions was written in Latin and intended for academic debate before a university audience. A close reading of them reveals that Luther rejects neither indulgences as such, nor purgatory, nor the sacrament of penance. Their importance lies in the fact that they were a small initial step that stirred up an international furor and thereby set in motion the dramatic events that followed.

> Out of love for the truth and the desire to bring it to light, the following propositions will be discussed at Wittenberg, under the presidency of the Reverend Father Martin Luther, Master of Arts and of Sacred Theology, and Lecturer in Ordinary on the same at that place. Wherefore he requests that those who are unable to be present and debate orally with us may do so by letter.
>
> In the Name our Lord Jesus Christ. Amen.

1. Our Lord and Master Jesus Christ, when He said Poenitentiam agite, willed that the whole life of believers should be repentance.
2. This word cannot be understood to mean sacramental penance, i.e., confession and satisfaction, which is administered by the priests.
3. Yet it means not inward repentance only; nay, there is no inward repentance which does not outwardly work divers mortifications of the flesh.
4. The penalty [of sin], therefore, continues so long as hatred of self continues; for this is the true inward repentance, and continues until our entrance into the kingdom of heaven.
5. The pope does not intend to remit, and cannot remit any penalties other than those which he has imposed either by his own authority or by that of the Canons.
6. The pope cannot remit any guilt, except by declaring that it has been remitted by God and by assenting to God's remission; though, to be sure, he may grant remission in cases reserved to his judgment. If his right to grant remission in such cases were despised, the guilt would remain entirely unforgiven.
7. God remits guilt to no one whom He does not, at the same time, humble in all things and bring into subjection to His vicar, the priest.
8. The penitential canons are imposed only on the living, and, according to them, nothing should be imposed on the dying.
9. Therefore the Holy Spirit in the pope is kind to us, because in his decrees he always makes exception of the article of death and of necessity.
10. Ignorant and wicked are the doings of those priests who, in the case of the dying, reserve canonical penances for purgatory.
11. This changing of the canonical penalty to the penalty of purgatory is quite evidently one of the tares that were sown while the bishops slept.
12. In former times the canonical penalties were imposed not after, but before absolution, as tests of true contrition.
13. The dying are freed by death from all penalties; they are already dead to canonical rules, and have a right to be released from them.

14. The imperfect health [of soul], that is to say, the imperfect love, of the dying brings with it, of necessity, great fear; and the smaller the love, the greater is the fear.
15. This fear and horror is sufficient of itself alone (to say nothing of other things) to constitute the penalty of purgatory, since it is very near to the horror of despair.
16. Hell, purgatory, and heaven seem to differ as do despair, almost-despair, and the assurance of safety.
17. With souls in purgatory it seems necessary that horror should grow less and love increase.
18. It seems unproved, either by reason or Scripture, that they are outside the state of merit, that is to say, of increasing love.
19. Again, it seems unproved that they, or at least that all of them, are certain or assured of their own blessedness, though we may be quite certain of it.
20. Therefore by "full remission of all penalties" the pope means not actually "of all," but only of those imposed by himself.
21. Therefore those preachers of indulgences are in error, who say that by the pope's indulgences a man is freed from every penalty, and saved;
22. Whereas he remits to souls in purgatory no penalty which, according to the canons, they would have had to pay in this life.
23. If it is at all possible to grant to any one the remission of all penalties whatsoever, it is certain that this remission can be granted only to the most perfect, that is, to the very fewest.
24. It must needs be, therefore, that the greater part of the people are deceived by that indiscriminate and highsounding promise of release from penalty.
25. The power which the pope has, in a general way, over purgatory, is just like the power which any bishop or curate has, in a special way, within his own diocese or parish.
26. The pope does well when he grants remission to souls [in purgatory], not by the power of the keys (which he does not possess), but by way of intercession.
27. They preach man who say that so soon as the penny jingles into the money-box, the soul flies out [of purgatory].
28. It is certain that when the penny jingles into the money-box, gain and avarice can be increased, but the result of the intercession of the Church is in the power of God alone.
29. Who knows whether all the souls in purgatory wish to be bought out of it, as in the legend of Sts. Severinus and Paschal.
30. No one is sure that his own contrition is sincere; much less that he has attained full remission.
31. Rare as is the man that is truly penitent, so rare is also the man who truly buys indulgences, i.e., such men are most rare.
32. They will be condemned eternally, together with their teachers, who believe themselves sure of their salvation because they have letters of pardon.

33. Men must be on their guard against those who say that the pope's pardons are that inestimable gift of God by which man is reconciled to Him;

34. For these "graces of pardon" concern only the penalties of sacramental satisfaction, and these are appointed by man.

35. They preach no Christian doctrine that teaches that contrition is not necessary in those who intend to buy souls out of purgatory or to buy confessionalia.

36. Every truly repentant Christian has a right to full remission of penalty and guilt, even without letters of pardon.

37. Every true Christian, whether living or dead, has part in all the blessings of Christ and the Church; and this is granted him by God, even without letters of pardon.

38. Nevertheless, the remission and participation [in the blessings of the Church] which are granted by the pope are in no way to be despised, for they are, as I have said, the declaration of divine remission.

39. It is most difficult, even for the very keenest theologians, at one and the same time to commend to the people the abundance of pardons and [the need of] true contrition.

40. True contrition seeks and loves penalties, but liberal pardons only relax penalties and cause them to be hated, or at least, furnish an occasion [for hating them].

41. Apostolic pardons are to be preached with caution, lest the people may falsely think them preferable to other good works of love.

42. Christians are to be taught that the pope does not intend the buying of pardons to be compared in any way to works of mercy.

43. Christians are to be taught that he who gives to the poor or lends to the needy does a better work than buying pardons;

44. Because love grows by works of love, and man becomes better; but by pardons man does not grow better, only more free from penalty.

45. Christians are to be taught that he who sees a man in need, and passes him by, and gives [his money] for pardons, purchases not the indulgences of the pope, but the indignation of God.

46. Christians are to be taught that unless they have more than they need, they are bound to keep back what is necessary for their own families, and by no means to squander it on pardons.

47. Christians are to be taught that the buying of pardons is a matter of free will, and not of commandment.

48. Christians are to be taught that the pope, in granting pardons, needs, and therefore desires, their devout prayer for him more than the money they bring.

49. Christians are to be taught that the pope's pardons are useful, if they do not put their trust in them; but altogether harmful, if through them they lose their fear of God.

50. Christians are to be taught that if the pope knew the exactions of the pardon-preachers, he would rather that St. Peter's church should go to ashes, than that it should be built up with the skin, flesh and bones of his sheep.
51. Christians are to be taught that it would be the pope's wish, as it is his duty, to give of his own money to very many of those from whom certain hawkers of pardons cajole money, even though the church of St. Peter might have to be sold.
52. The assurance of salvation by letters of pardon is vain, even though the commissary, nay, even though the pope himself, were to stake his soul upon it.
53. They are enemies of Christ and of the pope, who bid the Word of God be altogether silent in some Churches, in order that pardons may be preached in others.
54. Injury is done the Word of God when, in the same sermon, an equal or a longer time is spent on pardons than on this Word.
55. It must be the intention of the pope that if pardons, which are a very small thing, are celebrated with one bell, with single processions and ceremonies, then the Gospel, which is the very greatest thing, should be preached with a hundred bells, a hundred processions, a hundred ceremonies.
56. The "treasures of the Church," out of which the pope grants indulgences, are not sufficiently named or known among the people of Christ.
57. That they are not temporal treasures is certainly evident, for many of the vendors do not pour out such treasures so easily, but only gather them.
58. Nor are they the merits of Christ and the Saints, for even without the pope, these always work grace for the inner man, and the cross, death, and hell for the outward man.
59. St. Lawrence said that the treasures of the Church were the Church's poor, but he spoke according to the usage of the word in his own time.
60. Without rashness we say that the keys of the Church, given by Christ's merit, are that treasure;
61. For it is clear that for the remission of penalties and of reserved cases, the power of the pope is of itself sufficient.
62. The true treasure of the Church is the Most Holy Gospel of the glory and the grace of God.
63. But this treasure is naturally most odious, for it makes the first to be last.
64. On the other hand, the treasure of indulgences is naturally most acceptable, for it makes the last to be first.
65. Therefore the treasures of the Gospel are nets with which they formerly were wont to fish for men of riches.
66. The treasures of the indulgences are nets with which they now fish for the riches of men.

67. The indulgences which the preachers cry as the "greatest graces" are known to be truly such, in so far as they promote gain.

68. Yet they are in truth the very smallest graces compared with the grace of God and the piety of the Cross.

69. Bishops and curates are bound to admit the commissaries of apostolic pardons, with all reverence.

70. But still more are they bound to strain all their eyes and attend with all their ears, lest these men preach their own dreams instead of the commission of the pope.

71. He who speaks against the truth of apostolic pardons, let him be anathema and accursed!

72. But he who guards against the lust and license of the pardon-preachers, let him be blessed!

73. The pope justly thunders against those who, by any art, contrive the injury of the traffic in pardons.

74. But much more does he intend to thunder against those who use the pretext of pardons to contrive the injury of holy love and truth.

75. To think the papal pardons so great that they could absolve a man even if he had committed an impossible sin and violated the Mother of God—this is madness.

76. We say, on the contrary, that the papal pardons are not able to remove the very least of venial sins, so far as its guilt is concerned.

77. It is said that even St. Peter, if he were now Pope, could not bestow greater graces; this is blasphemy against St. Peter and against the pope.

78. We say, on the contrary, that even the present pope, and any pope at all, has greater graces at his disposal; to wit, the Gospel, powers, gifts of healing, etc., as it is written in I. Corinthians xii.

79. To say that the cross, emblazoned with the papal arms, which is set up [by the preachers of indulgences], is of equal worth with the Cross of Christ, is blasphemy.

80. The bishops, curates and theologians who allow such talk to be spread among the people, will have an account to render.

81. This unbridled preaching of pardons makes it no easy matter, even for learned men, to rescue the reverence due to the pope from slander, or even from the shrewd questionings of the laity.

82. To wit:—"Why does not the pope empty purgatory, for the sake of holy love and of the dire need of the souls that are there, if he redeems an infinite number of souls for the sake of miserable money with which to build a Church? The former reasons would be most just; the latter is most trivial."

83. Again:—"Why are mortuary and anniversary masses for the dead continued, and why does he not return or permit the withdrawal of the endowments founded on their behalf, since it is wrong to pray for the redeemed?"
84. Again:—"What is this new piety of God and the pope, that for money they allow a man who is impious and their enemy to buy out of purgatory the pious soul of a friend of God, and do not rather, because of that pious and beloved soul's own need, free it for pure love's sake?"
85. Again:—"Why are the penitential canons long since in actual fact and through disuse abrogated and dead, now satisfied by the granting of indulgences, as though they were still alive and in force?"
86. Again:—"Why does not the pope, whose wealth is to-day greater than the riches of the richest, build just this one church of St. Peter with his own money, rather than with the money of poor believers?"
87. Again:—"What is it that the pope remits, and what participation does he grant to those who, by perfect contrition, have a right to full remission and participation?"
88. Again:—"What greater blessing could come to the Church than if the pope were to do a hundred times a day what he now does once, and bestow on every believer these remissions and participations?"
89. "Since the pope, by his pardons, seeks the salvation of souls rather than money, why does he suspend the indulgences and pardons granted heretofore, since these have equal efficacy?"
90. To repress these arguments and scruples of the laity by force alone, and not to resolve them by giving reasons, is to expose the Church and the pope to the ridicule of their enemies, and to make Christians unhappy.
91. If, therefore, pardons were preached according to the spirit and mind of the pope, all these doubts would be readily resolved; nay, they would not exist.
92. Away, then, with all those prophets who say to the people of Christ, "Peace, peace," and there is no peace!
93. Blessed be all those prophets who say to the people of Christ, "Cross, cross," and there is no cross!
94. Christians are to be exhorted that they be diligent in following Christ, their Head, through penalties, deaths, and hell;
95. And thus be confident of entering into heaven rather through many tribulations, than through the assurance of peace.

Source: Adolph Spaeth, et al., trans. and eds., *Works of Martin Luther*, with introductions and notes, 6 vols. (Philadelphia: A. J. Holman Company, 1915–1932), 1:29–38.

Document 3: Martin Luther's response to the ultimatum issued by the Imperial authorities at the Diet of Worms, 18 April 1521: "Here I Stand."

In 1520, Pope Leo X officially condemned Martin Luther's (1483–1546) Protestant views as heretical in the bull *Exsurge Domine*. On 17 April 1521, Luther stood before Emperor Charles V and the Estates of the Empire at the Diet of Worms where Johann von Eck, assistant to the Archbishop of Trier, acted as spokesman for the emperor. Expected to retract his theological views before the Diet, Luther's books were placed on a table, and he was asked if they were his works and whether he wanted to recant any of the information the books contained. Luther requested time so that he might think over his reply. The next day, the emperor, the princes and the theologians demanded a clear yes or no answer. Luther responded:

> Because then Your Imperial Majesty, Electoral and Princely Graces, desire a plain, simple, and truthful answer, I will give it, an answer without horns or teeth, namely this: unless I am persuaded and convinced with testimonies from Holy Scriptures or with obvious, clear, and irrefutable reasons and arguments— because I believe neither the pope or councils alone, for it is clear that they have often erred and contradicted themselves—I am bound by the Scriptures that I have quoted; my conscience is bound by the Word of God, so that I cannot and I will not revoke because it is neither safe nor sound to act against conscience. I can do nought else; here I stand, God help me, amen.

Source: D. Martin Luthers Werke, 70 vols. (Weimar: H. Bohlau, 1883–2000), 7:838, as cited in Martin Brecht, *Martin Luther*, trans. Claude R. Foster, Jr. (New York: Oxford University Press, 1991), 206.

Document 4: Excerpts from the Ecclesiastical Ordinances of Geneva, 1541

The Geneva City Council had expelled John Calvin (1509–1564) and his reforming associates from Geneva in 1538 when the reformers tried to enforce Protestant church discipline in the city. In his absence, Geneva experienced increasing religious and political turmoil. After several pleas from the Geneva City Council, Calvin agreed to return in September 1541. In November the Ecclesiastical Ordinances (*Ordonnances Ecclésiastiques*), a new church order, was adopted by the City

Council. This was the price of Calvin's second coming. The Church of Geneva was to be organized in accordance with this set of regulations. Since the Genevans believed that church and state were but two sides of the same commonwealth, these Ordinances also ordered civic life in the town. The aim was to bring all of life under "God's law" and to "Christianize" the social order. The following excerpt illustrates how the Church was to be organized and how religious, social and political matters interlocked. Notice Calvin's concern with "good order." Also, note that the words in brackets were modifications of Calvin's draft ordinances that were made at the insistence of the Geneva City Council before these regulations were enacted.

> In the name of God Almighty, we Syndics, Little and Great Council, together with our people assembled at the sound of the trumpet and great bell, according to our ancient custom, having determined that the matter is worthy of recommendation above all others, that the doctrine of the Holy Gospel of our Lord may be well preserved in its purity, and the Christian Church duly maintained, that the young may be faithfully instructed for the future, the hospital well run in good order for the sustentation of the poor, which cannot be done except there be a strict rule and regulations by which each one shall understand the duties of his office; for these reasons it has seemed good to us that the spiritual government which our Lord taught and instituted by his Word, be observed among us. And thus we have ordered and decreed that in our city and territories the regulations that follow shall be observed and kept, inasmuch as it seems to us that they are taken from the Gospel of Jesus Christ.
>
> First there are four orders of offices instituted by our Saviour for the government of his Church: namely, the pastors, then the doctors, next the elders [nominated and appointed by the government,] and fourthly the deacons. If we wish to see the Church well-ordered and maintained we ought to observe this form of government.

The Duty of Pastors

> Pastors are sometimes named in the Bible as overseers, elders and ministers. Their work is to proclaim the Word of God, to teach, admonish, exhort and reprove publicly and privately, to administer the sacraments and, with the elders or their deputies, to issue fraternal warnings.

The Examination of Pastors

> This consists of two parts. The first concerns doctrine—to find out if the candidate has a good and sound knowledge of the

Bible; and, secondly, comes his suitability for expounding this to the people for their edification.

Further, to avoid any danger of his having any wrong ideas, it is fitting that he should profess to accept and uphold the teaching approved by the Church.

Questions must be asked to find out if he is a good teacher and he must privately set forth the teaching of our Lord.

Next, it must be ascertained that he is a man of good principles without any known faults.

The Selection of Pastors

First the ministers should choose someone suitable for the position [and notify the government]. Then he is to be presented to the council. If he is approved, he will be accepted and received by the council [as it thinks fit]. He is then given a certificate to be produced when he preaches to the people, so that he can be received by the common consent of the faithful. If he is found to be unsuitable and this demonstrated by evidence, there must be a new selection to find another.

As to the manner of introducing him, because the ceremonies previously used led to a great deal of superstition, all that is needed is that a minister should explain the nature of the position to which he has been appointed and then prayers and pleas should be made that our Lord will give him grace to do what is needed.

After election he must take an oath of allegiance to the government following a written form as required of a minister.

Weekly Meetings to Be Arranged

In the first place it is desirable that all ministers should meet together once a week. This is to maintain purity and agreement in their teaching and to hold Bible discussions. Attendance shall be compulsory unless there is good reason for absence. As for the preachers in the villages under the control of the government, it is for the city ministers to urge them to attend whenever possible. . . .

What Should Be Done in Cases of Difference about Doctrine?

If any differences of opinion concerning doctrine should arise, the ministers should gather together and discuss the matter. If necessary, they should call in the elders and commissioners [appointed by the government] to assist in the settlement of any difficulties.

There must be some means available to discipline ministers . . . to prevent scandalous living. In this way, respect for the ministry can be maintained and the Word of God not debased by any minister bringing it into scorn and derision. Those who deserve it must be corrected, but at the same time care must be taken to deal with gossip and malicious rumours which can bring harm to innocent parties.

But it is of first importance to notice that certain crimes are quite incompatible with the ministry and cannot be dealt with by fraternal rebuke. Namely heresy, schism, rebellion against Church discipline, open blasphemy deserving civil punishment, simony and corrupt inducement, intriguing to take over one another's position, leaving the Church without special permission, forgery.

There Follows the Second Order Which We Have Called the Doctors

The special duty of the doctors is to instruct the faithful in sound doctrine so that the purity of the gospel is not corrupted by ignorance or wrong opinion.

As things stand at present, every agent assisting in the upholding of God's teaching is included so that the Church is not in difficulties from a lack of pastors and ministers. This is in common parlance the order of school teachers. The degree nearest the minister and closely joined to the government of the Church is the lecturer in theology.

Establishment of a College

Because it is only possible to profit from such teaching if one is first instructed in languages and humanities, and also because it is necessary to lay the foundations for the future ... a college should be instituted for instructing children to prepare them for the ministry as well as for civil government.

In the first place suitable accommodation needs to be provided for the teaching of children and others who want to take advantage of it. We also need a literate, scholarly and trained teacher who can take care of the establishment and their education. He should be chosen and paid on the understanding that he should have under his charge teachers in languages and logic, if they can be found. He should also have some student teachers (bachelors) to teach the little ones....

All who are engaged must be subject to the same ecclesiastical ordinances as apply to the ministers.

There is to be no other school in the city for small children, although the girls are to have a separate school of their own as has been the case up to now.

No one is to be appointed without the approval of the ministers—essential to avoid trouble. [The candidate must first have been notified to the government and then presented to the council. Two members of the "council of 24" should be present at all interviews.]

Here Follows the Third Order, or Elders

Their duty is to supervise every person's conduct. In friendly fashion they should warn backsliders and those of disorderly life. After that, where necessary, they should report to the Company [of pastors] who will arrange for fraternal correction. . . .

As our Church is now arranged, it would be most suitable to have two elected from the "council of 24," four from the "council of 60" and six from the "council of 200." They should be men of good repute and conduct. They should be chosen from each quarter of the city so that they can keep an eye on the whole of it.

Method of Choosing the Elders

Further we have decided upon the machinery for choosing them. The "council of 24" will be asked to nominate the most suitable and adequate men they can discover. In order to do this, they should discuss the matter with the ministers and then present their suggestion to the "council of 200" for approval. If they are found worthy land [and approved], they must take an oath in the same form as it is presented to the ministers. At the end of the year and after the elections to the council, they should present themselves to the government so that a decision can be made as to whether they shall be re-appointed or not, but they should not be changed frequently and without good cause provided that they are doing their work faithfully.

The Fourth Order of Ecclesiastical Government, Namely, the Deacons

There have always been two kinds of these in the early Church. One has to receive, distribute and care for the goods of the poor (i.e., daily alms as well as possessions, rents and pensions); the other has to tend and look after the sick and administer the allowances to the poor as is customary. [In order to avoid confusion], since we have officials and hospital staff, [one of the four officials of the said hospital should be responsible for the whole of its property and revenues and he should have an adequate salary in order to do his work properly.]

Concerning the Hospital

Care should be taken to see that the general hospital is properly maintained. This applies to the sick, to old people no longer able to work, to widows, orphans, children and other poor people. These are to be kept apart and separate from others and to form their own community.

Care for the poor who are scattered throughout the city shall be the responsibility of the officials. In addition to the hospital for those visiting the city, which is to be kept up, separate arrangements are to be made for those who need special treatment. To this end a room must be set apart to act as a reception room for those that are sent there by the officials.

Further, both for the poor people in the hospital and for those in the city who have no means, there must be a good physician and surgeon provided at the city's expense. . . .

As for the plague hospital, it must be kept entirely separate.

Begging

In order to stop begging, which is contrary to good order, the government should use some of its officers to remove any beggars who are obstinately present when people come out of Church.

And this especially if it should happen that the city is visited by this scourge of God.

Of the Sacraments

Baptism is to take place only at sermon time and is to be administered only by ministers or their assistants. A register is to be kept of the names of the children and of their parents: the justice department is to be informed of any bastard.

Since the Supper was instituted by our Lord to be more often observed by us and also since this was the case in the early Church until such time as the devil upset everything by setting up the mass in its place, the defect ought to be remedied by celebrating it a little more frequently. All the same, for the time being we have agreed and ordained that it should be administered four times a year, i.e., at Christmas, Easter, Pentecost and the first Sunday in September in the autumn.

The ministers shall distribute the bread in orderly and reverent fashion and no other person shall offer the chalice except those appointed (or the deacons) along with the ministers and for this reason there is no need for many plates and cups.

The tables should be set up close to the pulpit so that the mystery can be more suitably set forth near by.

Celebration should take place only in church and at the most suitable time.

Of the order which must be observed in obedience to those in authority, for the maintenance of supervision in the Church

A day should be fixed for the consistory. The elders, should meet once a week with the ministers, on a Thursday, to ensure that there is no disorder in the Church and to discuss together any necessary remedial action.

Since they have neither the power nor the authority to use force, we have agreed to assign one of our officials to them to summon those whom they wish to admonish.

If any one should deliberately refuse to appear, the council is to be informed so as to take action.

If any one teaches things contrary to the received doctrine he shall be summoned to a conference. If he listens to reason, let him be sent back without any scandal or disgrace. If he is obstinate, he should be admonished several times until it is apparent that greater severity is needed: then he shall be forbidden to attend the communion of the Supper and he shall be reported to the magistrates.

If any one fails to come to church to such a degree that there is real dislike for the community of believers manifested, or if any one shows that he cares nothing for ecclesiastical order, let him be admonished, and if he is tractable let him be amicably sent back. If however he goes from bad to worse, after having been warned three times, let him be cut off from the Church and be denounced to the magistrate. . . .

[All this must be done in such a way that the ministers have no civil jurisdiction nor use anything but the spiritual sword of the word of God as St Paul commands them; nor is the authority of the consistory to diminish in any way that of the magistrate or ordinary justice. The civil power must remain unimpaired. In cases where, in future, there may be a need to impose punishments or constrain individuals, then the ministers and the consistory, having heard the case and used such admonitions and exhortations as are appropriate, should report the whole matter to the council which, in turn, will judge and sentence. . . .

Source: J.-F. Bergier and R. M. Kingdon, eds., *Registres de la Compagnie des Pasteurs de Genève au temps de Calvin*, 2 vols. (Geneva: Droz, 1962–1964), 1:1–13. Translated by G. R. Potter and Mark Greengrass, in *Jean Calvin*, Documents of Modern History Series (New York: St. Martin's Press, 1983), 71–76.

Document 5: Excerpts from John Calvin's *Institutes of the Christian Religion* on *Civil Government*, 1559

John Calvin (1509–1564) was deeply interested in civil government because he believed that it was a part of God's domain as much as was the church. He taught that the two realms were separate but interlocking and mutually supportive. Always concerned with the fate of his co-religionists in his native France, much of the political commentary of his *Institutes* seems to be aimed at the French monarchy and its treatment of Reformed believers in France. Therefore, it is not surprising that he spends the last section of his *Institutes of the Christian Religion* discussing civil government. The last few pages of this last section contain dire warnings for those who misuse their power to persecute God's people: "Let the princes hear and be afraid." He also opens the door to political resistance in certain highly circumscribed circumstances by alluding to historical examples of lesser but legitimate magistrates who restrained misguided kings. All of these teachings helped to provide some of the bricks and mortar for the foundation of what became a full-blown Calvinist resistance theory in the generation following his death.

31. Constitutional Defenders of the People's Freedom

But however these deeds of men are judged in themselves, still the Lord accomplished his work through them alike when he broke the bloody scepters of arrogant kings and when he overturned intolerable governments. Let the princes hear and be afraid.

But we must, in the meantime, be very careful not to despise or violate that authority of magistrates, full of venerable majesty, which God has established by the weightiest decrees, even though it may reside with the most unworthy men, who defile it as much as they can with their own wickedness. For, if the correction of unbridled despotism is the Lord's to avenge, let us not at once think that it is entrusted to us, to whom no command has been given except to obey and suffer.

I am speaking all the while of private individuals. For if there are now any magistrates of the people, appointed to restrain the willfulness of kings (as in ancient times the ephors were set against the Spartan kings, or the tribunes of the people against the Roman consuls, or the demarchs against the senate of the Athenians; and perhaps, as things now are, such power as the three estates exercise in every realm when they hold their chief assemblies), I am so far from forbidding them to withstand, in accordance with their duty, the fierce licentiousness of kings, that, if they wink at kings who violently fall upon and assault the lowly common folk, I declare that their dissimulation involves nefarious perfidy, because they dishonestly betray the freedom of the people, of which they know that they have been appointed protectors by God's ordinance.

32. Obedience to Man Must Not Become Disobedience to God

But in that obedience which we have shown to be due the authority of rulers, we are always to make this exception, indeed, to observe it as primary, that such obedience is never to lead us away from obedience to him, to whose will the desires of all kings ought to be subject, to whose decrees all their commands ought to yield, to whose majesty their scepters ought to be submitted. And how absurd would it be that in satisfying men you should incur the displeasure of him for whose sake you obey men themselves! The Lord, therefore, is the King of Kings, who, when he has opened his sacred mouth, must alone be heard, before all and above all men; next to him we are subject to those men who are in authority over us, but only in him. If they command anything against him, let it go unesteemed. And here let us not be concerned about all that dignity which the magistrates possess; for no harm is done to it when it is humbled before that singular and truly supreme power of God.... As if God had made over his right to mortal men, giving them the rule over mankind! Or as if earthly power were diminished when it is subjected to its Author, in whose presence even the heavenly powers tremble as suppliants! I know with what great and present peril this constancy is menaced, because kings bear defiance with the greatest displeasure, whose "wrath is a messenger of death" [Prov. 16:14], says Solomon. But since this edict has been proclaimed by the heavenly herald, Peter—"We must obey God rather than men" [Acts 5:29]—let us comfort ourselves with the thought that we are rendering that obedience which the Lord requires when we suffer anything rather than turn aside from piety. And that our courage may not grow faint, Paul pricks us with another goad: That we have been redeemed by Christ at so great a price as our redemption cost him, so that we should not enslave ourselves to the wicked desires of men—much less be subject to their impiety [I Cor. 7:23].

Source: John Calvin, *Institutes of the Christian Religion*, ed. John T. McNeill, trans. Ford Lewis Battles, 2 vols. (Philadelphia: Westminster Press, 1960), 2:1518–1521.

Document 6: John Knox, Excerpt from his *History of the Reformation Within the Realm of Scotland*, 1644

The story of the Scottish Reformation is inextricably linked with the name of John Knox (1513–1572). He is often described as "a stormy petrel" and "the thundering Scot," and for good reason. He was a forceful speaker and persuasive debater, both on and off the platform. He records a confrontation with the recently returned Mary, Queen of Scots, in his monumental *History of the Reformation*

Within the Realm of Scotland, written during the last years of his life but not published in its entirety until 1644. This excerpt gives Knox's account of the first of three interviews with the queen in 1561–1562, following her return to Scotland from France. The exchange between the two is spirited and revealing of their respective temperaments. In the end, perhaps they were too much alike. In any case, Knox carried the day with the Scottish nobility and people, and Mary fled to England in 1567, where she remained in exile for the remainder of her life.

> From the return to Scotland of Mary, Queen of Scots, on 19th August 1561, to the rise of David Rizzio in 1564.
>
> Whether it was by counsel of others, or of Queen Mary's own desire, we know not, but the Queen spake with John Knox at Holyrood and had long reasoning with him, none being present except the Lord James Stewart, while two gentlewomen stood in the other end of the house.
>
> The Queen accused John Knox that he had raised a part of her subjects against her mother and against herself; that he had written a book against her just authority,—she meant the treatise against the Regiment of Women—which she should cause the most learned in Europe to write against; that he was the cause of great sedition and great slaughter in England; and that it was said to her, that all which he did was by necromancy.
>
> To the which the said John answered:—'Madam, may it please Your Majesty patiently to hear my simple answers? First, if to teach the Truth of God in sincerity, if to rebuke idolatry and to will a people to worship God according to His Word, be to raise subjects against their Princes, then can I not be excused; for it hath pleased God of His Mercy to make me one among many to disclose unto this Realm the vanity of the Papistical Religion, and the deceit, pride, and tyranny of that Roman Antichrist. But, Madam, if the true knowledge of God and His right worshipping be the chief causes, that must move men from their heart to obey their just Princes, as it is most certain they are, wherein can I be reprehended? I am surely persuaded that Your Grace has had, and presently has, as unfeigned obedience of such as profess Jesus Christ within this Realm, as ever your father or other progenitors had of those that were called Bishops.
>
> 'And, touching that Book which seemeth so highly to offend Your Majesty, it is most certain that I wrote it, and I am content that all the learned of the world judge of it. I hear that an Englishman hath written against it, but I have not read him. If he hath sufficiently improved [disproved] my reasons, and established his contrary propositions with as evident testimonies as I have done mine, I shall not be obstinate, but shall confess my error and ignorance. But to this hour I have thought, and

yet think, myself alone to be more able to sustain the things affirmed in my work, than any ten in Europe shall be able to confute it.'

Queen Mary: 'Ye think then that I have no just authority?'

John Knox: 'Please Your Majesty, learned men in all ages have had their judgments free. They have most commonly disagreed from the common judgment of the world. Such also have they published, both with pen and tongue, and yet, notwithstanding, they themselves have lived in common society with others, and have borne patiently with the errors and imperfections which they could not amend. Plato, the philosopher, wrote his book of *The Commonwealth*, in the which he damneth many things that then were maintained in the world, and requireth many things to be reformed. Yet, he lived under such policies as then were universally received, without further troubling of any estate. Even *so*, Madam, am I content to do in uprightness of heart, and with testimony of a good conscience. I have communicated my judgment to the world. If the Realm finds no inconvenience from the government of a woman, that which they approve shall I not further disallow than within my own breast, but shall be as well content to live under Your Grace as Paul was to live under Nero. My hope is, that so long as ye defile not your hands with the blood of the Saints of God, neither I nor that book shall either hurt you or your authority. In very deed, Madam, that book was written most especially against that wicked Jezebel of England' [*Queen Mary Tudor*].

Queen Mary: 'But ye speak of women in general?'

John Knox: 'Most true, Madam. Yet it appeareth to me that wisdom should persuade Your Grace, never to raise trouble for that, which to this day hath not troubled Your Majesty, neither in person nor yet in authority. Of late years many things which before were holden stable have been called in doubt; yea, they have been plainly impugned. Yet, Madam, I am assured that neither Protestant nor Papist shall be able to prove, that any such question was at any time moved in public or in secret. Now, Madam, if I had intended to have troubled your estate, because ye are a woman, I might have chosen a time more convenient for that purpose, than I can do now, when your own presence is within the Realm.

'But now, Madam, shortly to answer to the other two accusations. I heartily praise my God through Jesus Christ, if Satan, the enemy of mankind, and the wicked of the world, have no other crimes to lay to my charge, than such as the very world itself knoweth to be most false and vain. In England I was resident the space of five years. The places were Berwick, where I abode two years; so long in Newcastle; and a year in London. Now, Madam, if in any of these places, during the time that I was there, any man shall be able to prove that there was either battle, sedition, or mutiny, I shall confess that I myself was the malefactor and the shedder of the blood. I shame not, Madam, to affirm, that God so blessed my weak labors, that in Berwick—where commonly before there used to be slaughter by reason of quarrels among soldiers—there was as great quietness, all the time that I remained there, as there is this day in Edinburgh. And where they slander me of magic, necromancy, or of any other art forbidden of God, I have witnesses, besides my own conscience—all congregations that ever heard me—to what I spake both against such arts and against those that use such impiety.'

Queen Mary: 'But yet ye have taught the people to receive another religion than their Princes can allow. How can that doctrine be of God, seeing that God commandeth subjects to obey their Princes?'

John Knox: 'Madam, as right religion took neither original strength nor authority from worldly princes, but from the Eternal God alone, so are not subjects bound to frame their religion according to the appetites of their princes. Princes are oft the most ignorant of all others in God's true religion, as we may read in the Histories, as well before the death of Christ Jesus as after. If all the seed of Abraham should have been of the religion of Pharaoh, to whom they were long subjects, I pray you, Madam, what religion should there have been in the world? Or, if all men in the days of the Apostles should have been of the religion of the Roman Emperors, what religion should there have been upon the face of the earth? Daniel and his fellows were subjects to Nebuchadnezzar and unto Darius, and yet, Madam, they would not be of their religion; for the three children said: "We make it known unto thee, O King, that we will not worship thy Gods." Daniel did pray publicly unto his God against the expressed commandment of the King. And so, Madam, ye may perceive that subjects are not bound to the religion of their princes, although they are commanded to give them obedience.'

Queen Mary: 'Yea, but none of these men raised the sword against their princes.'

John Knox: 'Yet, Madam, ye can not deny that they resisted, for those who obey not the commandments that are given, in some sort resist.'

Queen Mary: 'But yet, they resisted not by the sword?'

John Knox: 'God, Madam, had not given them the power and the means.'

Queen Mary: 'Think ye that subjects, having the power, may resist their princes?'

John Knox: 'If their princes exceed their bounds, Madam, no doubt they may be resisted, even by power. For there is neither greater honour, nor greater obedience, to be given to kings or princes, than God hath commanded to be given unto father and mother. But the father may be stricken with a frenzy, in which he would slay his children. If the children arise, join themselves together, apprehend the father, take the sword from him, bind his hands, and keep him in prison till his frenzy be overpast—think ye, Madam, that the children do any wrong? It is even so, Madam, with princes that would murder the children of God that are subjects unto them. Their blind zeal is nothing but a very mad frenzy, and therefore, to take the sword from them, to bind their hands, and to cast them into prison, till they be brought to a more sober mind, is no disobedience against princes, but just obedience, because it agreeth with the will of God.'

At these words, the Queen stood as it were amazed, more than the quarter of an hour. Her countenance altered, so that Lord James began to entreat her and to demand, 'What hath offended you, Madam?'

At length she said to John Knox: 'Well then, I perceive that my subjects shall obey you, and not me. They shall do what they list, and not what I command; and so must I be subject to them, and not they to me.'

John Knox: 'God forbid that ever I take upon me to command any to obey me, or yet to set subjects at liberty to do what pleaseth them! My travail is that both princes and subjects obey God. Think not, Madam, that wrong is done you, when ye are willed to be subject to God. It is He that subjects peoples under princes, and causes obedience to be given unto them. Yea, God craves of Kings that they be foster-fathers to His Church, and commands Queens to be nurses to His people. This subjection, Madam, unto God, and unto His troubled Church, is the greatest dignity that flesh can get upon the face of the earth; for it shall carry them to everlasting glory.'

Queen Mary: 'Yea, but ye are not the Kirk that I will nourish. I will defend the Kirk of Rome, for it is, I think, the true Kirk of God.'

John Knox: Your will, Madam, is no reason; neither doth your *thought* make that Roman harlot to be the true and immaculate spouse of Jesus Christ. Wonder not, Madam, that I call Rome an harlot; for that Church is altogether polluted with all kind of spiritual fornication, as well in doctrine as in manners. Yea, Madam, I offer myself to prove, that the Church of the Jews which crucified Christ Jesus, was not so far degenerate from the ordinances which God gave by Moses and Aaron unto His people, when they manifestly denied the Son of God, as the Church of Rome is declined, and more than five hundred years hath declined, from the purity of that religion which the Apostles taught and planted.'

Queen Mary: 'My conscience is not so.'

John Knox: 'Conscience, Madam, requireth knowledge; and I fear that right knowledge ye have none.'

Queen Mary: 'But I have both heard and read.'

John Knox: 'So, Madam, did the Jews who crucified Christ Jesus read both the Law and the Prophets, and heard the same interpreted after their manner. Have ye heard any teach, but such as the Pope and his Cardinals have allowed? Ye may be assured that such will speak nothing to offend their own estate.'

Queen Mary: 'Ye interpret the Scriptures in one manner, and they in another. Whom shall I believe? Who shall be judge?'

John Knox: 'Ye shall believe God, that plainly speaketh in His Word; and further than the Word teacheth you, ye shall believe neither the one nor the other. The Word of God is plain in itself. If there appear any obscurity in one place, the Holy Ghost, which is never contrarious to Himself, explaineth the same more clearly in other places; so that there can remain no doubt, but unto such as obstinately will remain ignorant.

'Take one of the chief points, Madam, which this day is in controversy betwixt the Papists and us. The Papists have boldly affirmed that the Mass is the ordinance of God, and the institution of Jesus Christ, and a sacrifice for the sins of the quick and the dead. We deny both the one and the other. We affirm that the Mass, as it is now used, is nothing but the invention of man, and, therefore, is an abomination before God, and no sacrifice that ever God commanded. Now, Madam, who shall judge betwixt us two thus contending? It is no reason that either of the parties be further believed, than they are able to prove by insuspect witnessing. Let them prove their affirmatives by the plain words of the Book of God, and we shall give them the plea granted. What our Master Jesus Christ did, we know by His Evangelists; what the priest doeth at his Mass, the world seeth. Now, doth not the Word of God plainly assure us, that Christ Jesus neither said Mass, nor yet commanded Mass to be said, at His Last Supper, seeing that no such thing as their Mass is made mention of within the whole Scriptures?'

Queen Mary: 'Ye are ower sair [too hard] for me, but if they were here whom I have heard, they would answer you.'

John Knox: 'Madam, would to God that the learnedest Papist in Europe, and he that ye would best believe, were present with Your Grace to sustain the argument; and that ye would patiently abide to hear the matter reasoned to the end! Then, I doubt not, Madam, but ye should hear the vanity of the Papistical Religion, and how small ground it hath within the Word of God.'

Queen Mary: 'Well, ye may perchance get that sooner than ye believe.'

John Knox: 'Assuredly, if ever I get that in my life, I get it sooner than I believe. The ignorant Papists can not patiently reason, and the learned and crafty Papist will never come in your audience, Madam, to have the ground of their religion searched out. They know that they are never able to sustain an argument, except fire and sword and their own laws be judges.'

Queen Mary: 'So say you; but I can [not] believe that.'

John Knox: 'It hath been so to this day. How oft have the Papists in this and other Realms been required to come to conference, and yet could it never be obtained, unless themselves were admitted for Judges. Therefore, Madam, I must say again that they dare never dispute, but when they themselves are both judge and party. Whensoever ye shall let me see the contrary, I shall grant myself to have been deceived in that point.'

With this, the Queen was called upon to dinner, for it was afternoon. At departing, John Knox said unto her: 'I pray God, Madam, that ye may be as blessed within the Commonwealth of Scotland, if it be the pleasure of God, as ever Deborah was in the Commonwealth of Israel.'

Of this long conference, whereof we only touch a part, were diverse opinions. The Papists grudged, and feared that which they needed not. The godly, thinking at least that the Queen would have heard the preaching, rejoiced; but they were all utterly deceived, for she continued in her Massing, and despised and quietly mocked all exhortation.

John Knox, his own judgment being by some of his familiars demanded, what he thought of the Queen? 'If there be not in her,' said he, 'a proud mind, a crafty wit, and an indurate heart against God and His truth, my judgment faileth me.'

Source: John Knox, *The History of the Reformation of Religion within the Realm of Scotland*, edited for popular use by C. J. Guthrie (London: Adam and Charles Black, 1905), 271–283.

Document 7: The Act of Supremacy, 1534

After long and complex maneuvering to solve Henry VIII's (1509–1547) marital problems, an English ecclesiastical court presided over by Archbishop Thomas Cranmer finally annulled his marriage to Catherine of Aragon in 1533. Pope Clement VII thereupon excommunicated Henry, who responded in 1534 by having Parliament pass the Act of Supremacy. This legal repudiation of papal authority in England capitalized on existing anti-Roman feelings as well as growing Protestant sentiment, and required a loyalty oath to the king. Refusal to sign the oath was a capital crime and invoked the death penalty.

Albeit the King's Majesty justly and rightfully is and ought to be the supreme head of the Church of England, and so is recognized by the clergy of this realm in their Convocations, yet nevertheless for corroboration and confirmation thereof, and for increase of virtue in Christ's religion within this realm of England, and to repress and extirp all errors, heresies and other enormities and abuses heretofore used in the same:

Be it enacted by authority of this present Parliament that the King, our sovereign lord, his heirs and successors, kings of this realm, shall be taken, accepted and reputed the only supreme head in earth of the Church of England, called *Anglican Ecclesia*; and shall have and enjoy, annexed and united to the imperial crown of this realm, as well the title and style thereof, as all honors, dignities, pre-eminences, jurisdictions, privileges, authorities, immunities, profits and commodities to the said dignity of supreme head of the same Church belonging and appertaining; and that our said sovereign lord, his heirs and successors, kings of this realm, shall have full power and authority from time to time to visit, repress, redress, reform, order, correct, restrain and amend all such errors, heresies, abuses, offenses, contempts and enormities, whatsoever they be, which by any manner, spiritual authority or jurisdiction ought or may lawfully be reformed, repressed, ordered, redressed, corrected, restrained or amended, most to the pleasure of Almighty God, the increase of virtue in Christ's religion, and for the conservation of the peace, unity and tranquillity of this realm, any usage, custom, foreign law, foreign authority, prescription or any other thing or things to the contrary hereof notwithstanding.

Source: "The Act of Supremacy, 1534," *English History in the Making*, vol. 1, ed. William L. Sachse (New York: John Wiley and Sons, 1967), 187–188.

Document 8: An Eyewitness Account of the Execution of Archbishop Thomas Cranmer in Oxford, 21 March 1556

Henry VIII (1509–1547) made Thomas Cranmer (1489–1556) Archbishop of Canterbury in 1533. During the reign of Henry's son, Edward VI (1547–1553), Cranmer continued as archbishop and laid the foundations for the edifice of English Protestantism. By the time that Mary I (1553–1558) came to the throne, he was a fully committed Protestant and a Lutheran in theology. The new regime condemned him to death for treason but the sentence was not carried out. Under the renewed heresy laws of 1555, he was tried at Oxford, convicted and degraded of his ecclesiastical offices. After much pressure, he signed a number of recantations of his Protestant faith. However, on the eve of his execution his courage returned, and he went to the stake denying his recantations as he died for his faith. This first-hand account describes his final agony and ecstasy.

And because the morning was rainy, the sermon appointed by Mr Dr Cole to be made at the stake was made in St Mary's church.

When he had ended his sermon, he desired all the people to pray for him, Mr Cranmer kneeling down with them and praying for himself. I think there was never such a number so earnestly praying together. For they that hated him before now loved him for his conversion and hope of continuance. They that loved him before could not suddenly hate him, having hope of his confession again of his fall. So love and hope increased on every side....

When praying was done, he [Cranmer] stood up, and having leave to speak said, 'Good people, I have intended to desire you to pray for me, which, because Mr Dr hath desired and you have already done, I thank you most heartily for it. And now will I pray for myself, as I could best devise for mine own comfort, and say the prayer, word for word, as I have here written it.' And he read it standing, and after kneeled down and said the Lord's Prayer, and all the people on their knees devoutly praying with him.... Then rising he said....

'And now I come to the great thing that troubleth my conscience more than any other thing that ever I said or did in my life; and that is, the setting abroad of writings contrary to the truth. Which here now I renounce and refuse as things written with my hand, contrary to the truth which I have in my heart, and writ for fear of death and to save my life, if it might be: and that is all such bills which I have written or signed with mine own hand since my degradation, wherein I have written many things untrue. And forasmuch as my hand offended in writing contrary to my heart, therefore my hand shall first be punished. For if I may come to the fire, it shall be first burned. And as for the Pope, I refuse him as Christ's enemy and Antichrist, with all his false doctrine.'

And here being admonished of his recantation and dissembling, he said, 'Alas, my Lord, I have been a man that all my life loved plainness and never dissembled till now against the truth, which I am most sorry for.' He added hereunto, that for the Sacrament, he believed as he had taught in his book against the Bishop of Winchester. And here he was suffered to speak no more....

Coming to the stake with a cheerful countenance and willing mind, he put off his garments with haste, and stood upright in his shirt. And a Bachelor of Divinity, named Elye, of Brasenose College, laboured to convert him to his former recantation, with two Spanish friars. But when the friars saw his constancy, they said in Latin one to another, 'Let us go from him; we ought not to be nigh him, for the devil is with him.' But the Bachelor of Divinity was more earnest with him. Unto whom he answered, that as concerning his recantation he repented it right sore, because he knew it to be against the truth, with other words more. Whereupon the Lord Williams cried, 'Make short, make short.' Then the Bishop took certain of his friends by the hand. But the Bachelor of Divinity refused to take him by the hand, and blamed all others that did so, and said he was sorry that ever he came in his company. And yet again he required him to agree to his former recantation. And the Bishop answered (showing his hand), 'This is the hand that wrote it, and therefore shall it suffer first punishment.'

Fire being now put to him, he stretched out his right hand and thrust it into the flame, and held it there a good space, before the fire came to any part of his body, where his hand was seen of every man sensibly burning, crying with a loud voice, 'This hand hath offended.' As soon as the fire was got up, he was very soon dead, never stirring or crying all the while.

Source: Harleian MS. 422, cited in Hans J. Hillerbrand, *The Reformation: A Narrative History Related by Contemporary Observers and Participants* (New York: Harper and Row, 1964), 353–354.

Document 9: Excerpts from The Schleitheim Confession of Faith, Adopted by a Conference of the Swiss Brethren, 24 February 1527

This confession of faith was the first major expression of consensus among Anabaptist leaders. It was drafted and adopted at the town of Schleitheim in present-day Switzerland in February 1527. The soon to be martyred Michael Sattler (1490–1527), a former Benedictine prior, presided over the meeting and is considered by many historians to be the principal architect of the document. The confession was not intended to be a doctrinal formulation but a statement concerning order and discipline within the various Anabaptist congregations. The ban mentioned in the document was the Anabaptist method of congregational discipline. Those who strayed from the high moral code of the Anabaptists were banned from fellowship with the faithful (or shunned) until they repented and turned back to the path of righteousness. In any case, this confession expresses the Anabaptist ethos during the early years of the movement's existence.

Brotherly Union of a Number of Children of God Concerning Seven Articles

First. Observe concerning baptism: Baptism shall be given to all those who have learned repentance and amendment of life, and who believe truly that their sins are taken away by Christ, and to all those who walk in the resurrection of Jesus Christ, and wish to be buried with him in death, so that they may be resurrected with him, and to all those who with this significance request it [baptism] of us and demand it for themselves....

Second. We are agreed as follows on the ban: The ban shall be employed with all those who have given themselves to the Lord, to walk in his commandments, and with all those who are baptized into the one body of Christ and who are called brethren or sisters, and yet who slip sometimes and fall into error and sin, being inadvertently overtaken....

Third. In the breaking of bread we are of one mind and are agreed [as follows]: All those who wish to break one bread in remembrance of the broken body of Christ, and all who wish to drink of one drink as a remembrance of the shed blood of Christ, shall be united beforehand by baptism in one body of Christ which is the Church of God and whose head is Christ....

Therefore it is and must be [thus]: Whoever has not been called by one God to one faith, to one baptism, to one Spirit, to one body, with all the children of God's Church, cannot be made [into] one bread with them, as indeed must be done if one is truly to break bread according to the command of Christ.

Fourth. We are agreed [as follows] on separation: A separation shall be made from the evil and from the wickedness which the devil planted in the world; in this manner, simply that we shall not have fellowship with them [the wicked] and not run with them in the multitude of their abominations. This is the way it is: Since all who do not walk in the obedience of faith, and have not united themselves with God so that they wish to do his will, are a great abomination before God, it is not possible for anything to grow or issue from them except abominable things. For truly all creatures are in but two classes, good and bad, believing and unbelieving, darkness and light, the world and those who [have come] out of the world, God's temple and idols, Christ and Belial; and none can have part with the other.

To us then the command of the Lord is clear when he calls upon us to be separate from the evil and thus he will be our God and we shall be his sons and daughters....

Fifth. We are agreed as follows on pastors in the Church of God: The pastor in the Church of God shall, as Paul has prescribed, be one who out-and-out has a good report of those who are outside the faith. This office shall be to read, to admonish and teach, to warn, to discipline, to ban in the Church, to lead out in prayer for the advancement of all the brethren and sisters, to lift up the bread when it is to be broken, and in all things to see to the care of the body of Christ, in order that it may be built up and developed, and the mouth of the slanderer be stopped. . . .

Sixth. We are agreed as follows concerning the sword: The sword is ordained of God outside the perfection of Christ. It punishes and puts to death the wicked, and guards and protects the good. In the Law the sword was ordained for the punishment of the wicked and for their death, and the same [sword] is [now] ordained to be used by the worldly magistrates.

In the perfection of Christ, however, only the ban is used for a warning and for the excommunication of the one who has sinned, without putting the flesh to death—simply the warning and the command to sin no more. . . .

Seventh. We are agreed as follows concerning the oath: The oath is a confirmation among those who are quarreling or making promises. In the Law it is commanded to be performed in God's name, but only in truth, not falsely. Christ, who teaches the perfection of the Law, prohibits all swearing to his [followers], whether true or false—neither by heaven, nor by the earth, nor by Jerusalem, nor by our head—and that for the reason which he shortly thereafter gives, for you are not able to make one hair white or black. So you see it is for this reason that all swearing is forbidden: we cannot fulfill that which we promise when we swear, for we cannot change [even] the very least thing on us. . . .

Dear brethren and sisters in the Lord: These are the articles of certain brethren who had heretofore been in error and who had failed to agree in the true understanding, so that many weaker consciences were perplexed, causing the name of God to be greatly slandered. Therefore there has been a great need for us to become of one mind in the Lord, which has come to pass. To God be praise and glory! . . .

Keep watch on all who do not walk according to the simplicity of the divine truth which is stated in this letter from [the decisions of] our meeting, so that everyone among us will be governed by the rule of the ban and henceforth the entry of false brethren and sisters among us may be prevented.

Eliminate from you that which is evil and the Lord will be your God and you will be his sons and daughters.

Source: Hans J. Hillerbrand, *The Reformation: A Narrative History Related by Contemporary Observers and Participants* (New York: Harper and Row, 1964), 235–238.

Document 10: Excerpt from Menno Simons' *Foundation of Christian Doctrine*, 1540

Menno Simons (1496–1560) became the leader of the Dutch Anabaptists after leaving the Roman Catholic priesthood in 1536. He undoubtedly did more than any other single individual to rescue Dutch Anabaptism from its earlier radical tendencies and to launch it on a peaceful evangelical path. Eventually, the movement took his name as its own: Mennonites. In this excerpt from the conclusion of Menno's major theological work, he summarizes the Anabaptist position and pleads for toleration and understanding.

Dear sirs, friends, and brethren, we have indicated briefly on what foundation and Scriptures we rest, what we seek and intend, and how with the Word of the Lord we rebuke all abominations, sects, and wickedness of the whole world with both great and small, without any respect of persons, and point out to everyone the pure and blessed truth. Let the God-fearing read and judge.

I have not done this as though the cross of Christ may thereby be avoided; in no wise. For I know and am persuaded that the lamb will never be at peace with the wolf, the dove with the eagle, and Christ with Belial. Truth will be hated, even if spoken by Christ Himself from heaven. And neither Scripture nor piety, neither Christ nor apostle, neither prophet nor saint, neither life nor property, will prevail upon men. All those who rebuke in pure and honest zeal this haughty, avaricious, proud, idolatrous, blood-drunken world, all who diligently seek their happiness and eternal welfare, must suffer and tread the winepress.

You shall be hated of all men for my name's sake, says Christ. Through much tribulation you must enter into the kingdom of God. Christ Himself had to suffer and so enter into His glory.

But I have written in order that the noble, pure truth might be revealed; this or that man be won thereby; the blind pointed to the right way; the hungry fed with the Word of God; the erring directed to Christ their Shepherd; the ignorant taught; God's kingdom extended, and His holy name magnified and praised. And all this together with our innocence shall testify on the day of judgment against all bloodthirsty tyrants, against all deceivers, false prophets, and all the proud and impenitent, that to them the truth has been declared. But if you refuse to hear, then your sins will be upon you. God's Spirit, Word, truth, ordinance, and will I have declared unto you according to my small gifts, and have pointed out to you righteousness. Whosoever has ears to hear, let him hear; and whosoever has understanding, let him perceive.

I confess my Saviour openly; I confess Him and dissemble not. If you repent not, and are not born of God, and become not one with Christ in Spirit, faith, life, and worship, then is the sentence of your condemnation on your poor souls already finished and prepared.

All who teach you otherwise than we have here taught and confessed from the Scriptures deceive you. This is the narrow way through which we all must walk and must enter the strait gate, if we would be saved. Neither emperor nor king, duke nor count, knight nor nobleman, doctor nor licentiate, rich nor poor, man nor woman, is excepted. Whosoever boasts that he is a Christian, the same must walk as Christ walked. If any man have not the Spirit of Christ, he is none of His. Whosoever transgresseth and abideth not in the doctrine of Christ, hath not God. II John 1:9. He that committeth sin is of the devil. I John 3:8. Here neither baptism, Lord's Supper, confession, nor absolution will avail anything. These and other Scriptures stand immovable and judge all those who live outside the Spirit and Word of Christ and who mind earthly and carnal things. They shall never be overthrown, perverted, nor weakened by angel or devil.

If with rebellious Israel you say, We will not hear the word which you have preached to us in the name of the Lord, but we will do as our fathers, our kings and princes have done for many years until the present time, then I answer with holy Jeremiah and say: Since you have pleasure in lies and do such abominations, therefore the Lord has taken your wickedness to heart and sent you one hard punishment after another. He has sent hunger, pestilence, storms, grief, misery, and the cruel, consuming sword, so that your land is turned to a waste, an amazement and a curse, as one may see in many places. This is because you perform strange worship, despise the Lord your God, reject His Word, shed innocent blood, walk according to your own wills, sin against God and walk not in His law, ordinance, and commands, as the mouth of the Lord has commanded.

And I say that the unprofitable and rebellious world is commonly warned and rebuked against its will, so that the majority of the prophets and the true servants of God are condemned and killed by the princes and magistrates as seditious mutinists, and persecuted by the priests and common people as deceivers and heretics. Therefore we have prepared ourselves both to teach and to suffer, expecting that we fare no better in the matter than did they. But we do say with Ezekiel, that when that which will come has come, you will discover that the undissembled, pure Word of the Lord has been presented and taught among you.

The merciful, gracious Father, through His loving Son, Christ Jesus, our Lord, grant to you all the gift and grace of His

Holy Spirit, so that you may hear and read these our Christian labors and service of true love, with such hearts that you may strive for, confess, believe, and follow after the pure truth with all your soul, and be eternally saved. Amen.

Dear noble lords, grant to your poor servants that we may fear the Lord from the heart and may preach the Word of God and do right. This we pray you for Jesus' sake.

O Lord, Father of all grace, be pleased to open the eyes of the blind so that they may see Thy way, Word, truth, and will, and walk therein with faithful hearts. Amen.

By me, M. S.

Source: Menno Simons, *The Complete Writings of Menno Simons*, trans. Leonard Verduin, ed. John C. Wenger (Scottdale, PA: Herald Press, 1956), 224–226.

Document 11: Ignatius de Loyola, "Rules for Thinking with the Church," 1548

Ignatius de Loyola (1491–1556) wrote *The Spiritual Exercises* between 1522 and 1524 when he was at the beginning of the spiritual pilgrimage that led to the creation of the Society of Jesus. It was published in its final form in 1548. Loyola saw that the Jesuit ideal of the contemplative in action required a new spirituality. Therefore, he wrote the *Exercises* for this purpose. It prescribed an intensive course of personal interior religious development that would ideally last for four weeks and that would be life-transforming for the serious practitioner. Many historians believe that his ideal of unstinting service for the Roman Church and absolute obedience to the papacy is best represented in this section of this slim volume: "Rules for Thinking with the Church."

1. Always to be ready to obey with mind and heart, setting aside all judgement of one's own, the true spouse of Jesus Christ, our holy mother, our infallible and orthodox mistress, the Catholic Church, whose authority is exercised over us by the hierarchy.
2. To commend the confession of sins to a priest as it is practised in the Church; the reception of the Holy Eucharist once a year, or better still every week, or at least every month, with the necessary preparation.
3. To commend to the faithful frequent and devout assistance at the holy sacrifice of the Mass, the ecclesiastical hymns,

the divine office, and in general the prayers and devotions practised at stated times, whether in public in the churches or in private.

4. To have a great esteem for the religious orders, and to give the preference to celibacy or virginity over the married state.

5. To approve of the religious vows of chastity, poverty, perpetual obedience, as well as to the other works of perfection and supererogation. Let us remark in passing, that we must never engage by vow to take a state (such e.g. as marriage) that would be an impediment to one more perfect.

6. To praise relics, the veneration and invocation of Saints: also the stations, and pious pilgrimages, indulgences, jubilees, the custom of lighting candles in the churches, and other such aids to piety and devotion.

7. To praise the use of abstinence and fasts as those of Lent, of Ember Days, of Vigils, of Friday, Saturday, and of others undertaken out of pure devotion: also voluntary mortifications, which we call penances, not merely interior, but exterior also.

8. To commend moreover the construction of churches, and ornaments; also images, to be venerated with the fullest right, for the sake of what they represent.

9. To uphold especially all the precepts of the Church, and not censure them in any manner; but, on the contrary, to defend them promptly, with reasons drawn from all sources, against those who criticize them.

10. To be eager to commend the decrees, mandates, traditions, rites and customs of the Fathers in the Faith or our superiors. As to their conduct; although there may not always be the uprightness of conduct that there ought to be, yet to attack or revile them in private or in public tends to scandal and disorder. Such attacks set the people against their princes and pastors; we must avoid such reproaches and never attack superiors before inferiors. The best course is to make private approach to those who have power to remedy the evil.

11. To value most highly the sacred teaching, both the Positive and the Scholastic, as they are commonly called.

12. It is a thing to be blamed and avoided to compare men who are living on the earth (however worthy of praise) with the Saints and Blessed, saying: This man is more learned than St. Augustine, and so forth.

13. That we may be altogether of the same mind and in conformity with the Church herself, if she shall have defined anything to be black which to our eyes appears to be white, we ought in like manner to pronounce it to be black. For we must undoubtedly believe, that the Spirit of our Lord Jesus Christ, and the Spirit of the Orthodox Church His Spouse, by which Spirit we are governed and directed to Salvation, is the same.

14. It must also be borne in mind, that although it be most true, that no one is saved but he that is predestinated, yet we must speak with circumspection concerning this matter, lest perchance, stressing too much the grace or predestination of God, we should seem to wish to shut out the force of free will and the merits of good works; or on the other hand, attributing to these latter more than belongs to them, we derogate meanwhile from the power of grace.

15. For the like reason we should not speak on the subject of predestination frequently; if by chance we do so speak, we ought so to temper what we say as to give the people who hear no occasion of erring and saying, 'If my salvation or damnation is already decreed, my good or evil actions are predetermined'; whence many are wont to neglect good works, and the means of salvation.

16. It also happens not unfrequently, that from immoderate preaching and praise of faith, without distinction or explanation added, the people seize a pretext for being lazy with regard to any good works, which precede faith, or follow it when it has been formed by the bond of charity.

17. Nor any more must we push to such a point the preaching and inculcating of the grace of God, as that there may creep thence into the minds of the hearers the deadly error of denying our faculty of free will. We must speak of it as the glory of God requires ... that we may not raise doubts as to liberty and the efficacy of good works.

18. Although it is very praiseworthy and useful to serve God through the motive of pure charity, yet we must also recommend the fear of God; and not only filial fear, but servile fear, which is very useful and often even necessary to raise man from sin.... Once risen from the state, and free from the affection of mortal sin, we may then speak of that filial fear which is truly worthy of God, and which gives and preserves the union of pure love.

Source: Henry Bettenson and Chris Maunder, eds., *Documents of the Christian Church*, 3rd ed. (New York: Oxford University Press, 1999), 272–274.

Document 12: Excerpt from St. Teresa de Avila's *The Interior Castle*, 1577

Catholic renewal in the sixteenth century found a profound expression in the life and thought of several Spanish mystics, of which St. Teresa de Avila (1515–1582) was the most important. A

Carmelite reformer, mystic and writer, she dreamed of martyrdom and doing great works for God. *The Interior Castle*, which many scholars regard as her most important work, delineates the life of prayer from meditation through mystical marriage and noting intermediate stages. This excerpt speaks of the beauty and dignity of the soul and how prayer is the gate to the spiritual castle.

1. While I was begging our Lord to-day to speak for me, since I knew not what to say nor how to commence this work which obedience has laid upon me, an idea occurred to me which I will explain, and which will serve as a foundation for that I am about to write.

2. I thought of the soul as resembling a castle, formed of a single diamond or a very transparent crystal, and containing many rooms, just as in heaven there are many mansions. If we reflect, sisters, we shall see that the soul of the just man is but a paradise, in which, God tells us, He takes His delight. What, do you imagine, must that dwelling be in which a King so mighty, so wise, and so pure, containing in Himself all good, can delight to rest? Nothing can be compared to the great beauty and capabilities of a soul; however keen our intellects may be, they are as unable to comprehend them as to comprehend God, for, as He has told us, He created us in His own image and likeness.

3. As this is so, we need not tire ourselves by trying to realize all the beauty of this castle, although, being His creature, there is all the difference between the soul and God that there is between the creature and the Creator; the fact that it is made in God's image teaches us how great are its dignity and loveliness. It is no small misfortune and disgrace that, through our own fault, we neither understand our nature nor our origin. Would it not be gross ignorance, my daughters, if, when a man was questioned about his name, or country, or parents, he could not answer? Stupid as this would be, it is unspeakably more foolish to care to learn nothing of our nature except that we possess bodies, and only to realize vaguely that we have souls, because people say so and it is a doctrine of faith. Rarely do we reflect upon what gifts our souls may possess, Who dwells within them, or how extremely precious they are. Therefore we do little to preserve their beauty; all our care is concentrated on our bodies, which are but the coarse setting of the diamond, or the outer walls of the castle.

4. Let us imagine, as I said, that there are many rooms in this castle, of which some are above, some below, others at the side; in the centre, in the very midst of them all, is the principal chamber in which God and the soul hold their most

secret intercourse. Think over this comparison very carefully; God grant it may enlighten you about the different kinds of graces He is pleased to bestow upon the soul. No one can know all about them, much less a person so ignorant as I am. The knowledge that such things are possible will console you greatly should our Lord ever grant you any of these favours; people themselves deprived of them can then at least praise Him for His great goodness in bestowing them on others. The thought of heaven and the happiness of the saints does us no harm, but cheers and urges us to win this joy for ourselves, nor will it injure us to know that during this exile God can communicate Himself to us loathsome worms; it will rather make us love Him for such immense goodness and infinite mercy.

5. I feel sure that vexation at thinking that during our life on earth God can bestow these graces on the souls of others shows a want of humility and charity for one's neighbour, for why should we not feel glad at a brother's receiving divine favours which do not deprive us of our own share? Should we not rather rejoice at His Majesty's thus manifesting His greatness wherever He chooses? Sometimes our Lord acts thus solely for the sake of showing His power, as He declared when the Apostles questioned whether the blind man whom He cured had been suffering for his own or his parents' sins. God does not bestow these favours on certain souls because they are more holy than others who do not receive them, but to manifest His greatness, as in the case of St. Paul and St. Mary Magdalen, and that we may glorify Him in His creatures.

6. People may say such things appear impossible and it is best not to scandalize the weak in faith by speaking about them. But it is better that the latter should disbelieve us, than that we should desist from enlightening souls which receive these graces, that they may rejoice and may endeavour to love God better for His favours, seeing He is so mighty and so great. There is no danger here of shocking those for whom I write by treating of such matters, for they know and believe that God gives even greater proofs of His love. I am certain that if any one of you doubts the truth of this, God will never allow her to learn it by experience, for He desires that no limits should be set to His work: therefore, never discredit them because you are not thus led yourselves.

7. Now let us return to our beautiful and charming castle and discover how to enter it. This appears incongruous: if this castle is the soul, clearly no one can have to enter it, for it is the person himself: one might as well tell some one to go into a room he is already in! There are, however, very

different ways of being in this castle; many souls live in the courtyard of the building where the sentinels stand, neither caring to enter farther, nor to know who dwells in that most delightful place, what is in it and what rooms it contains.

8. Certain books on prayer that you have read advise the soul to enter into itself, and this is what I mean. I was recently told by a great theologian that souls without prayer are like bodies, palsied and lame, having hands and feet they cannot use. Just so, there are souls so infirm and accustomed to think of nothing but earthly matters, that there seems no cure for them. It appears impossible for them to retire into their own hearts; accustomed as they are to be with the reptiles and other creatures which live outside the castle, they have come at last to imitate their habits. Though these souls are by their nature so richly endowed, capable of communion even with God Himself, yet their case seems hopeless. Unless they endeavour to understand and remedy their most miserable plight, their minds will become, as it were, bereft of movement, just as Lot's wife became a pillar of salt for looking backwards in disobedience to God's command.

9. As far as I can understand, the gate by which to enter this castle is prayer and meditation. I do not allude more to mental than to vocal prayer, for if it is prayer at all, the mind must take part in it. If a person neither considers to Whom he is addressing himself, what he asks, nor what he is who ventures to speak to God, although his lips may utter many words, I do not call it prayer. Sometimes, indeed, one may pray devoutly without making all these considerations through having practised them at other times. The custom of speaking to God Almighty as freely as with a slave—caring nothing whether the words are suitable or not, but simply saying the first thing that comes to mind from being learnt by rote by frequent repetition—cannot be called prayer: God grant that no Christian may address Him in this manner. I trust His Majesty will prevent any of you, sisters, from doing so. Our habit in this Order of conversing about spiritual matters is a good preservative against such evil ways.

10. Let us speak no more of these crippled souls, who are in a most miserable and dangerous state, unless our Lord bid them rise, as He did the palsied man who had waited more than thirty years at the pool of Bethsaida. We will now think of the others who at last enter the precincts of the castle; they are still very worldly, yet have some desire to do right, and at times, though rarely, commend themselves to God's care. They think about their souls every now and then; although very busy, they pray a few times a month, with minds generally filled with a thousand other matters,

for where their treasure is, there is their heart also. Still, occasionally they cast aside these cares; it is a great boon for them to realize to some extent the state of their souls, and to see that they will never reach the gate by the road they are following.

11. At length they enter the first rooms in the basement of the castle, accompanied by numerous reptiles which disturb their peace, and prevent their seeing the beauty of the building; still, it is a great gain that these persons should have found their way in at all.

12. You may think, my daughters, that all this does not concern you, because, by God's grace, you are farther advanced; still, you must be patient with me, for I can explain myself on some spiritual matters concerning prayer in no other way. May our Lord enable me to speak to the point; the subject is most difficult to understand without personal experience of such graces. Any one who has received them will know how impossible it is to avoid touching on subjects which, by the mercy of God, will never apply to us.

Source: St. Teresa of Avila, *The Interior Castle or the Mansions*, trans. the Benedictines of Stanbrook, rev. with notes and introduction by the Very Rev. Fr. Benedict Zimmerman, 3rd ed. (London: Thomas Baker, 1921), 38–45.

GLOSSARY OF SELECTED TERMS

Ascetic life. Leading a life of self-discipline and self-denial, especially for spiritual improvement. In the early church, ascetic refers to one who was devoted to a solitary and contemplative life, characterized by rigorous religious devotion, excessive self-denial, and perhaps self-mortification.

Baroque. A seventeenth-century European style of architecture, art, music and decoration, common in central Europe. Beginning in Rome during the Catholic Reformation, the style is characterized by oval spaces, curved surfaces, and conspicuous use of decoration, sculpture, and color. The exuberant works of the Baroque period tend to engage the viewer, both physically and emotionally, by means of highly dramatic lighting effects, creating a sense of theatricality, energy, and movement of forms. In paintings, color was manipulated for its emotional effects and a heightened sense of drama and religious ecstasy. Baroque music is lively and tuneful yet expresses the fundamental order of the universe.

Bourgeois. A term that originated in medieval France, which denoted the inhabitant of a walled-in town, or *bourg*. In the sixteenth century, it was mainly applied to the emerging middle class.

Broadsides. Also known as broadsheets, broadsides are one of the earliest products of the printing press. Gutenberg printed his first broadside in 1454. Most broadsides ranged from $17 \times 13^{1}/_{2}$ inches to more than 5 feet in length. They were notices written on disposable, single sheets of paper printed on one side only, which allowed for affixing them to walls and other structures for easy public viewing. The importance of broadsides, particularly in political or religious arenas, lay in their power to have an immediate impact on the public.

City upon a hill. Associated with Governor John Winthrop's shipboard sermon of 1630, "A Model of Christian Charity." In his sermon, Winthrop warned the Puritan colonists of New England who were about to establish the Massachusetts Bay Colony that their new community would be a "city on a hill," watched by the world, which would provide an example to England and the world of a truly godly society. The concept later was secularized and became central to the United States' perception of itself as a preeminent and ideal nation.

Commonwealth. The republican form of government under the leadership of Parliament that governed first England and then Ireland and Scotland from 1649 to 1660.

Congregationalism. A democratic system of church governance in which local congregations are independent and ecclesiastically autonomous. Beginning with the Anglo-American Puritan and Baptist Movements of the seventeenth century, congregationalist denominations are distinguished most clearly from episcopal polity, which is governance by a hierarchy of bishops, and distinct from presbyterian polity, in which congregational representatives exercise authority over individual congregations.

Conversion. A changing from or to a faith or belief, such as the turning of a sinner to God, or the act of changing from one denomination to another or one religion to another. In biblical parlance, it means renouncing sin and turning one's life over to Jesus Christ, the Savior, a process in which "the old has gone, the new has come." (2 Corinthians 5:17)

Donatists. North African Christians who flourished in the fourth and fifth centuries and who were deemed heretics by the Bishop of Rome and subversives by the Roman Emperor. Although the Catholic Church of the day taught that the sacraments remained valid and effective in spite of any unworthiness on the part of the officiating church leader, Donatists regarded as critical the worthiness of the leader. Therefore, those who had been baptized by someone who was tainted by immorality or what Donatists regarded as unbiblical beliefs had to be re-baptized upon confession of faith in Christ when they joined a Donatist church. Similarly, consecrations in such circumstances were null and void in Donatist eyes. Eventually condemnation of the Donatist practice of what was perceived as a second baptism was written into Roman Law and declared a capital crime.

Double predestination. A term Calvin never used but which his second-generation followers inferred from his teaching concerning the predestination of the elect to salvation, meant that God also foreordains certain souls to damnation.

Ecclesiastical. Of or pertaining to the church or the clergy, not secular.

Ecumenical. Of or relating to or representing the whole of a body of churches, also, promoting or tending toward worldwide Christian unity or cooperation.

Enlightenment. An intellectual movement characterized by belief in the supreme power of human reason and by innovations in religious, political and educational thought that arose in Europe in the eighteenth century (also called the Age of Reason). Many Enlightenment thinkers were hostile to organized religion while others embraced a religious view called Deism that advocated belief in a benevolent God who created the world but who has since remained indifferent to his creation while it operates according to natural law.

Episcopalism. A monarchical form of church government that recognizes a governing order of bishops (spiritual overseers) in ecclesiastical polity. In the Roman Catholic Church, the pope is "the bishop of bishops" while in the Anglican Communion bishops tend to be more co-equal in running the Church.

Eucharist. Literally "a thanksgiving," the Eucharist during Christian worship is a time of giving thanks to God for the sacrifice of Jesus Christ. It is considered a sacrament by many Christian churches, and a central act of worship in some, especially by the Roman Catholic Church and by Anglo-Catholics in the Anglican Communion. Protestants generally use such terms as Holy Communion or the Lord's Supper to describe the Eucharist.

Evangelical. A term coined by Martin Luther to describe the Protestant Movement as basically devoted to the spreading of the Gospel, referring to the New Testament Greek word *evaggelion*, that is, "the Evangel" (literally the "Good News") of God's redemptive grace in Jesus Christ. The basic message of this "Good News" was, of course, contained in the New Testament with its declaration of Christ's incarnation, teaching, death, resurrection and exaltation. All sixteenth-century Protestants were in this sense "Evangelicals."

Excommunication. The most severe form of censure by various organized expressions of Christianity. It means that the individual is deprived of the ministrations and privileges of church membership, especially of the Eucharist in the Roman Catholic and Anglican Churches. Churches in the presbyterian and congregational traditions usually simply expel and try to redeem the wayward member. In the Middle Ages and the sixteenth century, those individuals who died while excommunicated did so outside of a state of grace and, according to Church teaching, went to hell.

First Great Awakening. An evangelical awakening of major proportions that swept across British North America in the 1730s and 1740s, the Great Awakening (as it was called at the time) focused on reviving professed Christians from their spiritual lethargy and reaching out to non-believers with the message that Jesus saves people from their sins and gives them a new start in life. Jonathan Edwards, a Congregational minister in Connecticut, was the most famous of a number of powerful preachers who led this awakening.

Flagellation. From the Latin *flagellum*, meaning whip, flagellation is the beating with a whip or strap or rope as a form of punishment or a source of religious stimulation. Flagellation can be submitted to willingly or unwillingly, or performed on oneself in religious contexts.

Gathered community. A term used to describe the Anabaptist view of the true church. They believed that the Christian Church existed only in local congregations of baptized believers. Thus the local church was a "gathered community" of heartfelt believers who had made a free and measured decision to follow Christ.

Heresy. In the Roman Catholic Church, the willful and persistent rejection of any article of faith by a baptized member of the church. In a more general sense, a belief or theory in opposition to the established beliefs and customs of any religious group. In the sixteenth century, heresy was a capital crime under Roman Law.

Idolatry. In Judaism and Christianity, the worship of an image, idea or object, as opposed to the worship of the true God. In the Reformation Era, Protestants routinely denounced the Roman Catholic use of statuary and prayer beads and their veneration of Mary and the Mass as idolatrous.

Millennial enthusiasts. During the Reformation, certain Protestant groups over-emphasized the doctrine of Christ's second coming to set up his millennial kingdom at the expense of other evangelical doctrines. Some of these groups, such as the followers of Thomas Müntzer and the Münsterites, believed that God had called them to prepare the way for Christ's return by slaying the ungodly and setting up a place for Jesus' millennial rule.

Millennium. A period of 1,000 years in which, according to certain schools of Christian eschatology, Christ will return again to reign gloriously on earth. Based on Revelation 20, this has been a recurring theme in Christianity since the first century. During the Reformation, certain Anabaptist groups, such as the Melchiorites and the Münsterites, emphasized the second coming of Christ.

Monasticism. An organized form of religious life with an emphasis on asceticism, usually in a community under a common rule. Characterized by a vow of celibacy, poverty and obedience, the focus of Christian monasticism is on the ideal of the higher Christian life. Some forms of monasticism emphasize the solitary life, with some form of spiritual guidance from an abbot or prior. The Rule of St. Benedict of Nursia nurtured all of monastic life up to the time of the Reformation. One reason for the coming of the Reformation was the failure of many monastic groups to live up to St. Benedict's code.

Mysticism. A doctrine of spiritual intuition of truths believed to transcend ordinary understanding, or of a direct, intimate union of the soul with God through prayer and meditation capped by an ecstatic vision of the Almighty. The spiritual quest of all mystics is for a direct experience of God. Notable Christian mystics include St. Bernard of Clairvaux, St. Francis of Assisi, and St. Teresa de Avila.

Nuncio. In the Roman Catholic Church, a special papal envoy or diplomatic representative who has ambassadorial status, or a diplomatic representative of the pope at a foreign court or capital who is equal in status to ambassadors from secular governments.

Ordeal. An ancient form of trial to determine guilt or innocence by subjecting the accused person to fire, poison, or other serious danger, the result being regarded as a divine or supernatural judgment. In the Middle Ages, the validity of the ordeal depended upon divine intercession, which only a priest could be expected to call forth.

Papal Curia. Curia in medieval Latin usage meant "court" in the sense of a "royal court" rather than a court of law. The Roman Curia, then, was the Papal Court, which assisted the pope in carrying out his administrative functions as the head of the Roman Catholic Church.

Parish. In the Roman Catholic, Anglican and certain other churches, the parish is an administrative part of a diocese that has its own church building, or an ecclesiastical district having its own church building and member of the clergy.

Pilgrimage. A journey, especially a long one of great moral significance, usually made to some shrine or holy place. Members of nearly every major religion participate in pilgrimages of some kind. The Medieval Catholic Church considered pilgrimages as acts of merit and indulgences were promised to pilgrims to certain shrines, a practice often denounced by Protestant reformers as superstition.

Presbyterianism. A representative form of church government that is most prevalent within the Presbyterian and Reformed branch of Protestant Christianity. Based on the New Testament concept of eldership (*presbuterous* is the Greek word for elder in the New Testament), the churches of these kinds of denominations are governed like a republic by elders elected by local congregations who send their representatives to presbyteries that oversee the life of the congregations. In the presbyterian system, lay elders are specially commissioned non-clergy members who take part in local pastoral care and decision-making at all levels. The Reformed Church in John Calvin's Geneva as well as John Knox's Reformed Kirk of Scotland were presbyterian.

Protectorate. The government of England from 1653 to 1659 was called The Protectorate, which took the form of direct personal rule by Oliver Cromwell, and after his death that of his son Richard, as Lord Protector.

Puritans. Although never definitively defined, most historians use this term to describe those sixteenth- and seventeenth-century English Protestants who yearned for a further reformation of the Church of England in order to make it less Roman Catholic and more biblical in an evangelical sense. The movement began immediately after the return of the Marian Exiles in 1558 and acquired the name "Puritan" soon thereafter. It originally meant those serious Protestants who wanted to "purify" the English Church of what they regarded as "its papal trappings."

Rump Parliament. Since 1649, the term "rump parliament" has been used to refer to any parliament left over after the true parliament has formally dissolved. The original English Rump Parliament immediately followed the Long Parliament, elected in 1640, and took over after Pride's Purge of 6 December 1648 that removed those members of the original Parliament who resisted the plan to try King Charles I for high treason. The Rump ordered the execution of Charles I in 1649, and abolished the monarchy and the House of Lords, establishing a Commonwealth governed by the House of Commons in its place. When the Rump Parliament was no longer in the favor of the army, Oliver Cromwell dissolved it on 20 April 1653, and assumed the title of Lord Protector. The Rump was recalled in 1659 after the fall of the Protectorate, and dissolved itself in 1660, thus making way for the restoration of the monarchy.

Sacraments. From the Latin word *sacramentum*, to "make sacred," the more dogmatic and theologically oriented Christian churches and denominations regard a sacrament as a visible sign of inward grace. During the Middle Ages, the Roman Catholic Church declared a sacrament to be a visible sign instituted by Jesus to confer grace. The seven sacraments of the Roman and Greek Catholic Churches historically have been baptism, confirmation, the Eucharist, matrimony, holy orders, penance and last rites (formerly extreme unction). Protestants rejected all but two of these sacraments, baptism and the Eucharist, because, they said, they could not find them stated as such in the New Testament. Anabaptists and Baptists declined to accept the concept of sacramentalism altogether and retained only baptism and the Lord's Supper as "ordinances" instituted by Jesus to be celebrated by his people.

Scala Sancta. The Scala Sancta, or "Holy Stairs," consists of 28 white marble steps, now located at Rome, near the pope's Lateran Palace. The steps are, according to Roman Catholic tradition, the very staircase that once led to the praetorium of Pilate at Jerusalem. Hence, they are sanctified by the footsteps of Jesus during his Passion. Medieval tradition said that the Holy Stairs were brought from Jerusalem to Rome about 326 by St. Helena, mother of the Roman Emperor Constantine I.

Second Coming. Refers to the Christian belief in the return to earth of Jesus Christ at the end of the present age, an event that will fulfill aspects of Messianic prophecy such as the resurrection of the dead, the last judgment and full establishment of the Kingdom of God on earth. Views about the time and nature of Christ's return vary among Christians. Some believe that he will come to judge the living and the dead before the millennium (premillennialism), others that Jesus will fulfill the Messianic prophecies after the millennium (postmillennialism) and still others that the millennium is a spiritual kingdom and is really the age of the church from the resurrection of Christ until he comes again (amillennialism). Still others frankly admit that no human knows the day or the hour but only God, therefore there is no point in speculation. Most Reformation Era millennialists expected Christ's imminent return leading at once to the last judgment and the end of the present world.

Theatine. A member of a congregation of regular clerics founded in Italy on 3 May 1524 to promote higher morality among Roman Catholics and to combat Protestantism. The name Theatines comes from the fact that one of the key founders of the congregation was Giovanni Pietro Carafa, later the hard-line anti-Protestant Pope Paul IV (1555–1559), then Bishop of Chieti (Theate), a city in southern Italy.

Transubstantiation. The Roman Catholic doctrine of the Eucharist, affirming the belief that the bread and wine used during Mass are changed into the body and blood of Christ, who is, therefore, truly present in the elements. Belief in transubstantiation was declared to be dogma at the Fourth Lateran Council in 1215. The sixteenth-century Protestant reformers, however, rejected this interpretation. Transubstantiation was reaffirmed as dogma by the Council of Trent in 1551.

Usury. From medieval Latin *usuria* meaning "use," interest was defined originally as charging a fee for "the use" of money. This generally meant interest on loans, although charging a fee for changing money from one currency to another was included in the original meaning. Based on the Old Testament (e.g., Exodus 22:25 and Deuteronomy 23:19–20), medieval canon law forbade Christians to charge interest on loans to other Christians. Likewise, Martin Luther, Philip Melanchthon and Ulrich Zwingli all denounced usury as immoral. However, John Calvin permitted the taking of moderate interest on money loaned to those wealthy enough to pay it.

ANNOTATED BIBLIOGRAPHY

Print Sources

Augustijn, Cornelis. *Erasmus: His Life, Works, and Influence*. Toronto: University of Toronto Press, 1991. A recent and comprehensive biography, and a good place to begin a study of the great humanist.

Bainton, Roland H. *Here I Stand: A Life of Martin Luther*. New York: Abingdon Press, 1950. A brilliantly written, classic study that continues to be the best place to begin a study of Luther.

Benedict, Philip. *Christ's Churches Purely Reformed: A Social History of Calvinism*. New Haven, CT: Yale University Press, 2003. A comprehensive social history of Calvinism in the sixteenth and seventeenth centuries that incorporates the best recent scholarship.

Brecht, Martin. *Martin Luther*, 3 vols. Minneapolis: Fortress Press, 1985–1991. The most comprehensive recent biography of Luther that incorporates a vast amount of new Luther research.

Collinson, Patrick. *The Elizabethan Puritan Movement*. Oxford: Clarendon Press, 1990. An excellent introduction to early Puritanism by one of the foremost scholars of the movement.

Dickens, A. G. *The English Reformation*, 2nd edition. London: Batsford, 1989. Despite the recent spate of revisionist history in this field, Dickens' work still stands as the standard work on the subject.

Dickens, A. G., and John M. Tonkin. *The Reformation in Historical Thought*. Cambridge, MA: Harvard University Press, 1985. Survey of historical writing about the Reformation.

Elton, G. R. *Reform and Reformation: England, 1509–1558*. Cambridge, MA: Harvard University Press, 1977. Well-written survey by an outstanding Tudor scholar.

Estep, William R. *The Anabaptist Story: An Introduction to Sixteenth-Century Anabaptism,* 3rd edition. Grand Rapids, MI: Eerdmans, 1996. A bit weak on Menno but strong on all other aspects of Anabaptist history.

Heinz, Rudolph W. *Reform and Conflict: From the Medieval World to the Wars of Religion, A. D. 1350–1648.* Grand Rapids, MI: Baker Books, 2005. Splendid up-to-date survey of the period delineated by the title.

Hillerbrand, Hans J. *The Reformation: A Narrative History Related by Contemporary Observers and Participants.* New York: Harper and Row, 1964. An old but useful collection of source materials with lively introductions.

Janz, Denis R., ed. *A Reformation Reader.* Minneapolis: Augsburg Fortress Press, 1999. A balanced collection of source materials with judiciously written introductions.

Jedin, Hubert. *A History of the Council of Trent,* 2 vols. St. Louis, MO: Herder, 1957. The most thorough and perceptive study of the Council of Trent yet published.

Kingdon, Robert M. *Geneva and the Coming of the Wars of Religion in France, 1555–1563.* Geneva: Droz, 1956. This remains the best study of Calvin's work in promoting the spread of Protestantism beyond Geneva.

———. *Geneva and the Consolidation of the French Protestant Movement, 1564–1572.* Geneva: Droz, 1967. The companion piece to *Geneva and the Coming of the Wars of Religion* by one of today's preeminent Reformation scholars.

Lindberg, Carter. *The European Reformations.* Oxford: Blackwell, 1996. Clear and comprehensive introduction to the Reformations of the sixteenth century for university and college undergraduates with an emphasis on religious and intellectual history.

MacCulloch, Diarmaid. *Thomas Cranmer: A Life.* New Haven, CT: Yale University Press, 1996. A lively recent biography of this key player in the English Reformation.

McGrath, Alister. *A Life of John Calvin.* Oxford: Blackwell, 1990. A recent biography that is especially valuable because it points out Calvin's contribution to the development of Western Civilization.

———. *Reformation Thought: An Introduction,* 3rd edition. Oxford: Blackwell, 1999. A reliable introduction to the most important ideas of the Reformation Era.

McKee, Elsie A. *Katharina Schutz Zell: The Life and Thought of a Sixteenth-Century Reformer.* Leiden, Netherlands: E. J. Brill, 1999. A model study of an important female Protestant reformer.

Monter, E. William. *Calvin's Geneva.* New York: Wiley, 1967. Especially valuable for an understanding of how Geneva functioned while Calvin was a resident.

Olin, John C. *Catholic Reform from Cardinal Ximenes to the Council of Trent, 1495–1563*. New York: Fordham University Press, 1990. Useful introduction to the topic with illustrative documents.

O'Malley, John W. *The First Jesuits*. Cambridge, MA: Harvard University Press, 1993. The place to begin any study of Loyola and the early Jesuits.

Ozment, Steven. *When Fathers Ruled: Family Life in Reformation Europe*. Cambridge, MA: Harvard University Press, 1983. Although the title is a bit misleading (it is really about Germany), this is a classic work of social history.

Parker, Geoffrey, and Simon Adams, eds. *The Thirty Years' War*, 2nd edition. London: Routledge, 1999. Standard work on the subject with contributions by a number of leading scholars.

Parker, T. H. L. *John Calvin: A Biography*. Philadelphia: Westminster Press, 1975. If there is a standard biography of Calvin, this is it.

Paul, Robert S. *The Lord Protector: Religion and Politics in the Life of Oliver Cromwell*. Grand Rapids, MI: Eerdmans, 1955. An insightful study of Oliver Cromwell by a scholar who really understands his religion.

Pettegree, Andrew, ed. *The Reformation World*. London: Routledge, 2000. Includes articles by specialists on a variety of topics including culture.

Potter, G. R. *Zwingli*. Cambridge: Cambridge University Press, 1977. Standard biography in English.

Siggins, Ian. *Luther and His Mother*. Minneapolis: Fortress Press, 1981. A brief but delightful study of a neglected aspect of Reformation history.

Wendel, François. *Calvin: The Origins and Development of His Thought*. New York: Harper and Row, 1963. This remains the best single introduction to Calvin's thought.

Wiesner, Merry. *Christianity and Sexuality in the Early Modern World*. New York: Routledge, 2000. A thoughtful study of the place of women in the Reformation Era from a feminist perspective.

Williams, George H. *The Radical Reformation*, 3rd edition. Kirksville, MO: Sixteenth Century Journal Publishers, 1992. Massive work that remains indispensable for the study of the radical reformers, including the Anabaptists.

Web Sites

http://www.bbc.co.uk/history/state/church_reformation/index.shtml

An excellent source for more than just the Reformation, it contains many beautiful images and interactive content, such as Stained Glasses that traces the history, myths and techniques in four famous stained-glass windows. It is easy to navigate.

http://www.calvin.edu/meeter/

This site will allow students access to the marvelous resources of the H. Henry Meeter Center for Calvin Studies in Grand Rapids, Michigan.

http://www.eldrbarry.net/heidel/anabrsc.htm

This site contains Anabaptists, Enthusiasts, Spiritualists, Anti-Trinitarians, and several links to informative Web sites of published resources, as well as online resources, home pages, and bibliographical links. There is a wealth of information on this site and it is easy to navigate.

http://www.fordham.edu/halsall/mod/modsbook02.html

Provided by Fordham University, this site is an excellent place to begin research, especially on the Catholic Reformation and the Jesuits. It is well organized and easy to use, allows access to full texts, contains a search option, too many links to mention and an informative Studying History section.

http://history.hanover.edu/early/cath.html

From the Hanover College Department of History, this is a well-organized site that contains many links, some of which are The Council of Trent, Canons and Decrees, St. Ignatius of Loyola, and St. John of the Cross as well as a Resources link. It is easy to navigate.

http://history.hanover.edu/early/prot.html

An Internet archive of texts and documents provided by the Hanover College Department of History, this site contains many links, organized into Lutheran Reformations, Reformed Reformations, Radical Reformations, English Reformation and Scottish Reformation. It also has a section on resources and is easy to navigate.

http://www.library.yale.edu/div/

Provided by Yale University Divinity School, this is an excellent site for serious scholars of the Reformation. It contains a vast amount of information but it can be a bit complicated to access some of the collections and not all of the information is available for off-campus use.

http://www.mun.ca/rels/reform/

A general Reformation site, it contains well-organized links to Luther, Calvin, Zwingli, Melanchthon, Bullinger, Schwenkfelder and Catholic Reformation sources. It is easy to navigate and also features a picture gallery.

http://www.newadvent.org/cathen/index.html

This is the Web site of *The Catholic Encyclopedia*. As the Web page states, the purpose is "to give its readers full and authoritative information on the entire cycle of Catholic interests, action and doctrine." The site is easy to navigate and has a wealth of information that attempts to familiarize students with "all that Catholics have done."

http://bethelks.edu/mla

The Web site of the Mennonite Library and Archives associated with Bethel College in North Newton, Kansas, is the best place to begin a search for Mennonite and Anabaptist materials.

http://www.williamtyndale.com/0reformationtimeline.htm

Lists pre-Reformation, Reformation and post-Reformation time lines, and contains several useful links such as Why Were Our Reformers Burned?, History of the English Bible and Sir Thomas More's Controversy with Tyndale. Music plays and the site is easy to navigate.

INDEX

About the Author

ROBERT D. LINDER is Distinguished Professor of History at Kansas State University in Manhattan, Kansas. He is the author or editor of fifteen books, including *The History of the Church* (2002), *The Long Tragedy: Australian Evangelical Christians and the Great War, 1914–1918* (2000), and *A Dictionary of Christianity in America* (1990).